PROSPERITY AND THE COMING APOCALYPSE

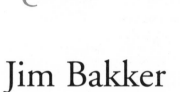

Jim Bakker

with Ken Abraham

THOMAS NELSON PUBLISHERS

Nashville

Published in association with the literary agency of Alive Communications, 1465 Kelly Johnson Blvd., Suite 320, Colorado Springs, CO 80920.

Published in Nashville, Tennessee, by Thomas Nelson, Inc., Publishers

Scripture quotations noted NKJV are from THE NEW KING JAMES VERSION. Copyright © 1979, 1980, 1982, Thomas Nelson, Inc., Publishers.

Scripture quotations noted KJV are from the KING JAMES VERSION.

Scripture quotations noted NIV are from the HOLY BIBLE: NEW INTERNATIONAL VERSION. Copyright © 1973, 1978, 1984 by International Bible Society. Used by permission of Zondervan Publishing House. All rights reserved.

Scripture quotations noted NASB are from the NEW AMERICAN STANDARD BIBLE®, © Copyright The Lockman Foundation 1960, 1962, 1963, 1968, 1971, 1972, 1973, 1975, 1977. Used by permission.

Scripture quotations noted TLB are from *The Living Bible,* copyright © 1971. Used by permission of Tyndale House Publishers, Inc., Wheaton, Illinois 60189. All rights reserved.

Library of Congress Cataloging-in-Publication Data
Bakker, Jim, 1940–
    Prosperity and the coming apocalypse / Jim Bakker with Ken Abraham.
      p. cm.
    Includes bibliographical references.
    ISBN 0-7852-7458-8
    1. Wealth—Religious aspects—Christianity. 2. Tribulation (Christian eschatology).
3. Bakker, Jim, 1940– . I. Abraham, Ken. II. Title.
BR115.W4B35   1998
241'.68—dc21

                        98-39749
                          CIP

Printed in the United States of America
1 2 3 4 5 6 BVG 03 02 01 00 99 98

In memory of my father, Raleigh Bakker (9-13-06 – 5-21-98)

Dedicated to my mother, Furnia Irwin Bakker
My daughter, Tammy Sue Bakker-Chapman, her husband, Doug
My grandsons, James and Jonathan
My son, Jamie Charles
My brother, Norman Bakker, and his wife, June
My sister, Donna Puckett

With special thanks to a wonderful Board of Directors
under whom I have the privilege of serving:
Pastor Tommy Barnett
Governor Julian Carroll
Rick Joyner
Dr. R. T. Kendall
Pastor Tommy Reid

And to those special people with whom I work on a daily basis:
My executive assistant for twenty-one years, Shirley Fulbright

Kendon Alexander
Doyle Borden
Bradford Bryson
Tess Burdios
Pastor Murray and Sally Cresswell
Connie Elling
Jamie and Rob Feist
Dominic and Debbie Gaccetta
Clayton Galligher
Michelle Grogan
Dave and Gina Hanley
Myrna Hernandez
Robert Jackson
Aaron Jayne
Todd Leader
Calvin McClary
Victoria and Richard McCue

Howard and Leanne Bailey
Willette, James, and B.J. Brown
Terri and Milt Bulian
Pastor Andrew Clay
Doug Diebele
Maria Evarts
Pastor Marco Friese
Henny Givens
Lynda Gray
Irene Gutierrez
Anthony Scott Harris
Melanie Hopson
Greg James
Chrissy Keeville
Jose Luna
Jamie and Danielle McClanaghan
Jennier McDevitt

Mike McMahon
Kelli Miller
Amanda Moses
Carolina Olsson
Leo Pitts
Robert Sayles
Louise and Carl Schlittenhart
Lynn and Dennis Smith
Jason Terry
Bobby and Ceci Tores
Margie and Don Watson
Scott Zoph

Allan and Joy Meyer
Rick Mills
Cynthia Ofnhausen
Dave and Debbie Peters
Armando Saavedra
Gene Schaefer
Ken and Beth Smith
Billy and Cheryl Soto
Katie Thompson
Pastor Julian Toriz
Wesley and Elaine Webb

My good friends, John and Joyce Caruso

*My good friend and senior pastor of Los Angeles International Church,
Matthew Barnett*

*All my New Covenant Fellowship friends and partners
All my friends at Los Angeles International Church*

And all my faithful friends who stood with me through the valley years

Contents

Appendix A

Appendix B

Foreword

IN THE FALL OF 1997 I was sitting in my mountain cabin reading the book of Revelation. I was especially interested in the message of chapters twelve through fourteen. I prayed and asked the Lord for understanding. A few minutes later there was a knock on the door. It was Jim Bakker. "I had a dream last night," he began. "I've got to show you some things from the Book of Revelation, especially chapters twelve through fourteen." He had my full attention! For several hours we went on a very interesting spiritual journey.

What Jim shared with me that day is the essence of what is written in this book. The Lord had prepared me to hear it. I already believed the general principles of almost everything he shared and had preached or written on many of them. Even so, much of it was still hard for me to hear. The message of this book will be like a cold slap in the face. However, the slap is not meant to hurt us, but to wake us up.

I do not like pain or problems. I try to get through life with as few of them as possible. I love peace, prosperity, and the country I live in, all of which I believe are blessings from God. I also love truth and the Word of God. Because I love the truth, I must accept the fact that the Scriptures make it clear that at the end of this age there is going to be a time of trouble such as the world has never known. If we cannot face this we have been deceived, and we are not building our lives on the truth of Scripture.

The Scriptures are also clear that in Christ we can not only be prepared for the times, but we can prevail through them. It is also a basic biblical truth that the Lord wants all of His people to be financially independent. That does not necessarily mean that we are to be wealthy according to the world's standards, but rather something even greater than that. It means that we should all have a lifestyle where we never have to base our decisions on whether we can afford to do something or not, but simply on the will of the Lord.

God does want His people to prosper. During the most difficult times that the world is going to go through God's people will be prospering. That is a part of the message of this book (though you may question that through the first few chapters). However, this book is also a necessary challenge to many popular definitions of prosperity and a call to establish our definition of prosperity on sound, biblical truth not popular trends or worldly philosophies that the Scriptures vehemently warn us to reject.

We also know by the Scriptures that one of the ultimate tests to come upon the whole world at the end of this age is going to deal with our relationship to money. The mark of the beast is an economic mark. That mark will determine who can buy, sell, or trade with the present system of the world. Many are hoping to avoid taking this mark by trying to figure out the form that it is going to come in, while they are building their lives on the very spirit of the beast every day.

Jesus said "the harvest is the end of the age." The harvest is the reaping of everything that has been sown, both the good and the evil. Good and evil will both be coming to their full maturity at the end. One of the ultimate idols of the human heart, and therefore one of the ultimate evils, is the love of money. An idol is not just something that people worship, but it is what they put their trust in instead of God. In 1 Timothy 6:10 we are told: "For the love of money is the root of all evil: which while some coveted after, they have erred from the faith, and pierced themselves through with many sorrows" (KJV).

The love of money is fundamental to evil, and doctrines that are promulgated which try to dilute this are helping to set up many people for the ultimate tragedy, "worshiping the beast." If we trust our bank accounts, our retirement accounts, our other worldly assets, more than God, we are building our lives on a trust in this present world more than in God, and are therefore "worshiping the beast."

If you are sincere seeker of truth, a simple test will determine whether you are building your life on a true faith in God or in this present world. Ask yourself, "Where do I get my encouragement, or discouragement, from?" Does it depress you when the stock market takes a jolt or when you hear other troubling economic news? If we are troubled when the world begins to shake, it is a revelation of what we have been building our lives on.

Hebrews twelve declares that everything that can be shaken will be shaken. Even so, as that chapter also declares, we have a kingdom that cannot be shaken. If we will build our lives on that kingdom, all of the kingdoms of this world can fall apart, but we will stand strong and confident.

If the message of this book angers you, especially the first few chapters, you are probably in the most desperate need of its message. If the latter chapters scare you, you are probably one of those who most needs to read them. This is not to imply that you must agree with everything that is said here, or the way it is said. There will forever be only one man whose message was perfect—Jesus. There is only one book that is infallible—the Bible. Even so, I believe that this is a message that is on time and critical for our time.

Jim Bakker is himself a message that we need to hear. His life has been a prophecy. Few people have ever experienced the kind of extremes that he has. He rode to the heights of popularity and material prosperity, and then sank to the lowest levels of reproach and poverty as a federal prisoner cleaning toilets. To the surprise of many, Jim not only survived this ordeal, he emerged stronger with a greater clarity of vision, and a much greater resolve to walk in sound biblical truth.

I did not know Jim before he went to prison. The few times that I saw Jim's PTL program it seemed very foreign to me. If I was asked to describe it in one word, I would have probably used the word *unreal.* I did not believe that it presented real Christianity. Since Jim's release from prison I have gotten to know him quite well. I confess to being very surprised to find him to be one of the most genuine, and sincere, Christians that I have ever met. He is also one of the most passionate seekers of truth, and devoted lovers of Scripture. I am constantly amazed by his depth of wisdom and knowledge. At times I cannot believe that he is the same person who used to host the PTL program, and then I realize that he isn't!

By his own admission, Jim had to go to prison to have enough time for God to speak to him. He had become so busy in ministry that he did not have time for God. If we will hear the message of Jim's life, we may be able to judge ourselves lest we be judged (1 Cor. 11:31). Jim had to be stripped of everything but God in order to truly learn that he did not need anything by God.

The Lord does not want this to happen to us, but it will, for our own good, if we do not hear the message of Jim's life and change many of our ways. Many churches, ministries, and individual Christians have been betrothed to Christ but are married to the spirit of the world. Many have already suffered shipwreck, and many others are drifting closer to the reefs. They will hit them if they do not make some very radical course changes. The message of this book, and the message of Jim's life, is intended to save us from the disasters that many are still headed for. It can even save many from the ultimate disaster—worshiping the beast.

The world can look at Jim Bakker's past and have good excuse not to listen to him. The early church could have looked at the apostles the same way. Did they not deny the Lord, abandon Him in His time of greatest need? Men could have had a greater excuse not to hear the apostle Paul. Did he not even persecute the church? However, those who come to truly know God come to understand that His primary business in this world is redemption. He loves revealing His strength through those who are weak, His wisdom through those who are foolish, and His nobility through those who have been shamed. Therefore, those who love His truth will also love redemption. If we know God's power of redemption in our own life, how can we keep holding others in bondage to their past?

I have watched Jim closely for the years since his release from prison. I knew that he was changed, but the changes that come from such circumstances are not always lasting, especially when the circumstances change. With Jim they have lasted. Every time I see him, I feel that he is closer to the Lord, has an even stronger grasp of truth, and has an even deeper love for people. After all that he has been through, I have yet to hear a bitter word come from him concerning anything that happened to him, or about anyone who betrayed or attacked him. I have seen him challenged by some of the most difficult circumstances without compromising the fruit of the Spirit. That is genuine Christianity, and Jim is one of the most genuine Christians that I know.

One of the great encouragements to me concerning the present state of the church has been the way that believers almost across the spectrum of Christianity have embraced Jim Bakker since his release from prison. Whether it has been Pentecostal, Charismatic, Baptist, traditional, or non-traditional churches, he has been constantly introduced to standing ovations.

He is listened to with genuine openness and respect. Large stadiums have been filled by people wanting to hear what he has to say. That has been a great encouragement. I have had Jim share in our conferences, our home congregation, and our school of ministry a number of times. I have watched people grow dramatically every time he comes—even those who disagree with him. As I told our ministry team, even if I disagreed with all of Jim's conclusions, I would still have him come. He imparts such an esteem for the Word of God, and for truth, that I know those who listen to him inevitably go away with a greater devotion to seek the Lord and know His word.

In the past, the church has not generally treated its leaders who have made mistakes very well, but it must if we do not want to fall ourselves, which Paul explained in Galatians 6:1:

> Brethren, even if a man is caught in any trespass, you who are spiritual, restore such a one in a spirit of gentleness; each one looking to yourself, lest you too be tempted. (NASB)

Here we are commanded to restore those who are caught in "any trespass" so that we will not ourselves be tempted. To *restore* means much more than just to forgive. Restoration is also a word that is linked strongly to these times. This is not just the end of the age; it is the beginning of the age in which Christ will reign over the earth and His people with Him. This reign is for the "restoration of all things" as Peter declared in his second sermon after the Day of Pentecost (Acts 3:20–21).

The church has been given the greatest message of hope that the world has ever known. The Lord is coming back! He is not coming back just to get even with those who rejected Him, though they will certainly mourn when they see Him. He is not coming back to destroy the world—He is coming back to restore it to its original condition of paradise. What we are coming to is not just an end—it is the beginning!

Even if you completely disagree with the message of this book, it is important for you to read it. Even if you completely agree with it, I encourage you to seek an even deeper understanding of it. At the very least, this will help you to sink your own roots deeper into the Word of God. It could save you from many troubles. It could save your life. The Lord's sheep know His voice, and we must all know His voice for ourselves.

I encourage you not to judge the entire book by any single section of it but by its whole. This message is going to go forth, and it is going to have a significant impact on the church.

—Rick Joyner
Founder of Morningstar Ministries
Author of The Final Quest
August, 1998

PART I

The Final Warning

1

A Reluctant Messenger

I fidgeted nervously as the officer at the airport security checkpoint stopped the conveyer belt and scanned the X-ray image of my briefcase. The man stared at the screen, glanced icily at me, then fixed his gaze again on the gray monitor in front of him. For a moment I wondered if perhaps he had guessed that I was carrying a package that was potentially far more earthshaking than any bomb he might ever discover.

Without saying a word, the security officer restarted the conveyer, and in a matter of seconds my briefcase emerged and slid down the stainless steel counter. I quickly gathered my carry-on luggage and, as discreetly as possible, looked inside the briefcase to make sure the package was intact. I shuffled some papers next to the volatile materials, zipped the case shut, and hurried toward the customs station, where I answered a few questions concerning the reason for my trip, and my bag received a thorough search by a U.S. Customs officer. When I finally boarded my flight to Singapore on December 17, 1997, I slumped into my seat like a fugitive on the run.

Before stowing my briefcase, I retrieved the package and held it warily in my hands. *Why, God?* I thought as I stared at the package. *Why have You given me this assignment? You know I'll do anything You instruct me to do; but I confess, I'm scared. I don't really want to be the one to deliver this. But I have promised to obey no matter what the cost, so I'll do it.*

I leaned back in the comfortable seat of the 747 and closed my eyes as I waited for takeoff. It would be a long flight, nearly thirty-two hours including transfers, as the huge airship carried its five hundred passengers literally to the other side of the world. Sometime tomorrow I was scheduled for a brief layover in Taiwan, then on to Hong Kong, the newly acquired jewel of the People's Republic of China. From there it was a direct flight to Singapore, another former British colony and one of the richest societies on the face of the earth. Yet even as I pressed the recline button on my seat, I knew that the very fabric of Singapore's society was about to change.

Indeed, life on our entire planet was about to change.

Nearly a day and a half later, as I unpacked my luggage in a hotel room in Singapore, I took the package out of my briefcase and opened its contents. Inside a leather three-ring notebook was a message—the most explosive, exciting, frightening, yet exhilarating message I had ever received from God. The message had been ten years in the making; five of those years I had spent in a federal prison while God got my undivided attention and brought me to the point where I was willing not only to hear this message and accept it as the truth, but to proclaim it.

After my release from prison, the message remained sealed in my heart, burning within me, refining my own thinking and lifestyle. It was not until a few days before Christmas 1997 that God gave me the go-ahead to speak it aloud.

It was not the kind of message most people want to hear. It was a warning from God, and I felt that He had called me—of all people—to sound the alarm.

A CHANGED MAN

A decade earlier, I would have been preparing for a gala celebration at Heritage USA, the twenty-three-hundred-acre Christian retreat center I had headed in Fort Mill, South Carolina, in the 1970s and 1980s. I would have been getting ready to preach a much different sort of message—a message that said, "God wants you to be happy. God wants you to be rich. God wants you to prosper, even as your soul prospers."

I preferred happy messages; I liked people to go away feeling good after hearing me speak or watching one of our PTL television programs beamed by satellite all around the world. On our television network I did not want to hear any bad news. I would not allow my staff to book a guest who was sick or having severe financial, emotional, or spiritual problems. If a guest had not come out on "the victory side of life," he was not asked to be on the air. I was not being cruel; I just wanted everyone to praise the Lord and be happy. Like a car salesman, I did not want anyone to see any defects in our "product." I wanted to put God and His people in a positive light. Although my own life was not perfect, and my wife and I at times were going through extreme marital stress, I still felt I had a responsibility to protect God's reputation somehow. I tried desperately to project an ideal image: "Everyone is happy; no problems; everything is grand; life is wonderful."

For at least half of my ministry, I had presented a Disneyland gospel, in which the good guys always get rich, the bad guys are defeated, and everyone lives happily ever after. I lived in, and attempted to promote, a spiritual fantasyland, where God's people are always blessed materially, physically, and of course, spiritually.

But by 1997 my message had changed. Now my heart burned with a new, imperative word. But it was not a message I would have chosen to carry. Actually, it was not even my message anymore. It was the Lord's. In prison, God had not only shown me how wrong my thinking had been, He had set my heart ablaze with the gospel I should have been preaching all along.

Still, I was reluctant to speak the word God had seared into my heart. After all, who wants to be known as a prophet of gloom? Who wants to be the bearer of bad news? My temperament is one that cries out for people to like me. I have never enjoyed confrontations, arguments, or battles (although I've been in more than my share). My personality is that of a peacemaker. It is simply not my nature to bring a negative message. My desire has always been to bring joy and encouragement, and that is what I tried to do in a variety of ways during most of my ministry.

Yet now, as I studied the Scripture and contemplated the warnings I believed God had placed in my heart and mind, I came to realize that even this dire word was a message of hope, an encouragement for the body of Christ, the family of God, the true church. But it was *genuine* hope based on sound doctrine, rather than foolish spiritual slogans propagated by pleasure-loving disciples. This message had been formulated by considering a mass of scriptural evidence rather than contrived concepts derived from one or two obscure passages or the twisting or shading of biblical truths to one's personal interpretation.

For those who heed this word from God, it will be life; those who do not pay attention to God's final warning will be sealing their own tombs.

A CHANGED MESSAGE

In a nutshell, the new message was this: the era of prosperity is over; perilous times are upon us, the end of the age is at hand. Get ready, not just for the second coming of Jesus Christ, but for a worldwide shaking, a sifting of epic proportions, far more devastating than anything men and women on earth have ever before experienced.

The specifics of God's message stirring in my heart grew more ominous with each passing day. I shuddered when I thought of what the Lord had shown me. Catastrophic calamities are coming upon the earth, not one of these days in the distant future, but soon—now! Torrential rains, unsettling weather patterns, violent storms, floods, famines, droughts, earthquakes increasing in frequency and intensity, volcanic eruptions, and a host of other signs of the times Jesus told us to watch for are happening *now.*

Moreover, the fulfillment of the prophecies in the book of Revelation are imminent: prophecies concerning the sun being darkened for long periods of time, wreaking devastation upon the earth; millions of people being killed by meteors impacting the earth, mountains falling into the sea, large portions of land being scorched; worldwide economic chaos and collapse, people willing to trade their treasures of a lifetime for a piece of bread to eat . . . all of this and more the Lord showed me, with the warning that these things will be happening soon and we need to get ready. As Jesus said concerning His second coming and the end of the world, "When you see all these things, know that it is near—at the doors! Assuredly, I say to you, this generation will by no means pass away till all these things take place" (Matt. 24:33–34 NKJV).

Most important, as I studied the words of Jesus for hours on end in prison—often sixteen hours a day, not closing my Bible until the sun came up and it was time for me to go to work—I came to a conclusion that shook me to my very foundations, a conclusion that was contrary to the teaching I had always accepted as fact and had presented to millions of people on television. But when I studied Scripture and allowed it to speak for itself, I realized, to my horror, that Jesus was not coming back *before* all these catastrophic calamities came upon the earth.

I had always believed that Christians would escape the difficult days our world is about to endure. I had been taught, and had preached, that before the awful tribulation period takes place, there would be a *rapture,* a great "catching away," in which all Christians would be caught up together to meet Jesus in the air. From there He would take us to heaven and we would, of course, all live happily ever after.

But as I pored over the Word of God, the Holy Spirit used the Scriptures to convince me that I, like so many of my former colleagues, had merely been preaching what I had heard other preachers say. I passed along things I had read in somebody else's books, rather than carefully examining the Scriptures to see what God had to say about the days in which we are now living. I had to admit that my hope in a pretribulational rapture was not based on an accurate understanding of the Bible, but on other people's opinions and ideas.

All of this weighed heavily on my mind as I prepared to preach in Singapore. I could see the tabloid headlines now: "Bakker Predicts End of the World—Earth to Be Destroyed by Giant Meteor." I had been caricatured often enough in the past two decades; I really did not care to become fodder for another round of jokes. On the other hand, when I lost Heritage USA and went to prison, I lost much more than houses, cars, and other material possessions. I lost my dignity, my pride, and my reputation. Maybe that's why God had selected me to carry such a potentially laughable message: I had no reputation left to protect.

Not that I welcomed being considered a spiritual kook. We've all seen sincere but misguided people carrying placards announcing, "The End Is Near" or, "Prepare to Meet Thy God." Hollywood loves to portray weirdos in long robes and bare feet, tramping up and down the posh streets of America's party towns, proclaiming a message of gloom and doom. Yet, ironically, I could identify more with the passion of the barefoot placard-bearer than I could the message now being proclaimed by many of America's most popular pulpiteers.

Who Wants to Hear Bad News?

By and large, most of the church in the United States does not want to hear an apocalyptic message. It wants a message of health and wealth, hope, healing, and financial prosperity mixed with a measure of blathering psychobabble focused on getting our needs met. Rarely does anyone talk about sacrifice, repentance of sin, or our failure to be what God has called us to be. When, for example, was the last time you heard a message on the cost of discipleship? When was the last time you heard someone preach on the judgment of God or the horrors of hell? How often have you heard a message encouraging Christians to bear one another's burdens?

No, we simply want to be happy Christians. Seeds of the prosperity gospel I helped plant years ago have now borne fruit . . . and the fruit is poisonous.

While I was in prison, God had showed me the error of my ways—not simply the mistakes in my lifestyle and attitudes, but more fundamentally, He showed me how wrong I had been in my understanding of the Bible. He showed me that although He has promised to bless His people, He does not promise to make all Christians rich in this world's goods. After my release from prison, I wrote a book called *I Was Wrong,* which chronicled how and why I had misled millions of people to seek after material gain, while I had missed God's truth in my own life.

When I began to proclaim that message across America in television interviews, in pastors' conferences, and from pulpits wherever I was invited to speak, many of my friends became upset. I was rocking their boat, and several let me know they did not appreciate it. One person labeled those who did not believe in the prosperity message as an "anti-prosperity cult." Another said, "If you don't believe that Jesus Christ was wealthy when He walked on the earth, you are a heretic." Others were kinder, simply telling me, "Oh, Jim, you'll balance back, once you've had a chance to get reacclimated to where the church is today."

God forbid! I've been to the top of that mountain made of sugar candy, and I now know that when the shaking comes and the hard rains come—and they are coming soon—that mountain will dissolve in an instant, and those whose hope is built upon it will be swept away in the syrupy tide.

SHOCKING CONFIRMATIONS

As I prepared to step behind the pulpit in Singapore, the dual messages I carried within my heart—that of the dangers of falling in love with material things instead of Jesus, and the message that the world was about to be shaken like never before—vibrated in my chest like a volcano ready to erupt. Bad enough that I had to be the bearer of bad news, but why, O God, did I have to start here, in one of the richest city-nations on earth, a place where the prosperity message had been preached and believed for years?

The services in Singapore were held in the city's large Indoor Stadium, an arena-like facility that seated thousands. We enjoyed an uplifting time of praise-and-worship music and then it was time for me to speak. As Rick Seaward, the host pastor, introduced me, I was shocked at his words. He said somberly, "God has brought Jim Bakker here to bring the last warning to Singapore."

I could hardly believe my ears! The last warning? That's all I needed to hear. I was already nervous knowing I had to warn the people of Singapore about the dangers concerning the love of money and material things. I had not discussed my message with the pastor. Nor had he asked me to speak on any particular subject, although I knew that the main reason he had invited me to Singapore was the destructive emphasis on prosperity that had been propagated in his homeland. I was planning to speak to that issue. Now, added to that burden, the pastor had unwittingly confirmed the word the Lord had been speaking to me, that it was time for the urgent message God had given me to be made public. The contents of the package in my briefcase would soon be exposed for all the world to accept or reject.

Actually, the pastor's introduction was the last straw in a series of recent confirmations I had encountered. On the plane a flight attendant had handed me a copy of the December 16, 1997, edition of *USA Today*. As I idly thumbed through the paper, a headline grabbed my attention. "Volcanoes stir concerns about L.A. water supply," the paper practically shouted at me. The Associated Press article said, "Recent earthquakes in the eastern Sierra Nevada, near the resort community of Mammoth Lakes, have raised fears of a volcanic eruption and the possible disruption of water that flows hundreds of miles southwest to Los Angeles."[1]

The article continued:

Geologists don't know when or how severe a volcanic eruption will be, but their concerns have been raised by recent earthquakes, believed to be caused by magma (the semi-liquid material below the earth's surface) fracturing rock or pressurizing liquid four miles underground. After a magnitude–4.9 earthquake struck the Mammoth Lakes area Nov. 30 [1997]—the strongest of more than 8,000 quakes since the summer— U.S. Geological Survey (USGS) scientists came close to declaring a yellow volcano "watch" for the region, indicating intense unrest.[2]

Intense unrest! As I read the report, I could not help feeling tense myself. I recalled what Jesus said: "When you see a preponderance of earthquakes in various places, get ready, because I'm coming back" (Matt. 24:7, paraphrased).

Other confirmations were quick in coming. While I was in prison, God had shown me that the economic systems of our world were about to take a tumble. Two years prior to my trip to Singapore, Pastor Seaward had given a prophetic word that the economy of his country would collapse in two years. On the day I stood to speak, the collapse had already begun— exactly two years to the week from the time Pastor Seaward had made that announcement. Many investors lost as much as seventy-five cents on the dollar, and some of them had invested millions. A few counted their losses in the billions of dollars as stocks continued to plunge on the Far East markets. One of the local pastors informed me that days before my arrival, three of the wealthiest businessmen in Singapore had committed suicide because of their enormous losses.

Signs in the weather patterns also confirmed what I knew in my heart. One report after another linked billions of dollars worth of property damage along the California coastline to weather patterns caused by El Niño, the warm water currents of the Pacific Ocean that create havoc in the air currents. Sunny California had turned to cloudy California as day after day of incessant rains saturated the soil to dangerous levels. By late 1997 Americans had become almost numb to more El Niño-related weather reports. But our nation was not alone in experiencing unusual weather patterns. The day I spoke in Singapore, I picked up that day's newspaper and read: "Moscow witnessed its coldest day in history on Tuesday."

"The Ukraine, a record minus thirty-five degrees Celsius." Meanwhile, in Mexico, "More than sixty people have died in a wave of savage weather that struck most of the country."[3]

It got worse.

The following day, Saturday, December 20, 1997, I opened the *Herald Tribune,* the leading newspaper in Singapore (published in conjunction with *The New York Times* and *The Washington Post,* and another headline jumped off the front page: "The Hunt For Meteor Is on in Greenland." The article, based on information supplied by the Niels Bohr Institute, associated with the University of Copenhagen, Denmark, in cooperation with the Tycho Brahe Planetarium, reported: "In the dead of the Arctic night on Dec. 9, flashes of light as bright as nuclear blasts lighted up the southern tip of Greenland, and Danish scientists have begun a search for what they believe was a gigantic meteor impact."[4]

According to the article, scientists thought the main impact of the meteor had occurred on the Greenland ice cap about fifty kilometers northeast of the coastal airport of Narsarsuag. Deep snowfall made their exploration more difficult, but what they had observed was disconcerting.

"The Bohr Institute reported, 'The flashes observed in conjunction with the meteorite were so bright as to turn night into daylight at a distance of 100 kilometers, and can be compared to the light of a nuclear explosion in the atmosphere.'"[5] The institute went on to stress that the flash had been caused by natural causes.

As I read the article, I sat in my chair, stunned. It felt as though every drop of blood had drained from my body, and I could not move. A few days before embarking on my trip to Singapore, I had viewed a video, *Fire From the Sky,*[6] which featured the work of renowned astronomers Gene Shoemaker and David Levy. Together, Shoemaker and Levy had shocked the scientific world in 1993, when they discovered a comet and a series of asteroids on a collision course with the planet Jupiter. The comet did indeed impact Jupiter, in a rapid progression of sixteen direct hits over six days. The impacts created a fireball the size of Earth. The energy released by these impacts was equivalent to one atomic bomb going off every second for several years, and the devastation to the planet caused a debris cloud that rose over two thousand miles high and hung there for more than a year.

Scientists estimate that if a similar meteor ever impacted Earth, millions of people would die; the dust and debris cloud, hundreds of times worse than that created by the volcanic eruption of Mount Saint Helens, would plunge the earth into darkness for more than a year. We have already experienced a few known "near misses" in which asteroids came close to colliding with Earth.

My, Lord! These things are happening already, I thought as I put down the paper and tried to regain my composure.

A NEW MANDATE

That weekend in Singapore I presented the message God had given me in prison, a mandate to warn the church of Jesus Christ that we have become so enamored with material prosperity that we are in danger of missing what God is doing in these last days.

Quite candidly, I fear that many Christians have fallen more in love with this present world, and the things of this world, than with Jesus. Yet the Bible warns us:

> Do not love the world or the things in the world. If anyone loves the world, the love of the Father is not in him. For all that is in the world—the lust of the flesh, the lust of the eyes, and the pride of life—is not of the Father but is of the world. And the world is passing away, and the lust of it; but he who does the will of God abides forever. (1 John 2:15–17 NKJV)

Sadly, I must take responsibility for some of the complacency I see in parts of the body of Christ today. For it was through my misguided, mistaken, materialistic theology—the health-and-wealth gospel, "name it and claim it," prosperity gospel, or whatever else you care to label it—that many sincere Christians were misled into hoping for riches in this world rather than in heaven. Consequently, and it grieves me to say this, I see far too few Christians nowadays who are heavenly minded.

On the contrary, most contemporary Christians are too attached to this world. They not only ignore signs of our Lord's soon return, they have been lulled into thinking that it is okay, perhaps even preferable, to lay up treasures in this world rather than in heaven. Though few would admit it, we have subtly adopted the world's slogans as our creeds:

- You only go around once in life.

- Go for the gusto.

- Life is short, live it up.

- The one who dies with the most toys wins.

Many younger Christians say, "I know Jesus is coming back, but I hope He doesn't come soon. After all, I'd like to enjoy this life for a while. I have my career to think about, I'd like to get married" . . . and on and on. Those things may be fine, but when our love for this world surpasses our love for Jesus, it is a clear indication that our priorities are out of whack.

Meanwhile, we have compromised our families, our faith, and our future in the futile quest to acquire more material possessions. The end-time prophecies recorded in Revelation are coming to pass right before our eyes, yet many Christians are so drunk and sated by the pleasures of this life, they are ignoring the red warning flags all around us.

That is what compels me to write this book: to warn you of the things to come, and to urge you to fall in love with Jesus. In the pages to follow I will reveal to you how I came to know what God is saying about the times in which we live. I will retrace my personal road to Revelation, in which my own eyes were opened concerning the dangers of prosperity in light of the approaching apocalypse. And I will describe in detail where I believe we are on God's timetable, and some of the things that will soon come to pass.

Please understand, I am not a prophet in the predictive sense of that title. I am simply a student of Scripture, one who has studied intensely for the past ten years as God has prepared my heart and mind to present this message.

Nor do I wish to be an alarmist. But as you will see in the chapters to follow, some of the things I will describe are, in fact, more than alarming. They are terrifying. Yet at the same time they are encouraging, because Jesus said, "Now when these things begin to happen, look up and lift up your heads, because your redemption draws near" (Luke 21:28 NKJV).

The confidence I have in the truth of that statement is also part of what motivates me to impart this message to you. I do not want you to be caught off guard at this crucial juncture in human history. After listing the apocalyptic signs of His return, Jesus put it this way: "But take heed to yourselves, lest your hearts be weighed down with carousing, drunkenness, and cares of this life, and that Day come on you unexpectedly" (Luke 21:34 NKJV).

I have no doubt that this message, in part or in whole, will be panned by some people and misconstrued by others. You may choose to mock, laugh, or make fun of me or this message. You may write me off as another extremist. That is your prerogative. But when the earth begins to crumble beneath our feet, it may be too late for any more warnings.

Would it not be better for you to consider now the possibility that what I am about to tell you is an accurate presentation of the near future? If only a small portion of what God has shown me through His Word comes to pass in our lifetimes, it will be more devastating, more terrifying, than the worst horror movie ever imagined. *Now* is the time to get ready.

If you consider this message seriously and carefully examine the scriptural evidence, it will help you align your priorities in these last days. It might just save your life and the lives of your loved ones. More important, it will point you to the One—the only One—Jesus Christ, who can save your soul eternally.

PART II

The Prosperity Message:
A False Gospel

2

My Road to Revelation

Early in my incarceration in federal prison, I was walking across the prison yard when I noticed a rather disheveled young inmate approaching me on the sidewalk. I tried to ignore him, as I had been instructed to do by my prison mentors. "If you hope to survive in prison," they told me, "it is best not to get involved in a confrontation." I was warned that I could get into a fight, or worse yet, I could be killed for invading another inmate's space. Consequently, anytime I was in the "public" areas of the compound, I usually walked hurriedly with my eyes riveted to the ground, hoping to avoid making eye contact with anyone.

This young man, however, would not allow me to pass without a confrontation. He came right up to me and stopped me on the sidewalk. "Hey, Bakker," he said. "I have a question for you."

The boy seemed sad and distraught more than dangerous. "Okay, what's your question?" I replied nervously, not sure I really wanted to know.

He told me that before his imprisonment he had watched a television preacher who encouraged his viewers to send in money as a step of faith in God's power to bless them. "That TV preacher said that if I gave a thousand-dollar pledge, I would get a huge return on my money. Well, I made that pledge and nothing happened."

The boy's words had an accusatory tone, as though he were accusing me, too, of letting him down. "Why didn't God answer my prayer?" he asked. "If He did it for all those other people, why didn't He do it for me? The TV preacher said that everything was going to work out okay, that I was going to get a good job, make a lot of money. Nothing happened. In fact, everything went wrong in my life and I wound up here in prison."

As I looked at the boy's face, I saw a combination of disappointment, hurt, discouragement, and anger toward God . . . and toward me, since in his mind, at least, I represented God.

His words indicted me. They crushed me like a wrecking ball falling on my heart. For the first time I saw the other side of the message I had preached to so many people at Heritage USA and over the airwaves on the PTL television network. Prior to this, all I had ever heard were glorious testimonies of how God had financially blessed people who had given money to PTL. Now, suddenly, I stood face to face with living evidence that the principles I had preached so passionately did not work for everyone. In the years to follow I would come to realize that this young man represented an entire category of people who had given to God's work, expecting miraculous returns on their money, but who had in fact received little or no tangible return they could put in their bank accounts.

My heart ached for the boy, but I did not know how to answer him. I mumbled something about how much God really loved him, and tried to hurry on my way.

Although I had not been the preacher the boy had heard on television, I felt responsible for the prosperity message's negative effects in his life, because I had preached a give-to-get message too. I had encouraged people to send money to our ministry in anticipation that God would bless them. I was not intentionally deceiving the audience. I honestly believed that the Bible taught the hundredfold blessing, that God would return thirty, sixty, and even a hundred times the amount someone gave to His work.

Now I wondered, *How many other people watched my programs and had experiences like this boy? How many others had given to God's work, thinking God was going to give them a 100 percent return on their gift, only to be disappointed?*

The boy's words haunted me throughout the first two years of my lengthy prison sentence. But because I was still struggling through my own valley of despair and loneliness, shell-shocked from the events that had landed me in prison, I had few answers for him or for myself.

THE DREAM THAT CHANGED MY LIFE

As I languished in my cell, I could not even hear God's voice anymore. I truly felt He had abandoned me, that perhaps my sins were too awful, the repercussions too great. I tried praying, but it seemed that God did not hear me. I even prayed what I now call "stupid prayers." I would say, "Please, God, make the leaves on this plant wiggle." Or, "Please send an angel to me. Do anything. Just let me know You haven't given up on me." The leaves never budged and an angel never came . . . that I know of.

I began crying out to God, "Please talk to me! Show me something, anything, Lord. Just let me know that You still care."

Then one night I had a dream unlike anything I had ever experienced before, a dream that totally transformed my life. The colors in the dream were so vivid, it was like dreaming in blazing Technicolor! In this dream, I was sitting next to Jesus. He was dressed in white and blue and He seemed to have a brilliance and depth like diamonds—yet like nothing I had ever seen in my life! (I'm now convinced that the colors of heaven far exceed anything mere mortals have experienced here on earth.)

As I sat there, Jesus reached up and pulled out a slice of His eye. It looked like a contact lens. He reached over and gently put the thin slice of His eye into mine and said, "I want you to see everything and everyone through My eyes."

Then, just as suddenly as the dream began, it was over and I woke up. I knew that something supernatural had happened, but what did it mean? How could I see everyone and everything through the eyes of Jesus?

The minute I woke up from the dream, I knew exactly what I had to do. The answer came, whether from God or my conscience or my own mind, I couldn't tell. But it was crystal clear: *I had to go to the Word of God. I must read every word Jesus said, because if I know Him and His words, then I can see everything through His eyes.*

I began reading the gospels every day, concentrating on the words of Jesus. From the prison chapel library I got a red-letter edition of the Bible, the words written in red indicating the words of Jesus. I literally wrote down every word Christ spoke as recorded in the Scriptures. Then I wrote a condensed version of the verses to help me remember them. For instance, "Love God," "Love your neighbor," "Do not sin."

As I studied the Scripture, I began to see things in the Bible I had never seen before. One of the most obvious reasons was that I was now taking time to study, not simply picking up the Bible for a quick dose of inspiration. In the past I had naturally gravitated toward those passages in the Bible that supported what I wanted to say or do. I found it easy to skip certain verses, passages, and sometimes even whole books, such as the book of Revelation. I had made up my mind now, however, that I would not skip over any part of the Scriptures. And I was going to ask God all the difficult questions I had skirted during my busy years. I had time—nothing but time—to listen and learn from the Lord.

The more I studied the words of Jesus, the more convinced I became that much of what is being presented as "gospel" in many contemporary Christian circles is not consistent with the actual message of Jesus Christ. Worse yet, as I read, dissected, and wrote down the words of Christ, the study raised serious questions in my own mind concerning many of the things I had believed and taught while at PTL.

For instance, I had taught for years that Christianity was not a religion of "dos and don'ts." But when I began to examine the recorded words of Christ closely, I learned that much of what Jesus expected of me fell into the category of "do this" or "don't do that." Jesus was not encouraging legalism; He was simply instructing me how to live.

I discovered at least three hundred specific instructions in the words of Jesus. When taken at their face value, the words of Jesus clearly explain what a Christian is supposed to do and not to do.

"EVERY WORD"

One of the most important principles I learned from the words of Jesus was something I had read hundreds of times yet had somehow missed. After Jesus had been fasting in the wilderness for forty days, Satan tempted Him to turn a stone into bread to satisfy His hunger. Jesus resisted the temptation and rebuked the devil by quoting an Old Testament passage, Deuteronomy 8:3, saying, "It is written, 'Man shall not live by bread alone, but by every word that proceeds from the mouth of God'" (Matt. 4:4 NKJV). I had read this passage, quoted it, and preached on it, but suddenly the word *every* practically leaped off the page toward me.

I had missed the point of Jesus' statement. He was not saying that we are to live by one biblical principle; nor was He implying that it is okay to pick out our favorite verses from the Bible and make those our guiding lights. *"Every* word," He said.

While in prison, I heard a guest on Dr. James Dobson's radio program. The gist of what the guest said was, "One of the problems with our preaching and teaching nowadays is that we have too many 'longhorn' sermons. A longhorn sermon is a point here and a point there, and a lot of bull in between!"

I chuckled at the man's joke, but I began to realize that I had been guilty of preaching longhorn sermons. As my ministry had gotten bigger and busier, I had fallen into the trap of taking a verse here and a verse there and making the Bible say what I wanted, rather than what God wants. I am now convinced that one of the reasons false doctrine has infiltrated many churches today is that we have taken verses out of context and built our theologies on them.

In Matthew 4:4, Jesus says that we are to live by *every* word of God; we are to take the Scriptures as a whole rather than build our theologies on a particular verse or phrase that suits our needs at the moment. When I took the time to search the Scriptures, I discovered that God's Word is consistent with itself from Genesis to Revelation.

Maybe that's why I was so shocked when I discovered what Jesus had to say about money.

A FRESH REVELATION

To my surprise, after months of studying Jesus, I concluded that He did not have one good thing to say about money. Most of Jesus' statements about riches, wealth, and material gain were negative. Even The Prodigal Son, one of my favorite stories Jesus told, took on new meaning when I noticed that the story began with the younger brother saying to the father, "Give me! Give me my part of the inheritance" (Luke 15:12). He didn't even say, "Please give me." He simply demanded his portion of his father's wealth.

Before long that young man landed in the pigpen. I began to see that the fastest route to the pigpen begins with "Give me." And as I often tell audiences today, the fastest route to the "big pen," the federal penitentiary, often begins with the same phrase: "Give me!"

I was amazed at this "new" revelation, but beyond that, I was deeply concerned. As the true impact of Jesus' words regarding money impacted my heart and mind, I became physically nauseated. I realized I had been teaching the opposite of what Jesus had said. That is what broke my heart; when I came to the awareness that I had actually been contradicting Christ, I was horrified.

For years I had embraced and espoused a gospel that skeptics had branded as a "prosperity gospel." I didn't mind the label; on the contrary, I was proud of it. "You're absolutely right! I preach it and live it," I would say to critics and friends alike. "I believe in a God who wants to bless His people. Look at all the rich saints in the Old Testament. And the New Testament clearly says that above all, God wants us to prosper even as our souls prosper. If your soul is prospering, you should be prospering materially as well!"

I even got to the point where I was teaching people at PTL,

Don't pray, "Lord, Your will be done," when you are praying for health or wealth. You already know it is God's will for you to have those things! To ask God to confirm His will in a matter, when He has already told you what His will is, is an insult to God. It is as though you don't really trust Him, or believe that He is as good as His Word. Instead of praying, "Thy will be done," when you want a new car, just claim it. Pray specifically; tell God what kind you want, and be sure to specify what options and what color you want too!

Such arrogance! Such foolishness! Such sin! The Bible says we are not to presume upon God. We should not even say that we are going to a certain city tomorrow, but we should say, "If the Lord wills, we shall live and do this or that" (James 4:15 NKJV). Sadly, not long ago, I heard a well-known television preacher replicating my mistake. The preacher told his audience, "You don't need to pray The Lord's Prayer. That was only for the disciples. It is a lack of faith to pray, 'Lord, Thy will be done.' Just tell God what you want."

What a shock to realize that I had helped propagate an impostor, not a true gospel, but another gospel—a gospel that subtly implied and often overtly stated that God wants you to be rich! Christians should have the best because we are children of God—"King's Kids," as I often put it. And shouldn't the King's Kids have the best this world has to offer?

The more I studied the Bible, however, I had to admit that the prosperity message did not line up with the tenor of Scripture. My heart was crushed to think that I had led so many people astray. I was appalled that I could have been so wrong, and I was deeply grateful that God had not struck me dead as a false prophet!

WHAT DOES JESUS REALLY SAY ABOUT MONEY?

How could I have taught and even written books on the subject of how to get rich, when Jesus spoke so clearly about the dangers of earthly riches? One of the statements of Jesus that kept echoing in my head and heart was in The Parable of the Sower, where Jesus said that "the cares of this world, the deceitfulness of riches, and the desires for other things entering in choke the word, and it becomes unfruitful" (Mark 4:19 NKJV). *The deceitfulness of riches!* The more I thought about it, the more I had to admit that I had fallen into that snare. I had allowed the quest for material possessions, the deceitfulness of riches, and desires for other things to choke the Word of God in my own life, and in the lives of my family members and coworkers. As PTL grew larger, and our ministry more widespread, I had a financial tiger by the tail; just coming up with enough money to meet the daily budgets dominated my thoughts and my time.

Sitting in my dimly lit prison cell, I decided to dig into the Scriptures further to see what else Jesus had to say about money. For example, He said,

Do not store up for yourself treasures on earth, where moth and rust destroy, and where thieves break in and steal. But store up for yourselves treasures in heaven, where moth and rust do not destroy, and where thieves do not break in and steal. For where your treasure is, there your heart will be also. (Matt. 6:19–21 NIV)

It wasn't long until I began to understand that the real issue was all about *heart*. Jesus wants our love, 100 percent. The love of money and earthly treasures diverts our attention from Him. It is a thief, a harlot—the false lover—that steals our attention and hearts away from God.

Jesus makes this very clear in Matthew's gospel. "No one can serve two masters. Either he will hate the one and love the other, or he will be devoted to the one and despise the other. You cannot serve both God and Money" (6:24 NIV). In that same passage I discovered that God's priorities were much different than mine had been.

Jesus said,

> Therefore I tell you, do not worry about your life, what you will eat or drink; or about your body, what you will wear. Is not life more important than food, and the body more important than clothes? . . . So do not worry, saying, "What shall we eat?" or "What shall we drink?" or "What shall we wear?" For the pagans run after all these things, and your heavenly Father knows that you need them. But seek first his kingdom and his righteousness, and all these things will be given to you as well. (Matt. 6:25, 31–33 NIV)

How could I have been teaching people how to get rich when Jesus said we are not even to worry about what we are going to eat, drink, or wear?

Jesus had little good to say about the rich. In fact, He said, "But woe to you who are rich, / for you have already received your comfort" (Luke 6:24 NIV). Prosperity teaching emphasizes comfort and ease. There is little discussion of denying oneself. But real Christianity involves sacrifice, and Jesus makes it clear that for true followers of Christ, self-denial is a basic ingredient. "Then Jesus said to his disciples, 'If anyone would come after me, he must deny himself and take up his cross and follow me'" (Matt. 16:24 NIV). This verse dramatically illustrates the stark contrast between what Jesus taught and what I had been teaching. I had taught that Christians could have the best of both worlds, the best this world has to offer and heaven too. Yet Jesus said, "Deny yourself."

Today I certainly do not teach that Christians should live in poverty, or that God does not bless His people. But I can no longer teach people to seek after wealth when Jesus said it is almost impossible for the rich to enter into heaven.

Jesus taught, "How hard it is for the rich to enter the kingdom of God! Indeed, it is easier for a camel to go through the eye of a needle than for a rich man to enter the kingdom of God" (Luke 18:24–25 NIV). Unwittingly, I had tried to explain this verse away with the help of modern scholarship. I had taught people that the "eye of the needle" of which Jesus spoke was a low arch in the city walls common in the Holy Land. Supposedly, a camel carrying a heavy load had to get down on its knees to slip through the "eye of the needle." This was the explanation I had heard from other prosperity teachers whom I admired and respected, so I simply passed on their explanation as fact, without really examining the verse carefully. Nor had I consulted any Bible dictionaries or encyclopedias. If I had done so, I might have found that not a shred of reputable archeological or historical evidence supports the camel-through-the-arch theory.

I had always wondered how those camels could walk on their knees. In our Passion Play at Heritage USA, we had three camels, and they were some of the most cantankerous animals I had ever seen. We had a hard time getting them to walk across the stage, much less get down on their knees and walk.

When I took time to study the meaning of Jesus' words in the original Greek language, I discovered that Jesus was not talking about camels walking on their knees at all! The word He used was one commonly used to describe a *sewing needle,* not an archway. In other words, the verse meant exactly what it said: it may not be impossible for a rich man to enter heaven, but apart from a miracle of God, he doesn't stand a chance. Jesus emphasized how hard it is for a rich person to enter the kingdom of heaven, not because it is any more difficult for the Lord to save a wealthy person, but because so many rich people see themselves as self-sufficient, with no need of a Savior. No wonder Jesus referred to the deceitfulness of riches.

In The Parable of the Sower, Jesus warned again about the seed (the good news) that is so easily choked out in our lives by our love of money. "Now the ones that fell among thorns are those who, when they have heard, go out and are choked with cares, riches, and pleasures of life, and bring no fruit to maturity" (Luke 8:14 NKJV).

Jesus also cautioned, "Watch out! Be on your guard against all kinds of greed; a man's life does not consist in the abundance of his possessions" (Luke 12:15 NIV).

Even more sobering, I read where Jesus said that unless we forsake all that we have, we cannot be His disciples (Luke 14:33). The words of Jesus truly cut my heart like a two-edged sword. I was in a prison cell, determined not to run away from the Word anymore. I was determined to listen to the full counsel of Christ's teaching and no longer just focus on the words that felt good.

In almost every story Jesus told in which He refers to a rich person, Jesus placed the wealthy person in a negative context. For example, when Jesus told a story concerning the awfulness of eternity in hell without God, He told of Lazarus, a poor man, who went to heaven, and a rich man who went to hell (Luke 16:19–31).

Jesus did not dislike or avoid rich people. On the contrary, when He saw Zaccheus, the tax collector, perched in a tree to get a better look at Him, Jesus offered Zaccheus an up-close opportunity to get to know Him. Something about Jesus, however, caused Zaccheus immediately to realize the dichotomy created by his desiring a relationship with Christ and holding onto his ill-gotten gain. "And Zaccheus stopped and said to the Lord, 'Behold, Lord, half of my possessions I will give to the poor, and if I have defrauded anyone of anything, I will give back four times as much'" (Luke 19:8 NASB). Undoubtedly, Zaccheus made the right choice.

Contrary to encouraging people to seek riches, Jesus actually elevates the status of the poor. He loved the poor. In fact, He said that He came to preach the gospel to the poor. When Jesus saw the rich putting their gifts into the temple treasury and He also saw a poor widow put in two very small copper coins, Jesus was impressed not by the size of her gift, but by the size of her heart. "'I tell you the truth,' he said, 'this poor widow has put in more than all the others. All these people gave their gifts out of their wealth; but she out of her poverty put in all she had to live on'" (Luke 21:3–4 NIV). In Jesus' view it wasn't how much she had, but what she did with what she had that mattered.

In prosperity teaching, the poor are made to feel guilty. One prominent prosperity teacher proclaims, "How dare we be satisfied earning just enough to get us by?" Some teachers even go so far as to say that a person who is poor must not have enough faith, or worse yet, may have hidden sin in her life. Funny, Jesus didn't see it that way at all.

The more I studied the Bible, the more I had to face the awful truth: I had been preaching false doctrine for years and hadn't even known it. Tragically, too late, I recognized that at PTL I had done just the opposite of Jesus' words by teaching people to fall in love with money. Jesus never equated His blessings with material things, but I had. I laid so much emphasis upon materialism, I subtly encouraged people to put their hearts into things, rather than into Jesus. I should have taught them to fall in love with Jesus. He is the only One who will never leave us or forsake us when the money and possessions are gone.

When I realized the truth, I was deeply grieved and repented over my error. How could I have been so wrong? How could I have missed Christ's true message so completely? His statements about material possessions in general, and money in particular, were clear. How could I have had the audacity to twist Jesus' statements into the opposite of what He had taught?

I am now convinced that I did the body of Christ a great disservice. God can take care of His people. He promises to supply all our needs, and He has all the riches of heaven at His disposal. He can and does bless us, but our main focus should never be on material blessings. Our focus must be on Jesus and our total love for Him.

By preaching "another gospel," with its emphasis on ease of living, material wealth, and sensational miracles, prosperity preachers and teachers have unwittingly set the Christian community up for the arrival of the Antichrist.

3

Another Jesus, Another Gospel

In October 1995 I spoke at First Assembly of God Church in Fort Myers, Florida. It was one of my first speaking engagements after being released from prison. The pastor of the church, Dan Betzer, had written to me in prison and now welcomed me with open arms. That morning I shared how I had lost everything, but God had never left me. At the close of the service, I invited people who wanted to pray to come forward to the front of the sanctuary. Many people responded to the invitation.

I noticed one woman praying along with her young children. She was crying profusely, so I quickly knelt down in front of her and asked her if there was something I could pray with her about. I've learned the importance of listening to people and bearing their burdens. It's not enough to say, "God bless you, Sister (or Brother), go in peace" (James 2:15–16). We need to enter into their pain, to pray and believe God with them. We don't have to have all the answers; sometimes we just need to be good listeners.

That morning in Fort Myers, the woman, a first-time visitor to the church, began to tell me how her life had completely fallen apart. Her husband had walked out, leaving her to raise the children alone. A series of heartbreaking events had transpired in her life since then, the most recent of which was an auto accident in which her car was badly damaged. She sobbed, "I feel that God has turned His back on me. He must not love me anymore."

I well understood that woman's feelings of discouragement and abandonment. I had felt the same way when I went to prison and lost my home, cars, bank accounts, insurance policies, retirement money, my relationships with many "friends," and eventually, even my wife. According to my concepts of the gospel, these things should not have happened. Where was God?

Answer: the same place He had always been. He had not moved or changed His mind or His message. I was the one who had equated His material blessings with what I called "abundant life."

I prayed with the woman at the altar, and I also pointed out to her that some of the things happening to her might be the result of satanic attack, others might have been the consequences of sin—hers or her husband's—and some of the things she was enduring were simply God's refining fire at work in her life.

Then I showed her the Scripture, "For whom the LORD loves He chastens, / And scourges every son whom He receives" (Heb. 12:6 NKJV). At first she was a bit uncomfortable with the idea that God disciplines His children, but she was a good mother who understood that discipline is an integral part of love. She left that morning encouraged, not because her circumstances had changed, but because her concept of God's love and blessing had changed. And I left encouraged because I had an opportunity to help someone who had been damaged by the kind of materialistic message I used to preach.

A DECEPTIVE AND DESTRUCTIVE MESSAGE

Why is the modern emphasis on materialism so insidious? Why is it so dangerous in these last days before the return of Christ? Simply this: it is "another gospel," not the true gospel.

The term *another gospel* comes from the apostle Paul's second letter of correction and encouragement addressed to the church in Corinth. He wrote:

> But I fear, lest somehow, as the serpent deceived Eve by his craftiness, so your minds may be corrupted from the simplicity that is in Christ. For if he who comes preaches another Jesus whom we have not preached, or

if you receive a different spirit which you have not received, or a different gospel [another gospel, KJV] which you have not accepted—you may well put up with it! (11:3–4 NKJV)

Basically Paul was saying, "Just as the devil subtly deceived Eve, you too might be thrown off track by someone who comes preaching a message that is different than the message I presented to you." What really seems to concern the apostle is that the Corinthians might be gullible enough in their faith to accept such an impostor.

Paul had a similar concern for the Christians at Galatia. These believers had started out well, but then had gotten sidetracked into legalism. Paul was amazed that the Galatians could allow that to happen so easily. He wrote:

I marvel that you are turning away so soon from Him who called you in the grace of Christ, to a different gospel, which is not another; but there are some who trouble you and want to pervert the gospel of Christ. But even if we, or an angel from heaven, preach any other gospel to you than what we have preached to you, let him be accursed. As we have said before, so now I say again, if anyone preaches any other gospel to you than what you have received, let him be accursed. (1:6–9 NKJV)

Whew! Do you get the impression that the apostle was seriously concerned about the danger of someone perverting the gospel? Absolutely. Paul was saying, "I don't care who it is, or how nice a person he or she might be; even if it is me, or one of my close associates, or an angel from heaven. If that person tells you anything that contradicts or perverts the gospel I preached to you—the true gospel of Jesus Christ—let that person be accursed!"

Paul was concerned about the Galatians believing a different gospel, one in which they accepted a mixture of salvation through legalistic works with a belief in salvation through Christ alone. Paul was saying, "Hey, folks. The two don't mix."

Unfortunately, by mixing the quest for money with a relationship with God, many preachers and Bible teachers in our day have perpetrated a perversion equally as destructive. By giving the impression that God wants all of His people to be rich materially, we have diluted the true gospel and foisted upon the public a deceptively false substitute. We have been preaching "another Jesus, another gospel." And the church today, like that in Galatia, is putting up with it.

Worse yet, the church is welcoming these false doctrines. Herds of sincere Christians with "itching ears" (2 Tim. 4:3 NKJV) follow pastors and evangelists who tell them what they want to hear, and these believers are being duped into accepting "another gospel"—the prosperity gospel.

WHAT IS THE PROSPERITY MESSAGE?

In a nutshell, the prosperity message promises that Christians should expect to achieve health, wealth, success, happiness, and personal fulfillment—not just in heaven to come, but during this life on earth. While only the most blatant prosperity teachers are willing to say "God wants you to get rich," the message with its various subtleties has been propagated so thoroughly for the past few decades, it has seeped into the hearts and minds of many Christians who would not consider themselves advocates of a prosperity gospel. Many of these are sincere believers who congregate in churches supposedly centered on the Word, fellowships based on a serious exposition of the Logos, the Word of Christ. Others are attracted to full-gospel fellowships, congregations that espouse a deeper experience with God, in which the believer is filled with the Holy Spirit subsequent to his salvation experience. Fairly or unfairly, many of the groups emphasizing God's material blessings have been lumped into the general categories of charismatic or pentecostal fellowships.

But the Christian obsession with materialism is not confined to those whose spiritual experience leans toward a more ecstatic, euphoric worship style. Just take a look in the parking lots of most mainstream denominational churches, and you will notice the same status symbols equated with material success in "worldly" circles. No longer do Christians feel uncomfortable about driving expensive cars, living in luxurious homes, wearing the best clothes, or eating the finest foods. Even many pastors have succumbed to the temptation to "have it all" in this life. While most pastors in America are underpaid and often underappreciated, others live like kings. I recently heard of a pastor's salary that rivaled (and exceeded!) that of the corporate CEOs in his congregation.

Granted, the responsibilities of pastoring are enormous, but just how many hundreds of thousands of dollars should a pastor receive from his congregation?

No doubt someone will be quick to point out, "Jim, you didn't seem to mind when you were receiving large sums of money as salaries and bonuses as the pastor of Heritage Village Missionary Church (PTL)." And that is correct. *But I should have.* As I discussed in *I Was Wrong,* one of the most serious mistakes I made at Heritage USA was to accept the exorbitant remunerations the board of directors voted to give me. Were the salaries and bonuses legal? Absolutely. Were they right? Absolutely not. They allowed me to live out the errors of the prosperity gospel I was preaching.

Many Christians who hold to a prosperity doctrine are quick to point to Jesus' words in John 10:10, "I have come that they may have life, and that they may have it more abundantly" (NKJV).

"See," the prosperity teacher says, "it is obvious that Jesus wants His people to prosper. He wants to give us a good life, abundant in quality and quantity."

I used to tell people the same thing. Speaking about John 10:10, I told the studio audience at PTL,

> Somehow our modern thinking has managed to twist this truth around to make it appear like the opposite is true—that God is the thief, to say "no, no" to all our fun and adventure . . . To think that God doesn't want your life to be rich, exciting, and full of adventure is the greatest lie that I know. The word *abundant* that Jesus uses here in verse ten literally means to excel and superabound both in quality and quantity. God wants us to superabound in every part of our life.[1]

At first glance, it's easy to see how such a verse could be interpreted to imply that God wants us to enjoy material prosperity. The word for *life* in this verse, however, is *zoe,* a word indicating "life in the spirit and soul." Another Greek word, *bios,* from which we get our word *biology,* also means "life"; but *bios* is the word used to refer to physical, material life. Of the two words, *zoe* is usually considered the more noble, higher concept of life. Jesus was saying this: "I want you to have an abundant life in the spirit, which is My highest and best for you."

Actually, John 10:10 has nothing to do with material prosperity. If abundant life meant having expensive houses and cars, parties and entertainment, then it would be legitimate to say that many non-Christians are experiencing abundant life. By that criteria, members of the Mafia, movie stars, and Wall Street financial wizards would certainly be considered blessed.

Though nonbelievers and believers alike may have an abundance of riches, that in itself is no sign that they are experiencing the abundant life Jesus promised. Besides, if you are equating God's love for you with how much money you have, how big a house you live in, or what kind of car you drive, what happens when all of those things are gone? Does that mean God no longer loves you? Sadly, I have met many sincere but deceived Christians who now believe just that.

THE "KEY" TO PROSPERITY

One of the key verses most frequently used to bolster the prosperity message is 3 John 2. It is also one of the most misunderstood verses in the Bible. The verse reads: "Beloved, I wish above all things that thou mayest prosper and be in health, even as thy soul prospereth" (KJV).

I had preached on this verse for most of my ministry. It seemed to say exactly what I had believed: that God wanted His people to prosper. And I interpreted it to mean prosper financially and materially; in other words, to get rich.

I had even written books instructing people how they could guarantee material success. In an attempt to encourage Christians to trust God for more material blessings, I once wrote:

As a child of God, you ought to live in victory. Christianity is a winning way of life. God intends for you to be successful in every part of your living.

Unfortunately, many Christians do not realize this. They somehow have been conditioned to accept—indeed, to expect—failure. Surrounded by an atmosphere of negativism and self-pity, they resign themselves to being second- or third-class citizens, inferior, end of the line.

This attitude is not scriptural. This lifestyle is not Christian.

God is not defeated. He is not a failure. His resources are not limited.

Why, then, should His children, the citizens of His kingdom, live in defeat, failure, and want?

God's will for you is good. He has declared in His Word, "Beloved, I wish above all things that thou mayest prosper and be in health, even as thy soul prospereth" (3 John 2 KJV). He *expects* you to be successful. He has canceled the claim of sin and death on your life and placed all the power and resources of heaven at your disposal.

So it's not God's fault if you're not successful!

Don't blame God for your failure—He's given you all you need to be a winner. Through His love, His blessings, His Word—in every conceivable way—He constantly assures you that you can make it.[2]

Please understand, I was not attempting to deceive anyone. I honestly believed what I wrote. I taught it and I lived it, and my lifestyle reflected the theology that said God is pleased with material prosperity. Fancy cars, beautiful homes, stylish clothes, staying in the finest hotels in the world—such extravagances may not be wrong for some people, but for me these things were wrong because they were the outward manifestations and the logical extension of my misinterpretation of Scripture.

I never really examined the true meaning of the text in 3 John 2. I never looked up any of the words in a Greek-English dictionary, or consulted a learned theologian concerning its meaning. Nor did I ever seriously consider why this verse seemed to contradict so much of what the New Testament said in other places. I simply pulled the verse out of context and used it to justify my God-wants-you-rich theology.

Part of the problem is that the King James translation of the Bible obscures the true meaning of the verse. First, the phrase *above all things* creates confusion for many Christians. The words make it sound as though our prosperity is at the top of God's priority list for us. But wait a minute. *Above all?*

Does that mean even above our salvation? Of course not. In fact, when a fellow asked Jesus what He thought was number one on God's top ten list, Jesus' answer included no reference to material prosperity at all.

And Jesus answered him, The first of all the commandments is, Hear, O Israel; the Lord our God is one Lord: And thou shalt love the Lord thy God with all thy heart, and with all thy soul, and with all thy mind, and with all thy strength: this is the first commandment. And the second is like, namely this, Thou shalt love thy neighbor as thyself. There is none other commandment greater than these. (Mark 12:29–31 KJV)

Jesus was saying that our number one concern is to love God supremely; after that we are to love our neighbors as ourselves. Jesus did not even hint that material prosperity has anything to do with His priorities for our lives. Why, then, would the apostle John say that "above all" we should have prosperity?

He didn't.

What Does It Mean to Prosper?

The word *prosper* has various forms, and if you look them up in an English dictionary, you will get the impression that the words have one meaning in common: "to increase in wealth." But the word *prosper* as translated into English from the original New Testament Greek has quite a different meaning. The word translated *prosper* in the King James Version comes from a Greek word, *euodoo,* which is made up of two root words, *eu,* which means "good," and *hodos,* which means "road, or route, a progress, or journey." It can also mean "to be led in a good way."[3]

Besides 3 John 2, the word *euodoo* is used only two other times in the New Testament, and in no place does it refer to vast sums of money, riches, or material gain. Granted, it *can* be accurately translated *prosper* in 1 Corinthians 16:2, where the apostle Paul is encouraging the church to prepare an offering for the suffering saints in Jerusalem. He suggests that the believers contribute a portion of their income each week, so they will not have to take a special collection when he arrives in Corinth. Rather than setting a specific amount that each person should give in the offering, Paul gave the Corinthian Christians a general principle that they should give as they had prospered: "On the first day of the week let each one of you lay something aside, storing up as he may prosper, that there be no collections when I come" (NKJV).

To infer that the prosperity Paul mentions here meant that the Corinthian Christians were rolling in money is an assumption we have no right to make. While there may have been some wealthy Christians in the Corinthian church, it is highly doubtful that Paul was hoping for a few "big-bucks" donors to carry the load. Most likely, he expected each person to give in proportion to what they had received, which would add up to a generous gift for the Jerusalem church.

In his second letter to the Corinthians, Paul further explains, "For I do not mean that others should be eased and you burdened; but by an equality, that now at this time your abundance may supply their lack, that their abundance also may supply your lack—that there may be equality" (8:13–14 NKJV). Notice that this biblical principle produces an equality in giving, yet no person is unduly burdened or pressured to give.

The word *euodoo* is also found in Romans 1:10, where Paul writes, "Making request, if by any means now at length I might have a prosperous journey by the will of God to come unto you" (KJV). This passage, however, has nothing to do with money or material possessions. On the contrary, Paul often took special care to make sure that his motivation for preaching the gospel could not be misconstrued or maligned because of money. It would be unthinkable for the apostle to say, "Please pray for me that somehow or other I might obtain wealth by coming to preach to you," or, "Please pray that I will make a lot of money on this trip." Yet that is how Romans 1:10 would have to be interpreted if we took the King James Version's translation of *euodoo* to mean wealth or material gain. Clearly, that was not the apostle Paul's intent. He was saying simply, "I sure hope God grants me an opportunity to visit you soon. Please pray that I will have a good journey on the road as I travel to see you."

The apostle John, the writer of 3 John 2, was saying something similar when he said, "Beloved, I wish above all things that thou mayest prosper and be in health, even as thy soul prospereth." It was a greeting, a prayerful desire of the apostle's, not a principle suggesting that Christians should be wealthy. John was saying simply, "I wish you a good, safe, and healthy journey throughout your life, just as your soul has a good and safe journey to heaven."

John was not saying "Above everything else, I want you to get rich. Above all, you should prosper and make money." That is not even implied in the true meaning of the verse. Many highly respected Bible scholars, including William Barclay, Robert Jamieson, A. R. Fausset, and David Brown, believe that John is simply wishing his reader good physical health.[4] In the larger context of Scripture, how could any serious reader of the New Testament think that John would wish above all else that Christians get rich?

But like many other prosperity teachers, I taught for years that as one of Jesus' closest friends during His earthly ministry, John must have known what was important to the Lord.

"When John says that *'Above all things,* I pray that you prosper and be in health,' surely he was reflecting the heart of God," I said. "After all, John was writing under the inspiration of the Holy Spirit, so this message must be directly from the heart of God Himself. Obviously, God wants you to be wealthy!"

Consequently, good, hardworking, sincere people, men and women who regularly attend services in churches across America, are filing bankruptcy in record numbers. Why? Because they have mortgaged their futures for budget-busting houses and cars; they have run their credit cards to the max and are living paycheck to paycheck, not just in an attempt to get more material things, but to show how spiritual they are for having them! After all, if material prosperity is a sign of God's blessing, you don't want to be driving a beaten-up clunker or living in a house within your means in an ordinary neighborhood. You are a King's Kid, don't you know, and King's Kids deserve the best. At least, that is the message that has permeated many Christian circles.

CHASING SIGNS AND WONDERS

Along with the emphasis on money, the new materialistic Christianity places strong emphasis on the miraculous—signs and wonders, or some physical manifestation of a spiritual experience. Consequently, people are running to and fro, hoping to experience the latest Christian phenomenon.

If the Church of Jesus Christ really were the great *Ship of Zion,* as it has often been characterized in written and musical allegories, we would be named the *Titanic,* because every time some new spiritual wave occurs, many Christians run to the side of the ship where the outpouring is taking place, causing the ship to go under. Either that, or we would be known as the *Good Ship Lollipop,* because our decks are full of believers who will take all the sweet, sugary candy the "captains" want to pass out.

Some Christians rush to where they hear miracles are taking place; others rush to an experience of being "slain in the Spirit." Some rush to the experience of "laughing in the Spirit." In some circles, I have even heard of Christians barking like dogs. (Where is the scriptural validation for that one?)

Please understand, it is not my purpose to pass judgment on events taking place in many Christian meetings. I recognize that in these last days before Jesus comes, we can expect to see and hear of some unusual events; we should not be surprised when God does something in our midst that is not preplanned, structured, or printed in our church bulletins. But I would offer two cautions: First, we need to have a sound scriptural basis for whatever we adopt in our lifestyle and whatever we encourage others to experience. In this regard, too many of us have gotten the cart before the horse. Our experience needs to align with the Word of God rather than mere traditions; we must not try to twist something in the Word to validate our experiences.

Second, I would caution that these unusual manifestations should not become the main attraction. There is only one main attraction and His name is Jesus. I do not discount the unusual occurrences some Christians seem to be experiencing, but I consider them to be similar to what Jesus referred to as "birth pangs" before His coming. When I speak on this subject, I often ask from the podium, "Mothers, how many of you enjoyed your birth pangs?" The question usually elicits laughter from the fathers and rolled eyes from mothers.

Oddly, the church today is enamored with birth pangs. We are focusing on some curious and unusual sounds and experiences, rather than anticipating what God is about to bring to life. Instead of centering our attention on the outward expressions, we need to discover what God wants to do in and through us, what sort of church He wants to bring to life.

Clearly, our seeking after these unusual phenomena can easily distract us from the central Person of Jesus Christ and lead us to accept "another gospel." *Beware.* Be especially suspect of any experience or any message that is built on isolated Scriptures or twisted interpretations.

4

An Unwitting False Prophet

During a church service, a prosperity teacher rebuked a group of economically poor Christians for singing a particular Christ-exalting song before he got up to speak. It bothered the preacher that the congregation sang, "He's all I need; He's all I need; Jesus is all I need," because he felt the believers were using the song almost like a drug to dull the pain of their impoverished lives. Basing his incorrect deduction on Matthew 6:32, he told the congregation that their heavenly Father knew that they needed "all these things" (NKJV).

Instead, the congregation had it right: Jesus *is* all we need!

Near the time I was to be released from prison, a friend of mine visited me. "What have you learned from this experience, Jim?" he asked. "Tell me the three most important lessons."

I looked back at him and replied simply, "Jesus, Jesus, Jesus."

"Okay," he replied. "I understand that, but what else? Give me three other things you learned."

"The Word, the Word, the Word," I told him.

"Come on, Jim. Give me three more," he pleaded.

"Obey, obey, obey," I answered.

You see, I learned the hard way that Jesus really is all I need. He is the only Friend who was able to go with me through the prison gates. And He is the only One who can satisfy your soul—not money, not *stuff.*

Go ahead. Tell the Christian inmates inside America's prisons that God wants them to prosper. (Then run for cover!) Or go to a nursing home and preach a prosperity message to the dear saints of God who have been economically raped of everything they own, and tell them that God wants them to be materially blessed.

Similarly, materialistic Christianity simply does not compute for most Christians outside America's borders. Author Florence Bulle poignantly challenges, "Imagine [the late] Mother Teresa stooping over a dying beggar sprawled in the mud-and-dung-filled streets in India to inform him God wants him to be rich in this world's goods."[1]

When confronted with the glaring realities of the impoverished nations of the world, many materialistic Christians simply shrug their shoulders and say, "Well, wealth is relative." Either that, or they will blame the poor people's plight on their reluctance to accept the gospel, or their lack of faith. But what about the poor Christians in those places—men and women who love the Lord as much as we do, and who have as great a faith as we do (maybe greater!), but who are living in abject poverty? And what about the dedicated missionaries serving in poverty-stricken regions? Why doesn't materialistic Christianity work for them? Could it be because it is based on a theology steeped in error?

I believe it is. But it was not until I spent five years in prison—where I had plenty of time to study the Bible in its entirety—that I began to understand that I had built my prosperity theology on a few isolated, misinterpreted verses of Scripture.

Throughout my incarceration I asked myself again and again, *How could I have taught people to fall in love with material things?* The answer is that I did not have an accurate understanding of how to study and interpret the Bible properly.

A Proper Interpretation

Hermeneutics is the big word theologians use to describe the study of the principles of biblical interpretation. In their book *Introduction to Biblical Interpretation,* Dr. William W. Klein, Dr. Craig L. Blomberg, and Dr. Robert L. Hubbard Jr. provide several basic, but valuable, rules of hermeneutics that students of the Bible should keep in mind as they study. First, the authors caution, "We find no place for a self-structured theology that promotes its own self-serving agenda."[2]

That was exactly what I had been doing throughout the early years of my ministry. In much of my sermon preparation time, I simply picked out some motivational principles, then scanned through the Bible to find a verse or passage that supported what I wanted to say. Sadly, many other teachers have made the same mistake. As I listen to and read the materials of many contemporary teachers, I can now see that all too often they violate the basic principles of hermeneutics.

The authors of *Introduction to Biblical Interpretation* emphasize that if we are to be accurate in our doctrines, *we must "follow the sound exegesis of the appropriate texts* . . . [For] example, if theologians wish to formulate a theology of 'faith,' they must investigate all the passages that speak to that issue."[3] This was the point I began to understand when the Lord seared Matthew 4:4 into my heart: "Man shall not live by bread alone, but by every word that proceeds from the mouth of God" (NKJV). *Every word.*

God's Word, Not Our Own
The scholars' second key to biblical understanding is even more specific:

> *Theology must be based on the Bible's total teaching, not on selected or isolated texts.* For example, suppose we want to develop a theology of election and free will. We cannot develop a faithful and honest statement of this doctrine if we deny or discount texts that conflict with our preferred theory. If God authored the entire Bible and if its parts do not hopelessly contradict . . . then a valid theological statement about an issue must take into account *all* that God has said concerning it.[4]

Again, my method of teaching the Bible was shattered when I began to read the Book as a whole. When I studied all that Jesus said about money, for example, I could not ignore His statements concerning the dangers of riches.

Major on the Majors
A third rule of biblical interpretation is:

Legitimate theology considers and expresses the Bible's own emphases . . . theologians ought to strive to "major on the majors"—to stress what the
Bible portrays as most important—in their theologies. Theology should
grasp God's principle concerns in the Scriptures, rather than merely mir-
ror contemporary agendas and priorities.[5]

Certainly, the Bible promises that God will bless His people, that as
we obey His commands, He will provide for us; but is it really legitimate
for prosperity teachers to say that Jesus was rich? Yet many Bible teachers tell people it would have been impossible for Jesus to be poor! After
all, throughout the Old Testament, God promised material blessings to
anyone who would walk perfectly and uprightly before Him. Jesus certainly did just that. If God blessed the Old Testament saints such as
Abraham, Isaac, Jacob, Job, David, Solomon, and others—many of
whom were extremely wealthy by the standards of their societies—and
He had failed to bless Jesus financially, He would have been breaking His
own Word.

Was Jesus Really Rich?

Not long ago I was one of the speakers at a conference that drew over ten
thousand attendees. During one of my breaks, I decided to sit in and listen to another speaker about whom I had heard many good things. But as
I heard his message, I was shocked. The essence of the message was,

Jesus was rich. Jesus owned many houses. He had everything He needed
and more! He had a seamless garment, which was a sign of wealth. Jesus
didn't dress in drab attire. Nowadays, we would probably consider Jesus
a well-dressed man, wearing designer clothes. Obviously, His garment
was valuable because the soldiers gambled for it while Jesus hung on the
cross.

Another assumption on the part of the teacher, which supposedly proved
that Jesus was financially prosperous, sounded all too familiar: "Jesus had a
treasurer among His disciples, which showed that He had accumulated
large sums of money which needed to be managed. Enough money went
through that treasury for Judas to steal from it without the money being

missed." But the most ludicrous assumption the speaker made was yet to come. He said, "Jesus grew up wealthy. As a baby, the wise men brought Him expensive gifts, which His parents probably sold for great sums of money. They invested the cash, and as a result, Jesus probably grew up as a millionaire."

As I sat listening to the speaker's ridiculous theory, I could not believe my ears. I thought, *My Lord did not even have a pillow for His head!* Jesus described His own living conditions when He said, "Foxes have holes and birds of the air have nests, but the Son of Man has nowhere to lay His head" (Matt. 8:20 NKJV). Yet the prosperity teacher was convinced that Jesus had a nice home. "After all," he told the audience, "when Andrew and another disciple first heard John the Baptist acknowledge Jesus as the Lamb of God (John 1:29, 36), they hurried after Jesus and asked Him where he was dwelling."

> Then Jesus turned, and saw them following, and saith unto them, What seek ye? They said unto him, Rabbi, (which is to say, being interpreted, Master,) where dwellest thou? He saith unto them, Come and see. They came and saw where he dwelt, and abode with him that day: for it was about the tenth hour. (John 1:38–39 KJV)

Basically Andrew and the other disciple were asking where Jesus was staying. (That is exactly how the New King James Version translates this verse.) When Jesus encouraged them to come and see, He was not inviting them to vacation at His plush condo along the beach of Lake Galilee. Nothing in that passage indicates that Jesus had a posh home, or that He owned a home of any kind. Most likely, if this incident is consistent with other passages of Scripture, Jesus was staying with friends. He merely invited the inquirers to go there with Him. Or, they could have gone to some hillside campsite.

Regardless, the men stayed with Jesus until about four o'clock in the afternoon, the tenth hour. The passage does not necessarily indicate that they stayed with Jesus any longer than that. Although it is possible they may have stayed overnight, Middle Eastern hospitality being what it was, most modern translations of the Bible do not give that impression. The only people who seem obsessed with proving that Jesus invited the men to stay at His home are Bible teachers such as the conference speaker, who insist on reading their own interpretations into the biblical text.

Worse still, the audience at the conference enthusiastically received the misguided message as the truth, even though it violated the overall message of the Bible and calls Jesus a liar! The speaker was preaching "another gospel and another Jesus," and the crowd welcomed it! That is a very grave danger of poor hermeneutics.

The True Gospel Works

A fourth principle of biblical interpretation is that theologians must *"state theological points in ways that explain and illuminate their significance for the life and ministry of the church today."*[6] In other words, our doctrine must be relevant. It must work in the real world. Here again, what I formerly taught—and what many still teach—simply does not work for most believers. Many sincere Christians who are suffering with painful physical ailments, or struggling to make ends meet financially, or both, are given the impression that their lack of faith keeps them from being healed: "If I really believed, God would help me." Because they are not healed or financially prosperous, their pain is compounded. What false spiritual guilt we have heaped upon sincere believers who have discovered the truth that the prosperity gospel does not work in the real world.

Bible teachers who impose such cumbersome doctrines on their audiences are ignoring the fact that Scripture teaches that the trial of our faith is more precious than gold (1 Peter 1:7), and that whom God loves He chastens (Heb. 12:6).

Opinions Are Just Opinions

A fifth principle of biblical interpretation cautions against accepting what other people say about the Bible, even our spiritual ancestors, rather than allowing the Bible to speak for itself. *"Theology must be centered in what God has revealed,* not in what people, however enlightened, have devised in their own thinking."[7]

Unfortunately, like many other preachers of a God-wants-you-rich message, I got most of my sermon ideas from other preachers rather than from the Word itself. The prophet Jeremiah warned about such a practice: "I stand against these 'prophets' who get their messages from each other"

(23:30 TLB). Even if someone is a sincere man or woman of God, we dare not passively accept his or her interpretation of Scripture without studying it for ourselves.

Learning from Our Church Heritage

The sixth principle of biblical interpretation is the flip side of the fifth. While we dare not bow to man's brilliance, we should not ignore the fact that a lot of good, solid Bible study and exposition has already been done for us by our spiritual ancestors. *"Modern theologians cannot do their work as if in a vacuum, as if no Christians have ever considered these issues prior to their own time,"* the authors of *Introduction to Biblical Interpretation* tell us.[8]

We need to learn from our brothers and sisters who have walked in the faith before us, who have won great victories and suffered severe losses. Church traditions, creeds, dogmas, and denominational teachings all have something to offer us, even if, after we have studied them, we choose to reject them. On the other hand, some of Jesus' harshest words were directed toward the Pharisees who clung tenaciously to their traditions in the face of clear evidence that God was doing something wonderfully different, something supernatural and life-changing, through the presence of Jesus Christ among them.

Had I stopped to consider that the materialistic gospel I was preaching did not fit with most of the preaching and teaching of great Christians throughout church history, it might have tempered my message. Instead, I felt that I had the mind of God on the matter, and I foolishly preached another gospel to millions of people. It is relatively easy to make such a mistake, especially when prosperity theology is working for you. And don't let anyone convince you otherwise: prosperity theology does work . . . for those who are preaching it. It worked for me—for a while. As I encouraged people to sow their money into our ministry, I truly believed they would receive a harvest of blessings—spiritually, physically, and financially. And many of them were blessed, even as I was blessed as a result of their giving.

But the truth is that many who espouse a materialistic Christianity must do so to rationalize their own lavish lifestyles, and the lifestyles must be maintained to validate their theology. It is a vicious circle.

But consider this: If those who preach and teach a prosperity gospel truly believe their principles work for everyone, shouldn't those same teachers be some of the world's leading philanthropists? Shouldn't they be doing more than anyone else to feed and clothe the starving children around the world? Shouldn't they be sending more gospel ministries into the streets of our nation than anyone else? Instead of helping to alleviate the hurts and meet the needs of other people, many materialistic Christians are lining their own pockets and using their misguided biblical interpretations to get more goodies for themselves.

Granted, many materialistic Christians are greatly involved in missions projects and other humanitarian efforts. Many are generous givers. I will always be grateful to some of the best-known prosperity teachers who, without fanfare, quietly and inconspicuously gave me financial assistance when I was released from prison, simply to help me get on my feet again. So I must confess that I am faced with a dilemma in writing this book. Many of the prosperity teachers are my close friends and I love them dearly. I do not mean to impugn their reputations or their ministries in any way. Yet I feel compelled to warn this generation about the love of money.

Let me show you how, by being ignorant of the basic principles of Bible study I've just shared with you, I mistook a passage I had heard other preachers present as proof positive that God wants us to be wealthy. (Actually, the "proof positive" was more like "proof-texting," pulling a verse of Scripture out of its context, misapplying it, or building a pet doctrine around it.)

THE DANGERS OF POOR INTERPRETATION

The entire passage is found in Deuteronomy 8:1–18, but for years, I conveniently centered my attention only on verse 18, and I used it as the basis for countless messages and appeals for money. The verse reads, "But thou shalt remember the LORD thy God: for it is he that giveth thee power to get wealth, that he may establish his covenant which he sware unto thy fathers, as it is this day" (KJV).

Few verses in Scripture look so good on a television screen as Deuteronomy 8:18. At PTL I loved to quote it emphatically as the words appeared on the screen: "Remember the Lord thy God, for it is He that giveth thee power to get *WE . . . ALTH.*" I would often drag the word out longer than necessary: *"W-e-a-l-t-h!"* I would nearly shout with glee.

Many prosperity teachers continue to use this verse to "prove" their message. One popular teacher is fond of saying, "God signs your paycheck." I used to say things like that myself. Of course, I never meant that God literally takes a pen and signs anything, but I wanted people to know that any skill, trade, profession, vocation—any ability that helps you earn income—comes from God. I often told my audiences, "If you want to increase your capacity to earn income, then seek the Lord's will. Ask Him where you should go and what you should do to improve your skills. What better employment counselor could you have than your heavenly Father? After all, 'It is He that giveth thee power to get wealth.'"

What's wrong with that? you may be wondering.

Nothing . . . except that I was misusing the Scripture and laying the emphasis on human wisdom, cleverness, motivation, and our own effort to apply worldly success principles to whatever field of endeavor people were seeking.

The verse does seem to support the idea that God gives us the power to get rich. But if you read the verse in its context, you will quickly discover that the thrust of the passage has little to do with acquiring riches. God was saying to the Israelites, "When I bring you out of Egypt into the promised land and you are enjoying the blessings I have given you, don't think that you have been successful in your own strength. Don't say that it is your own power, that you did all this yourself." The Lord then warns His people to remember that He is the One who deserves the glory. All God was saying was, "When you get to the promised land, don't forget who brought you there and gave you everything you have."

Furthermore, the word translated *wealth* in this passage comes from a Hebrew word, *chayil,* which is used 232 times in the Old Testament. In almost every case the word is meant to imply "might, strength, power, ability, virtue, valor," and, oh, yes: "wealth." It is used most often to describe valiant men and women and armies.

God was not telling the Israelites that they were going to be rich in this world's goods. He was really saying, "Remember, it is God who has given you the power to receive everything you have. He is the One who has given you strength. He is the One who has given you houses, land, or other possessions, and He expects you to use those things for His honor. Remember to give Him thanks."

Admittedly, I had used this verse in the past to make it sound as though it was God's will to make everyone wealthy, and if any of His people were poor, it was probably due to their lack of faith or not applying the biblical "formulas" correctly. That was an improper interpretation of Scripture. Yes, it is God who gives us the power to receive all that we have, but to assume that God makes people wealthy, based on this Scripture, is an illegitimate extension of that truth. If it is God who makes people wealthy, and wealth is a sign of God's blessing, then some of the wickedest rock stars should be elders in our churches!

FORGET THE CURSES—GIVE ME THOSE BLESSINGS!

Another Old Testament passage often used to "prove" the prosperity message is Deuteronomy 28. This chapter is part of what is known as the blessings and the curses, for obvious reasons. Not surprisingly, I used to quote this passage frequently, always laying tremendous emphasis on the blessings. "Blessed shalt thou be in the city, / and blessed shalt thou be in the field. / Blessed shall be the fruit of thy body, / and the fruit of thy ground . . . Blessed shalt thou be when thou comest in, / and blessed shalt thou be when thou goest out" (vv. 3–4, 6 KJV). One passage that we often displayed on our PTL television monitors was verse 13, "And the LORD shall make thee the head, and not the tail; and thou shalt be above only, and thou shalt not be beneath" (KJV). Now that is a motivating verse! After all, we may not all want to be the head of something, but few of us want to be the tail.

The promised blessings of God are definitely real. But so are the curses. Yet when I preached a prosperity message from this passage, I never got around to mentioning the curses. I usually stopped at the fourteenth verse. Interestingly, after thirteen verses powerful enough to send your spirits soaring, the Scripture suddenly brings us back to earth with a resounding thud. Because in the fifteenth verse God says, "But it shall come to pass, if thou wilt not hearken unto the voice of the LORD thy God, to do all his commandments and his statutes which I command thee this day; that all these curses shall come upon thee, and overtake thee" (KJV).

From there, the prophetic Word sears through fifty-two verses loaded with curses, not on the *enemies* of God, but on God's *people* who do not do *"all* His commandments." Many of the curses are the exact opposite of the promised blessings. Why don't the prosperity teachers talk about that part of the equation? Could it be because curses don't bring in money? Who wants to donate to a ministry that tells you, "If you don't obey God, you are going to be cursed"?

Was God dangling a carrot He knew none of us could reach? Yes and no. The truth is that it is impossible for us to keep all of God's laws. Even the best of the Old Testament believers failed to live up to God's commands. The bad news is that if we don't keep *all* God's laws perfectly, we will discover what Adam and Eve found out—that it takes only one sin to separate us from God. Scripture says in James 2:10, "Whoever shall keep the whole law, and yet stumble in one point, he is guilty of all" (NKJV). The good news is that Jesus Christ came into the world and delivered us from the curse by becoming cursed Himself, dying on a cross. He who knew no sin became sin for you and me (2 Cor. 5:21). God's standards have not changed: He still expects perfection. Yet Jesus imputes His perfection to us, He puts His perfection in us. We can inherit the blessings, but most of His blessings have little to do with money.

5

"I Want My Hundred Houses"

In January 1997 I preached in San Juan, Puerto Rico, at the First Presbyterian Church, the congregation pastored by Dr. Mario E. Rivera. After I had spoken sternly concerning the deceitfulness of riches, a group of pastors asked if they could have lunch with me.

At the restaurant, they told me of the devastating toll materialistic Christianity had taken upon the church in that area. With a trembling voice one of them said,

> We are almost having a revolution in this country because of the prosperity teaching. The teachers tell the people that they are poor because they have sin in their lives. Since most of the people of Puerto Rico are poor, they live with mounds of guilt. Others desperately try to improve their lot, even to the point of doing foolish or sinful things to obtain money or the trinkets associated with having money, just to appear prosperous.

Another man told of a prosperity teacher from the mainland who, during his sermon, took a chair from the quaint, simply decorated church platform, and smashed it in front of the audience. "God deserves better than this junk!" the visiting preacher railed. The next day church leaders purchased several pulpit chairs, each one costing more than five hundred dollars, simply to give the impression of prosperity.

I did not know what to make of the pastors' stories, but they emphatically warned me, "Jim, if you keep preaching this message, the advocates of the prosperity gospel in this country will have you killed!"

Although less dramatic, the reaction to my message was similar throughout much of mainland America. When I first began speaking out about what I felt God had taught me concerning the dangers of money and materialism, many people listened to me with raised eyebrows. Some were appalled that I—a primary propagator of the prosperity message—had disavowed my former teaching. Others were skeptical, apparently thinking that my years in prison had skewed my perspective on the Christian life.

They said, "It's understandable that prison has had that sort of influence on Jim. He has nothing left. All his material possessions are gone; therefore, it's easy for him to believe that Christians should not worry about material things. We'll see how he feels once gets back in the mainstream of society."

They were wrong.

If anything, I am more convinced today than I was then that many contemporary Christians have fallen in love with things to the detriment of their relationship with Jesus Christ.

GIVING TO GET

It pains me to hear the prosperity gospel promoters encourage people to "give more so you can get more." You need more money, the message implies, not for your own selfish desires (Of course not! Never, not you!), but simply so you can live at the level the Lord intends for you. "The safest way to handle your money is to do as the old rhyme says, 'Do your giving while you're living, then you're knowing where it's going.' And what better place to invest your money than right here in our ministry? That way, you know for sure where it's going" . . . or at least you think you do.

The Scripture most frequently quoted in this regard comes directly from the mouth of Jesus. Tucked neatly into Luke's record of the Beatitudes and the Sermon on the Mount is Jesus' statement, "Give, and it shall be given unto you; good measure, pressed down, and shaken together, and running over, shall men give into your bosom. For with the same measure that ye mete withal it shall be measured to you again" (6:38 KJV). Interestingly, this verse is the culmination of Jesus' comments on loving our enemies unconditionally, forgiving rather than judging, and being merciful. Jesus was saying that in the same manner that you forgive, you will be forgiven. And, oh, yes, the context implies that it can be applied to the giving of money too.

This verse is often coupled with Paul's exhortation in 2 Corinthians 9:6, "He who sows sparingly will also reap sparingly, and he who sows bountifully will also reap bountifully" (NKJV). Materialistic Christians contend that this combination of verses provides a one–two punch proving that we should give and expect a financial return on our "investment in God's kingdom," which can often be translated as "an investment in my pet program or project."

This give-to-get principle is sometimes known as having "seed faith," based on the idea that whatever seed you plant is going to bring forth fruit, a valid scriptural principle when properly understood.

Frequently the give-to-get teaching appeals most enticingly to those who can least afford to give. One autumn evening in 1997 I was watching a Christian television program, and the more I watched, the more deeply grieved I became. A minister was encouraging people to send money to the television ministry. He promised people that if they would send (or pledge to send) a large financial gift to the television ministry, God would get them out of debt. Unfortunately, many of the people who respond to such appeals for money are facing overwhelming circumstances, and with their last bit of faith, they put their money in the mail.

While I appreciated the preacher's emphasis on Christians getting out of debt, God makes no such promises in His Word. He warns us that the borrower is a slave to the lender (Prov. 22:7), but if we do incur debts, we are to pay them. Yes, God will help you pay off your debts if you are willing to live according to His principles. But getting out of debt usually takes a lot of sacrifice as well as a change of lifestyle and priorities, not just a gift to a ministry offering another quick fix or an easy answer to a prolonged problem. I could not get away from the thought that the TV preacher was unwittingly fleecing God's flock, not feeding them.

The apostle Peter encouraged first-century spiritual leaders to "feed the flock of God which is among you, taking the oversight thereof, not by constraint, but willingly; not for filthy lucre, but of a ready mind; neither as being lords over God's heritage, but being examples to the flock" (1 Peter

5:2–3 KJV). Sadly, it seems that as soon as we ascend to some position of prominence in life, we quickly forget all those scriptural prohibitions against "filthy lucre" and all that it will buy.

The hook that grabs most people by their faith is the promise that no matter what they give, God will give back to them as much as thirty, sixty, or even one hundred times as much. This teaching links The Parable of the Sower (Matt. 13:1–9, 18–23) in which Jesus said the good seed brings forth a bountiful harvest, "some a hundredfold, some sixty, and some thirty" (Matt. 13:23 NASB), to financial blessings. Most materialistic Christians neglect to mention that in that passage Jesus is actually talking about the Word of God, not money. It is the *Word of God* that is represented by the seed; Jesus referred to it as "the word of the kingdom" in five successive statements (Matt. 13:19, 20, 21, 22, 23); nowhere does He imply that He is talking about a financial gift. And the Word, when it is planted in "good ground" (hearts that are receptive), does indeed bring forth an exponential harvest in comparison to the amount sown, sometimes as much as a hundredfold increase.

What's in It for Me?

This 100 percent return, known as the hundredfold blessing, is seized upon by prosperity teachers and often combined with the hundredfold increase Jesus talks about later in the gospels. Great emphasis is placed on Jesus' answer to Peter's cross question, "We have left everything and followed You; what then will there be for us?" (Matt. 19:27 NASB; see also Mark 10:28; Luke 18:28). We tend to cringe at Peter's blunt inquiry, as though none of us would ever ask such a question. Yet, in truth, most of us want to know the same thing: "What's in it for us?"

Interestingly, Peter put this question to Jesus immediately after Jesus had finished describing how hard it is for a rich person to get into heaven. Like Peter, some of us have to be hit right between the eyes with God's truth before we catch on.

Matthew records Jesus' answer this way:

And Jesus said to them, "Truly I say to you, that you who have followed Me, in the regeneration when the Son of Man will sit on His glorious throne, you also shall sit upon twelve thrones, judging the twelve tribes of Israel. And everyone who has left houses or brothers or sisters or father or mother or children or farms for My name's sake, shall receive many times as much, and shall inherit eternal life." (19:28–29 NASB)

The parallel passage in Luke is almost identical, but in describing the disciples' rewards, Luke includes the phrase, "many times as much *at this time* and in the age to come, eternal life" (18:30 NASB, emphasis mine). The King James Version translates the phrase, "manifold more in this present time." In other words, the disciples would receive at least part of their reward in this lifetime, with eternal life as the icing on the cake.

Mark's gospel is even more specific. Talking about the rewards that will be given to His followers who have left their homes, families, or land for the gospel's sake, Jesus is recorded as saying that "he shall receive a hundred times as much now *in the present age,* houses and brothers and sisters and mothers and children and farms, along with persecutions; and in the world to come, eternal life" (10:30 NASB, emphasis mine).

Jesus was saying, "Guys, if you think you have given up a lot for Me, let Me guarantee you that you will not be sorry when the final count is taken. But in the meantime, rest assured, you will be well taken care of in this life." It does not take a Bible scholar to see that Jesus is speaking in a comparative sense: compared to the reward you are going to receive, your sacrifice will seem almost negligible. The only people who insist on ignoring the obvious meaning of Jesus' statement seem to be the prosperity teachers.

Not long ago I participated in a conference, sitting next to a longtime friend who pastors a large church. He had written to me while I had been in prison, and we had met together since I had been released. I knew he disagreed with me at several points concerning my teaching about money. Now here we were seated together at a conference. Before long, we engaged in a lively conversation concerning our areas of disagreement. Together we looked up a variety of Scripture references concerning Jesus' attitude toward money. The pastor concurred with many of my conclusions, but when we came to Mark 10, he remained unconvinced.

"Jim," he kept pressing, "what about the hundred houses? Jesus promised us a hundredfold return. He said we would have a hundred houses in this present age. What about my one hundred houses, Jim?"

For a while I was stumped. The Scripture definitely does say that disciples who leave all for the gospel's sake will get a return one hundred times as great. But then I looked at the passage more closely. Jesus also talks about a hundredfold "return" on our brothers and sisters, mothers, and children, as well as our houses and lands (v. 30). Jesus mentions those who have sacrificed time with their wives for the gospel's sake. What about wives (v. 29)? Are we to get one hundred wives too? Such a conclusion from this passage would be ludicrous.

As the conference went on, I scribbled my musings on a piece of paper and pushed it toward my friend for him to peruse. He nodded his head, then whispered to me, "But what about my hundred houses?"

When I pause to consider Jesus' promise of a hundredfold blessing, I must admit that He has indeed kept His word to me. Since leaving home as a young man to follow Jesus, I have received back hundreds of times more than I ever gave up. Yes, I left my home and my family in Michigan to attend Bible college in Minnesota, but over the years God enriched my life with hundreds, even thousands, of dear "brothers and sisters in the Lord" who have befriended me. He has indeed given me hundreds of houses and acres of lands. No, I don't own a town known as Bakkersville. Nor am I referring to the millions of dollars' worth of projects I helped build at Heritage USA. But as I have traveled the world, God has allowed me to stay in the homes of hundreds of kind, loving families, who have treated me like royalty. He has given me "mothers and fathers" in the gospel ministry, women and men who have given me guidance and assistance. And, as an added blessing, God allowed my own parents, both of whom lived long, fruitful lives, to be an active, vital part of my ministry.

In my work nowadays, living in the inner city of Los Angeles, God has given me a larger "extended family" than I ever dreamed. I have brothers and sisters, and multitudes of kids who look to me as a father figure. Although I do not own a home today, nor do I have much money, God has indeed kept His Word to me. He has given me a hundredfold blessing, but it has had little to do with money in my bank account.

If Jesus had really intended for His disciples to have a hundredfold increase on what they had given up for the gospel's sake, then Peter, James, and John, and the other disciples should have been millionaires. After all, they really did leave all to follow Jesus, in a much more literal sense than most of us. Yet when a blind beggar hailed Peter and John as they were about to enter the Beautiful Gate to the Jewish temple, and asked them for a handout, Peter answered, "Silver and gold I do not have, but what I do have I give you: In the name of Jesus Christ of Nazareth, rise up and walk" (Acts 3:6 NKJV).

Either Peter was lying, or he really didn't have any money. Nor did John offer to dip into his deep pockets and pull out some cash. But what they had was far more valuable than money: they had the presence and power of the Holy Spirit pulsating through their lives, and they had a desire to see the man made well. No money was needed; no charge, no gimmicks; Peter and John did not encourage the man to make a donation to their ministry as a sign of his faith. They simply allowed God to work through them to help somebody who was hurting. The contrast between their simple, unadorned faith, which resulted in the healing of a man who had been crippled from birth and had been sitting by that same gate every day, probably for years, and our modern-day "Christian" hoopla and hype is stunning.

Similarly, if the hundredfold return Jesus promised was meant to be in material goods, then surely if anyone was to get rich off Jesus, it would have been His brother James. Skeptical of Jesus prior to the crucifixion, James later became a profound believer and a leader in the early church in Jerusalem. What did he get in return? A hundredfold blessing on his land, houses, and bank accounts? No way. James held the dubious distinction of leading the early church through years of near starvation, persecution from opposition outside the church, and doctrinal disputes within. In the midst of the difficulties, the members of the early church in Jerusalem did not get rich; on the contrary, they had all things in common. In fact, some of the more wealthy members of that church, such as a man named Barnabas, sold what they could and donated it to the church to help meet the needs of those who were less fortunate (Acts 4:34–37).

Concerning materialistic Christianity, James wrote,

Come now, you rich, weep and howl for your miseries which are coming upon you. Your riches have rotted and your garments have become moth-eaten. Your gold and your silver have rusted; and their rust will be a witness against you and will consume your flesh like fire. It is in the last days that you have stored up your treasure! . . . You have lived luxuriously on the earth and led a life of wanton pleasure; you have fattened your hearts in a day of slaughter. (5:1–3, 5 NASB)

Clearly, James had little time for materialistic Christians who simply wanted to hoard their money so they could spend more on themselves.

HUNDREDFOLD RETURN, ALONG WITH PERSECUTIONS

And what of that one phrase that is often omitted from the hundredfold return teaching based on Mark 10:30? Couched conspicuously in the same sentence in which Jesus promised the hundredfold return on houses, family, and lands is Christ's promise that His disciples would receive these things, "along with persecutions" (NASB). Few prosperity preachers speak about that part of the package. Yet Jesus promised that persecutions are as much a hallmark of the blessed Christian life as loving relationships and material possessions.

Those few prosperity teachers who dare touch that phrase are quick to explain it away, saying that, yes, Christians will be opposed and persecuted by people who despise them in this world, but that cannot diminish their wealth or their health.

In other words, you might anger some of your nonbelieving neighbors; they may be jealous because you are so successful. But that will not keep you from acquiring more of this world's goods, and these neighbors cannot hurt you physically. Not even the devil himself can lay a physical malady on you. Some prosperity teachers go so far as to claim they have not even had a headache since coming to understand God's principles of health and wealth.

Too bad the apostle Paul couldn't figure that out. He could have used such a spiritual bulletproof vest. Although there were times when Paul apparently had plenty, when he wrote to the Corinthians, he said of himself and his coworker Apollos,

To this present hour we are both hungry and thirsty, and are poorly clothed, and are roughly treated, and are homeless; and we toil, working with our own hands; when we are reviled, we bless; when we are persecuted, we endure; when we are slandered, we try to conciliate; we have

become as the scum of the world, the dregs of all things, even until now.
(1 Cor. 4:11–13 NASB).

Dressed in rags, homeless, considered the scum of the world, the dregs—
the bottom of the barrel—of society, such was the hundredfold blessing for
the great apostle Paul.

Paul was not living on easy street; his testimony was not that of a King's
Kid, at least not in the sense that I used to portray the prosperous
Christian life. I used to tell people, "God's hands are filled with gold, diamonds, and dollars for His kids. Who do you think He wants to have
those things—the devil's crowd? No! God never intended for the devil's
offspring to have all the good things in this world. Release your faith,
believe God, and receive all that He has for you. No weapon formed
against you shall prosper."

Quite the contrary, when Paul described himself and his closest associates, he said,

We are afflicted in every way, but not crushed; perplexed, but not
despairing; persecuted, but not forsaken; struck down, but not destroyed;
always carrying about in the body the dying of Jesus, that the life of Jesus
also may be manifested in our body. For we who live are constantly being
delivered over to death for Jesus' sake. (2 Cor. 4:8–11 NASB).

Hadn't Paul left all to follow Christ? Of course he had. Shouldn't he be
an ideal candidate to receive the hundredfold blessings Jesus promised? Of
course he should. Funny, though, when Paul reviewed his Christian experience, he did not mention anything about receiving a material blessing. In
fact, he revealed that he had served God

in much endurance, in afflictions, in hardships, in distresses, in beatings,
in imprisonments, in tumults, in labors, in sleeplessness, in hunger . . .
as sorrowful yet always rejoicing, as poor yet making many rich, as having nothing yet possessing all things. (2 Cor. 6:4–5, 10 NASB)

Later in the same letter, when compelled to defend his credentials as a
true apostle, Paul recalled that he had been

beaten times without number, often in danger of death. Five times I received from the Jews thirty-nine lashes. Three times I was beaten with rods, once I was stoned, three times I was shipwrecked, a night and a day I have spent in the deep. I have been on frequent journeys, in dangers from rivers, dangers from robbers, dangers from my countrymen, dangers from the Gentiles, dangers in the city, dangers in the wilderness, dangers on the sea, dangers among false brethren; I have been in labor and hardship, through many sleepless nights, in hunger and thirst, often without food, in cold and exposure. Apart from such external things, there is the daily pressure upon me of concern for all the churches. (11:23–28 NASB)

Ironically, rather than complaining that he had not received his hundredfold blessing, Paul offers one of the most humble expressions of understatement in the entire Bible. He said,

Therefore we do not lose heart, but though our outer man is decaying, yet our inner man is being renewed day by day. For momentary, light affliction is producing for us an eternal weight of glory far beyond all comparison, while we look not at the things which are seen, but at the things which are not seen; for the things which are seen are temporal, but the things which are not seen are eternal. (2 Cor. 4:16–18 NASB)

Did you catch that? Paul refers to the many tribulations he had endured for the sake of the gospel as "momentary, light afflictions."

Most of us would be howling to high heaven, "God, I want my hundred houses!"

6

The Love of Money

While in prison, I studied the temperaments of inmates who had committed violent crimes. Interestingly, I found that quite often these men were All-American types, who in a fit of rage committed a heinous crime. One such man was Mark Putnam, who lived across the hall from me during part of my stay at Rochester. Mark was a former FBI agent who had a sexual affair with a female informant. When Mark broke off with her, the woman threatened to tell the FBI and Mark's wife about their affair. She also claimed to be pregnant with Mark's child. When she went berserk and began beating wildly on Mark, he responded with an outburst of anger, and choked her to death in a matter of seconds.[1]

The casual observer would never have guessed Mark's crime. By all outward appearances he had it all together. He was a handsome, dedicated FBI agent with two beautiful children and an attractive wife who helped him up the ladder of success. In the prison visiting room, they looked like a perfect family. Mark did not speak, look, or act like the stereotypical killer. One angry moment had ruined his life and that of his family.

As I studied these men who had committed violent crimes, I found something even more basic than anger had gotten them into trouble. Something more insidious, more pervasive, something that I, too, had tried to cover and push aside in my own life—the love of money! The underlying reason some of the bankers, Wall Street businessmen, doctors, and others are in prison is that they did something wrong to get more money. Of the sixty percent of inmates who are in prison because of drug-related crimes, most are not there because of an addiction to drugs; they are there because of an addiction to the drug of money. It was their insatiable desire for wealth that led them to selling drugs, not a desire to ruin someone else's life by getting them hooked. Unimpeded, the lust for money carries the potential to destroy both the buyer and the seller.

Even Mark Putnam's case could possibly be attributed to money. When the woman threatened Mark's livelihood by saying she was going to expose him and ruin his career, the results were tragic.

MONEY MAKES THE WORLD GO WRONG

Money is at the heart of much that is wrong with our world today. No wonder that when the apostle Paul wrote a letter of advice, encouragement, and admonition to the young preacher Timothy, he emphasized:

> But those who desire to be rich fall into temptation and a snare, and into many foolish and harmful lusts which drown men in destruction and perdition. For the love of money is a root of all kinds of evil, for which some have strayed from the faith in their greediness, and pierced themselves through with many sorrows. (1 Tim. 6:9–10 NKJV)

The love of money! Paul states plainly that the love of money is the motivation behind the evil in our world. This passage clearly says that those who fall in love with money are asking for trouble. Why had I ignored the obvious truth of this passage for so many years? It did not support my preconceived notions of a materialistic Christianity that assumed God wanted to prosper His people financially. I didn't *want* to believe that the love of money and the material things it could purchase were evil, especially after I had immersed myself and my family in that materialistic lifestyle and had taught others to do the same.

Take a minute and read the 1 Timothy 6:9–10 passage again. Do you notice the awesome power of money? The making of money and the acquiring of material goods dominate the activities of many people during the day as well as their dreams at night. The problem is that most people can never get enough money to be satisfied. The answer to the question: "How much is enough?" invariably comes back: "Just a little more."

This Scripture passage indicates that greed and lust for the power purchased by money can control a person's thoughts, actions, and attitudes all the way to hell. Paul then goes a step further when he says that the love of money is behind much of the evil in our lives. The love of money, the quest for it, the extent to which we are willing to go for it, is a telling indicator of just how tight a hold money has on us. People often say there is nothing wrong with having money; it is when money has us that the problems occur. And that is true. Yet many of us tragically miscalculate the strength of the stranglehold money has on our lives, not to mention the tightness with which we clench our fists around our checkbooks. We think we control money, but the truth is that money is choking the life out of us, while we foolishly continue to grasp for it.

On the other hand, in most modern societies money is a basic necessity of life. Few civilized cultures function on a barter system nowadays. Consequently, we must all obtain a certain amount of money simply to survive, to buy food and clothing, to pay the rent or house payment, the electric and water bills, to put gas in the car, and to pay for a host of other ordinary expenses. Even if you have no desire to get rich, it still takes a substantial amount of money just to make ends meet each month, and for many people the money runs out long before the month does.

How Much Is "Rich"?

Actually, I think rich Christians have gotten a raw deal. It has been all too easy for "comfortably wealthy" Christians (which, in my estimation, includes any of us who have more than one change of clothing and have had something to eat today) to ignore the scriptural warnings about money because we have not considered ourselves wealthy. *Those admonitions about money are meant for the truly rich among us,* most of us think, *not for people like me. I'm just an average-income person.*

It is much too easy to cast spiritual stones at the wealthiest people among us and never examine our own motives. Yet most of us in Western countries are fabulously wealthy compared to the vast majority of the world's population. Our pets eat better and live in more comfortable conditions than millions of people on this planet.

Furthermore, the Bible does not direct its antimaterialism message merely to "super-rich" people. When Paul wrote that "those who desire to be rich fall into temptation and a snare" (1 Tim. 6:9 NKJV), he was saying that the pursuit of money puts us in danger. We run the risk of falling into foolish and harmful traps in this life, and spiritual ruin and destruction in the next.

Many Christians are derailed not by riches themselves, but by the desire to be rich in this world's goods. Indeed, some of the most selfish people you will ever meet are not rich folks, but people who want to be rich. They may be extremely poor, middle class, or moderately wealthy, but their insatiable desire for material wealth can turn them into conniving, pernicious people.

Is Christianity a Way to Get Rich?

Whether we are rich or poor, God does not want us to fall in love with material things, period. Whether we have much or little is irrelevant, if we seek material things more than God. Moreover, He does not want us to equate merely having money with godliness. Earlier in his letter to Timothy, Paul cautioned:

> If anyone teaches otherwise and does not consent to wholesome words, even the words of our Lord Jesus Christ, and to the doctrine which accords with godliness, he is proud, knowing nothing, but is obsessed with disputes and arguments over words, from which come envy, strife, reviling, evil suspicions, useless wranglings of men of corrupt minds and destitute of the truth, who suppose godliness is a means of gain. From such withdraw yourself. Now godliness with contentment is great gain. (1 Tim. 6:3–6 NKJV)

Notice the words, "who suppose that godliness is a means of gain." The implication is that some had confused the issue, equating material wealth with God's blessings. Unfortunately, we have given precisely the same impression in the church nowadays. One of the natural outgrowths of that misconception has been a desire on the part of some people to use their "godliness" as a means of making money. Have you ever been ripped off by a "Christian" insurance salesman or a "Christian" auto mechanic? Televangelists are not the only ones who have used their faith to profit financially.

Perhaps one of the clearest biblical examples of a person who supposed that godliness was a means of gaining financially was the man known as Simon in Acts 8:14–24. Shortly after the Holy Spirit had been poured out on the believers in Jerusalem on the Day of Pentecost, and supernatural events had begun to occur, Peter and John visited Samaria to assist the Christians in that area. As the apostles laid their hands on the believers, they received the Holy Spirit. Simon must have been intrigued by this because Scripture says,

> When Simon saw that the Spirit was bestowed through the laying on of the apostles' hands, he offered them money, saying, "Give this authority to me as well, so that everyone on whom I lay my hands may receive the Holy Spirit." (vv. 18–19 NASB)

Although we can't say for sure, many Bible scholars believe that Simon wanted to use the gift of God's Spirit to make more money for himself. Whatever Simon's ultimate goal was, Peter apparently perceived that Simon's motives were less than pure. Peter strongly rebuked him, saying,

> May your silver perish with you, because you thought you could obtain the gift of God with money! You have no part or portion in this matter, for your heart is not right before God. Therefore repent of this wickedness of yours, and pray the Lord that if possible, the intention of your heart may be forgiven you. For I see that you are in the gall of bitterness and in the bondage of iniquity. (vv. 20–23 NASB)

Simon had the good sense to repent of his error, something I fear we have not yet learned to do.

Not long ago I was watching a telethon for a Christian network. Having conducted numerous fundraising telethons in my day, I was aware that drumming up enthusiasm and evoking a response are part of the process.

Nevertheless, I was appalled at what I saw and heard. Repeatedly the appeal was made, "Send in your money, and be sure to give us the names of your family members who need to know Jesus, when you send your check." The not-so-subtle implication was that the TV ministers and their coworkers would pray for my family members, and God would move in my loved ones' lives, if and when I sent my check.

As I viewed the spiritual shenanigans employed to raise funds, I could almost hear the voice of Peter shouting, "May your money perish with you, because you thought that the gift of God could be purchased with money!" Shame on those TV fundraisers. Shame on the viewers who respond to such ploys. Shame on me for being a pioneer in using such methods to raise money, no matter how valid the cause.

A DANGEROUS MIXTURE

Mixing miracles and money can be dangerous. Understand, I am convinced that if we seek Jesus, we will indeed experience miracles. But we should not run after miracles, we should run after Jesus. If we will do what God commands, we will have what we need, without lowering ourselves to carnal methods.

An intriguing story in the Old Testament illustrates the dangers of desiring to be rich as well as the danger of mixing miracles and money. Naaman was the commander of the army of the king of Syria. He was a great man in the sight of his master and a highly regarded, valiant soldier. But Naaman had a serious problem; he had leprosy (2 Kings 5:1). Often compared to AIDS in our time, leprosy was the most dreaded disease known to man in biblical times. It was an incurable skin disease that initially turned the affected area white, and then slowly but surely ate its way through the body of the afflicted person. Lepers had no hope of ever reversing the disease, only surviving it in some way that made life tolerable.

The public's attitude toward lepers ranged from hysteria to revulsion. Polite society's fear of the debilitating effects of the disease forced most lepers into a demeaning, cloistered existence, living with their fellow lepers in an isolated colony. If a leper dared venture into the mainstream of society, by law he had to give advance warning of his approach by calling out loudly, "Unclean! Unclean!"

Imagine what an incredibly humbling act it was on Naaman's part to finally seek help from Elisha the prophet, an Israelite living in Samaria under the thumb of Syrian rule. But when Naaman, accompanied by the pomp and pride of his military procession, arrived at Elisha's home, the prophet did not so much as come out to greet him. Instead, Elisha sent his servant, Gehazi, to deliver instructions concerning how Naaman might be cleansed of his leprosy.

Naaman was furious. No doubt he had anticipated that the prophet would put on some sort of spiritual show for him (v. 11); the one thing he did not expect was to be ignored. Eventually though, Naaman's servants convinced him to give Elisha's plan a try; after all, if the prophet had asked him to do something difficult, he would have done it, but all Elisha had told him to do was to dip seven times in the Jordan River. What did he have to lose?

When Naaman complied, he was immediately cleansed of his leprosy. And that is where we usually stop in the retelling of the story, and when we do, we miss one of the most important lessons.

Overjoyed at his new lease on life, Naaman wanted to give Elisha a reward for his services, but the prophet refused. He was not in ministry for money. "The prophet answered, 'As surely as the LORD lives, whom I serve, I will not accept a thing.' And even though Naaman urged him, he refused" (v. 16 NIV).

When Elisha's servant, Gehazi, heard his master turn down what was likely to be a lucrative reward, his greed got the best of him. He probably thought, *Hey, maybe the old man doesn't want anything from Naaman, but I could sure use a few things!* At the first opportunity, Gehazi ran after Naaman, who had started on his way back home. Gehazi caught up to his caravan and told the commander a lie, that two Bible school students had just shown up at Elisha's place and were in need. (Students are almost always in need!) Could Naaman please give them a talent of silver and a couple of changes of clothing?

"Sure, take two talents of silver," the grateful Naaman replied.

In his best well-if-you-insist attitude, Gehazi accepted the "gift" and hurried home to hide it. Then he went back to Elisha.

What happened next should scare the socks off anyone who tries to use the Word of God as a means to get money or material possessions. When

Elisha asked Gehazi where he had been, the greedy servant lied again. "Oh, nowhere."

Isn't that amazing? The man had just witnessed one of the most incredible miracles, a leper cleansed of his leprosy. Wouldn't you have thought that Gehazi would have enough sense to realize that Elisha might have an inside line with God? The gall of the man! He stood there and lied again, this time to the man of God.

Scripture concludes the story with a pungent antipathy toward Gehazi:

> But Elisha said to him, "Was not my spirit with you when the man got down from his chariot to meet you? Is this the time to take money, or to accept clothes . . . ? Naaman's leprosy will cling to you and to your descendants forever." Then Gehazi went from Elisha's presence and he was leprous, as white as snow. (2 Kings 5:26–27 NIV)

Did you catch that? Not only Gehazi would live the remainder of his life as a leper, but his children and their children down through the generations. He had desired to make money from the power of God; instead, he brought a curse on himself and his family. Many of us have done something similar.

God says, "Don't charge for My miracles. Don't even hint about it!"

A corollary to that ought to be obvious to us: we do not need to pay for God's miracles. Unfortunately, just the opposite impression is often given by the proponents of materialistic, health-and-wealth Christianity.

At PTL, an evangelist who seemed to have powerful spiritual gifts was a frequent guest on our shows. I truly believe that God used him in some unusual ways, and many people actually experienced miraculous healings during his ministry. I cringed, however, when at the end of the service, he said, "Now, each one of you who brings a thousand dollars to me, I will pray over you and give you a word of knowledge."

That man is now dead. He died of AIDS, the modern-day leprosy.

SKINNING THE SHEEP

I believe Elisha's question to Gehazi is being asked again of many material-minded spiritual leaders: "Where have you been?"

Tragically, the answer is, "We have been skinning the sheep." In our desperation to maintain huge budgets, we have carelessly misused Scripture to our own advantage. In this regard, the prophet Ezekiel's warning to spiritual shepherds sounds as though it were written in our generation:

> Son of man, prophesy against the shepherds of Israel; prophesy and say to them: "This is what the Sovereign LORD says: Woe to the shepherds of Israel who only take care of themselves! Should not shepherds take care of the flock? You eat the curds, clothe yourselves with the wool and slaughter the choice animals, but you do not take care of the flock. You have not strengthened the weak or healed the sick or bound up the injured. You have not brought back the strays or searched for the lost. You have ruled them harshly and brutally. So they were scattered because there was no shepherd, and when they were scattered they became food for all the wild animals" (34:2–5 NIV).

Clearly, the anger of the Lord expressed through Ezekiel was a result of the spiritual leaders' callous concern for their own well-being, rather than being concerned about the needs of God's people. God wanted shepherds whose hearts' desire was to care for the sheep, not skin them alive. He still does.

One night while I was sleeping in a prison cell, God gave me another dream, a dramatic vision in which He showed me a picture of the church, the body of Christ. In the dream, the people of the church appeared as cattle being herded along in a line. I was horrified when I saw the sight, for these cattle had no skin! They were a bleeding, raw mass of flesh.

As I viewed the pitiful scene, I sensed God speaking to me. "This is what My leaders have done to My church—they have skinned them! They are being herded toward destruction by the shepherds; they are hurting and bleeding."

I awoke shuddering with fear and an attitude of repentance. I vowed, "Never again do I want to be associated with anything that even hints at impropriety. Never again will I even hint that godliness is a means of financial gain."

To Titus, Paul wrote of the requirements to be a spiritual leader, teaching that the bishop or overseer "must be above reproach as God's steward, not self-willed, not quick-tempered, not addicted to wine, not pugnacious, not fond of sordid gain" (1:7 NASB). Then, in an effort to alert Titus and other spiritual leaders to be on their guard against those teachers who were propagating false doctrine, Paul warned, "For there are many unruly and vain talkers and deceivers, specially they of the circumcision: Whose mouths must be stopped, who subvert whole houses, teaching things which they ought not, for filthy lucre's sake" (1:10–11 KJV).

Granted, Paul's main concern in this admonition was that spiritual leaders know sound doctrine so they could refute the errors being propagated by those believers who felt they should maintain the rituals of Judaism along with their newfound Christian faith; but it should not escape our notice that money was a motivating factor for the perpetrators of those false doctrines. It is still the same today. Money motivates much of the mixed-up, watered-down gospel messages being presented.

THE SUBTLE SEDUCTION OF MATERIALISM

Some of the greatest heroes of the Bible succumbed to the temptations associated with material success. For instance, God had given clear instructions concerning the kings of Israel. The fact that a monarchy existed at all was a concession; God seems to have preferred a theocracy, a nation ruled by God, rather than a monarchy. But He knew human nature, and long before the Israelites set foot in the promised land, the Lord spoke prophetically through Moses. He foretold that when the people became established in the land, they would want a king. Why? They would want a national leader so they could be like all the other countries around them.

Although God conceded and allowed the people to have a king, He laid down some specific rules concerning the king's conduct.

But he shall not multiply horses for himself, nor cause the people to return to Egypt to multiply horses, for the LORD has said unto you, "You shall not return that way again." Neither shall he multiply wives for himself, lest his heart turn away; nor shall he greatly multiply silver and gold for himself. (Deut. 17:16–17 NKJV)

Unfortunately, even the best of God's men betrayed this trust. For example, one of the first things David did after he realized that the Lord had established him as king over Israel was to take more concubines and wives from Jerusalem (2 Sam. 5:12–13). This was long before David met the bathing beauty named Bathsheba.

The wisest man in history was a fellow named Solomon, David's son. Not only was Solomon incredibly wise, he was fabulously wealthy. When Solomon first became king of Israel, the Lord allowed him to ask for anything he wanted. Solomon did not, however, ask for riches, wealth, honor, or long life. Instead, he asked for wisdom to lead God's people, which pleased the Lord so much that He gave Solomon both wisdom and wealth (2 Chron. 1:11). If anyone in the Bible could give us some positive input concerning material things, Solomon leads the pack. Yet Solomon's words directly contradict many modern-day messages concerning money and material blessings.

Solomon warned, "He who trusts in his riches will fall, / but the righteous will flourish like foliage" (Prov. 11:28 NKJV). Notice it does not say that he might fall; Solomon says *you can count on it.* The wise king also noted, "Better a little with the fear of the LORD, / than great wealth with turmoil" (Prov. 15:16 NIV). Have you ever noticed that the wealthiest people among us are not always the happiest? In fact, despite their big houses or other possessions, it is rare when they have true joy in their lives.

During the early years of our marriage, my wife and I loved to spend idyllic weekend afternoons driving around looking at big, beautiful homes. We were dirt poor, so all the houses looked like mansions to us. But we could dream: *Someday, maybe, we can have a big, beautiful home like that . . .*

Sometimes we would even be so bold as to attend open houses, pretending that we were prospective buyers, although we knew full well that we couldn't afford the lawn care at some of those huge homes, let alone the mortgage payments. Still, it was great fun to look and dream. After a while, though, we noticed a curious similarity among many of the fanciest homes for sale. When we inquired about the owner, the real estate agent often conceded that the home was being sold because the husband and wife who owned it were divorcing.

I thought, *Why would a couple who has everything money could buy want to divorce?* In my naivete I had not yet learned the lesson that Solomon taught: Money cannot buy happiness. Material things will never be the glue that holds a family together.

WHAT REALLY MATTERS?

I learned this the hard way in my relationship with my son, Jamie Charles—or lack of a relationship, I should say. I worked hard and wanted to give my son everything, anything he wanted. As a little boy growing up in the shadow of Heritage USA, he sometimes came to me needing money. I would give him the hundred-dollar bill I always carried in my wallet in case of emergencies. As Christmastime approached, I would tell him to circle the presents he wanted in a catalog. Then instead of taking the time to find out what he really wanted most, I simply gave the catalog to my assistant and said, "Go buy them all."

I failed to realize that he didn't want *things,* he wanted me! It was not until I went to prison that Jamie and I spent one entire day together in which I gave him my undivided attention. At the end of the day, sitting in a prison visiting room, my son said to me, "Dad, this has been the greatest day of my life! All I ever wanted was to have you all to myself for one whole day." How sad that I had to go to prison to spend one quality day with my boy!

Certainly, I had tried to be a good father to my daughter, Tammy Sue, and to my son, Jamie Charles. But I robbed Jamie, especially; I was so busy building Heritage USA, I rarely had any time to focus on Jamie alone. Like any good dad, I had taken him places, done fun things with him, and tried to create special memories. But I was so obsessed with raising money, doing what I thought was the "work of God," I had missed the painful, longing look in my little boy's eyes, the look that said, "I need my dad."

Don't lie to yourself, Mom and Dad. You may say, "I'm working so much because I am giving my kids all the things I didn't have as I was growing up." That's a con game from hell. What your kids really want is *you.*

Near the end of his life, Agur, the author of Proverbs 30, poignantly prayed:

> Two things I ask of you, O LORD;
>   do not refuse me before I die:

> Keep falsehood and lies far from me;
> > give me neither poverty nor riches,
> > but give me only my daily bread.
> Otherwise, I may have too much and disown you
> > and say, "Who is the LORD?"
> Or I may become poor and steal,
> > and so dishonor the name of my God. (Prov. 30:7–9 NIV)

The Bible does not tell us much about Agur, but one thing is certain: he was a perceptive fellow with a well-balanced attitude toward money and materialism. "If I have too much, I might forget about you, God, and get the notion that I can make it on my own. On the other hand, if I have too little, I might be tempted to do something dishonest, which would dishonor Your name just as badly. No, I don't need great wealth, Lord. I don't need a huge bank account or heavily loaded mutual funds. Just my daily bread will be enough."

Solomon, the man who had virtually overdosed on materialism for most of his life, found many of the material goals for which we seek to be ultimately meaningless. The richest man in recorded biblical history summarized the futility of it all as he neared death's door:

> Whoever loves money never has money enough;
> > whoever loves wealth is never satisfied with
> > > his income.
> > This too is meaningless.
> As goods increase,
> > so do those who consume them.
> And what benefit are they to the owner
> > except to feast his eyes on them?
> The sleep of a laborer is sweet,
> > whether he eats little or much,
> but the abundance of a rich man
> > permits him no sleep.
> I have seen a grievous evil under the sun:
> > wealth hoarded to the harm of its owner. (Eccl. 5:10–13 NIV)

During the first two years of my ministry, my budget was fifty dollars each week. By the time I lost PTL in 1987, I had to raise a million dollars every two days . . . and it wasn't enough. The more money I raised, the more we spent, and the more we needed to raise. I should have listened to Solomon, who gave us the key to true success. He said, "Now all has been heard; / here is the conclusion of the matter: / Fear God and keep his commandments, / for this is the whole duty of man" (Eccl. 12:13–14 NIV).

That's what really matters, not the accumulation of material things. Financial gain is no indication of God's pleasure. As Paul wrote to Timothy, "godliness with contentment is great gain" (1 Tim. 6:1 NKJV). Unfortunately, few people I have ever met are truly content; most of us have an insatiable appetite for more, more, more.

7

A Christian Work Ethic

In fairness, I must admit that I still believe God wants to prosper His people. No, God *does not* want us to become enamored by materialism; He does not want us to be possessive, sticky-fingered money-grubbers. But God *does* want to bless His people and take good care of us. We do not have to twist Scriptures or browbeat believers into giving money so God will meet the needs of His people. The Lord has promised to provide for us. As we honor Him by wisely using the resources He gives us, He will continue to pour out blessings upon us.

Speaking through the prophet Malachi, God challenges us to test His veracity in this area:

"Will a man rob God? Yet you have robbed Me! But you say, 'In what way have we robbed You?' In tithes and offerings. You are cursed with a curse, for you have robbed Me, even this whole nation. Bring all the tithes into the storehouse, that there may be food in My house, and try Me now in this," says the LORD of hosts, "if I will not open for you the windows of heaven and pour out for you such blessing that there will not be room enough to receive it. And I will rebuke the devourer for your sakes, so that he will not destroy the fruit of your ground, nor shall the vine fail to bear fruit for you in the field," says the LORD of hosts. (3:8–11 NKJV)

Not only do we rob God if we refuse to give Him "the tithe"—the first 10 percent of our resources, defined by many as not just our money, but our time, talents, and treasures—but when we refuse to give, we rob ourselves. The Lord invites us to prove Him, to test Him, to see if His promise of blessing is true. Furthermore, He promises to "rebuke the devourer" for those who will put Him first in their finances. I believe the devourer is the devil, who is trying to destroy the fruit of our labors. God promises that as we trust Him, the devil will be turned back. Why should we foolishly try to stand against the enemy in our own strength when God has promised that we can depend on His?

Yet many Christians do just that, and they end up getting devoured by debt, which often leads to their being devastated by the devil in other areas of their lives as well. If you are not giving a tithe of your time, talents, and treasure to God, through your local church, I strongly suggest that you begin to do so. But don't stop there. The tithe is a good place to start, but a poor place to stop in your giving; the tithe is a minimum requirement, not a maximum goal at which to shoot.

REAPING AND SOWING REALLY WORKS

God also gives us the principle of sowing and reaping: what we sow we are going to reap, whether it is physically, emotionally, spiritually, or financially. "He who sows sparingly will also reap sparingly, and he who sows bountifully will also reap bountifully" (2 Cor. 9:6 NKJV). Does this principle work? It certainly does. God does not, however, intend for this principle to foster lust for money and things or to support attitudes of greed and selfishness, both of which are totally contrary to the teachings of Christ. This principle does not give people a license to love money under the guise of sowing seed, reaping a huge personal harvest, and assuming that their gain is a sign of godliness. Remember, Scripture says we should withdraw ourselves from anyone who supposes that gain is godliness (1 Tim. 6:5).

We are to give generously and cheerfully, not stingily, and not because someone has made us feel guilty, or spiritually insecure, or has otherwise manipulated us into emptying our wallets or bank accounts. The Bible says, "Let each one give as he purposes in his heart, not grudgingly or under necessity; for God loves a cheerful giver" (2 Cor. 9:7 NKJV). And

God has wonderful ways of giving back to us. Wealthy King Solomon advised, "Cast your bread upon the waters, for you will find it after many days" (Eccl. 11:1 NKJV). I love the way the Living Bible paraphrases that verse, "Give generously, for your gifts will return to you later." And that is exactly what happens. It is the law of sowing and reaping.

John and Joyce Caruso of Burbank, California, are a couple who have proven that this law works. I met John one night after I had spoken on the subject of materialism at the Los Angeles International Church, a renovated old hospital known simply as the Dream Center to residents of midtown L.A. In describing the dangers of riches, I mentioned that I knew very few happy millionaires. In most cases their money had not brought them peace but more worries and concerns. After the service, John was waiting for me at the rear of the sanctuary.

"Hi, Jim," he said, his face beaming with the love of the Lord. "Meet a happy millionaire."

John Caruso grew up in the Queens section of New York City, where he became a journeyman carpenter by the age of fifteen. His family moved to California, and after leaving school, John honed his trade during a stint in the military. While still in the army, shortly after his twenty-first birthday, John met the Lord Jesus Christ. Upon completing his military obligations, John and Joyce married and set up their first home. They spent their entire savings—about five hundred dollars—on some bedroom furniture and started their marriage in the same manner as many American newlyweds. The couple was broke.

Nevertheless, they had a strong faith in God and a strong Christian work ethic, based on Colossians 3:23–24, "And whatever you do, do it heartily, as to the Lord and not to men, knowing that from the Lord you will receive the reward of the inheritance; for you serve the Lord Christ" (NKJV).

John worked hard and earned as much as two hundred fifty dollars per week, good money in 1956. John and Joyce started attending North Hollywood Assembly of God Church, where they were surprised to find a friend of John's family, Andrew Nelly, teaching a Sunday school class. The subject of the class was tithing. The couple began to incorporate Nelly's teachings into their lifestyle. From the earliest days of their marriage, John and Joyce gave a minimum of 10 percent of their income to the church.

And God blessed them! They continued working hard, and by their first anniversary, John and Joyce had paid off all their debts and saved one thousand dollars, tithing on every penny they earned. With five hundred dollars they started their own business, Aluminum Overhead Door Manufacturing Company.

"Is your dad coming to California to be your partner?" friends asked John. "No," John answered with a twinkle in his eye. "I already have a business partner—the Lord. With every dollar we take in, He gets the first 10 percent."

But the Carusos did not sit back and wait for the Lord to dump a pile of money on them. They combined wise financial principles with good, old-fashioned hard work. They bought properties and materials at low prices and sold them at higher prices. One of John's cardinal rules was, "Don't spend all you make," or in other words, "Stay out of debt." Whatever they wanted to buy, John and Joyce paid cash, or they put off the purchase until they could. "To this day," John quips, "Joyce gets upset if she has to pay interest or finance charges on anything."

As their business grew, the couple kept giving more of their resources to God's work, and the Lord continued to prosper them. Eventually they became bona fide millionaires, and built a beautiful home in the hills, overlooking the city of Burbank. With more money than they cared to spend, John and Joyce never lost touch with the Lord's work. Rather than attending a swanky, sophisticated church in the suburbs, they chose to join the inner city congregation at the Dream Center.

Besides tithing their money, they also tithed their time, devoting as much as fifteen daytime hours per week to serving in the church. They are still actively involved in the work of the Dream Center. Because of John and Joyce's hard work and faithful, obedient giving, they have prospered and the work of God has prospered.

GOD WILL SUPPLY WHAT YOU NEED

God has promised to bless those who put Him first in their lives. That principle has never changed; nor will it. God knows what we need, and He has promised to meet that need.

But we must remember what Jesus told us: "No one can serve two masters. Either he will hate the one and love the other, or he will be devoted to the one and despise the other. You cannot serve both God and Money" (Matt. 6:24 NIV). Almost as if He were giving us the other side of the story, Jesus continued by telling us not to worry about our lives, about what we will eat or drink, or about our bodies, what we will wear. "Is not life more important than food, and the body more important than clothes?" He asked (v. 25 NIV).

"Look at the birds of the air," Jesus said. "They do not sow or reap or store away in barns, and yet your heavenly Father feeds them. Are you not much more valuable than they?" (v. 26 NIV).

And what good is worrying anyway, especially about mundane things such as what you are going to wear?

Again, Jesus pointed us to a practical example of what He meant.

See how the lilies of the field grow. They do not labor or spin. Yet I tell you that not even Solomon in all his splendor was dressed like one of these. If that is how God clothes the grass of the field, which is here today and tomorrow is thrown into the fire, will he not much more clothe you, O you of little faith? (vv. 28–30 NIV)

Have you ever taken the time to appreciate a beautiful flower growing in a field? The same God who created such beauty can take good care of you.

Then Jesus gave us a wonderful word of encouragement. He said, "Your heavenly Father knows that you need them [food and clothes]. But seek first his kingdom and his righteousness, and all these things will be given to you as well" (vv. 32–33 NIV).

There it is—that's when we will find true contentment: when we seek God's kingdom first, and allow Him to take care of the details. Isn't that great? We can relax and stop worrying about how we are going to pay for the basic necessities of life. We can get off the vicious treadmill of trying to keep up the impressions of "prosperity." On the other hand, we do not need to feel guilty when God uses the gifts He has given to us to help finance His kingdom.

An Unusual Gift

Some people actually have a gift, it seems, of making money. And I am not just talking about the Donald Trumps, Ted Turners, or Rupert Murdochs of the world. In nearly every Christian congregation some businessmen and businesswomen seem to have a Midas touch. Everything they touch turns to gold. Where other entrepreneurs have failed, the natural money-makers among us may try the same idea and it proves fabulously successful. Obviously, we do not all produce the same results from the gifts God has given us.

This creates an interesting dilemma for wealthy Christians. They must deal with the dichotomy of knowing that Jesus said it is hard for a rich person to enter the kingdom of heaven, yet the very gift God has given them keeps them making money!

If this seems like one problem you'd love to have, stop and think about it for a moment. You might reconsider. It is generally agreed among Bible scholars outside the prosperity gospel ranks that Jesus was probably poor, as were most of the original disciples. So was the apostle Paul after his conversion to Christianity (although Paul acknowledged that he knew what it was like to be rich *and* to be poor). Similarly, many of the first-century Christians were in desperate financial straits, often as a result of their uncompromising faith in Christ. By the time the apostle Paul wrote his early letters to the Christians at Corinth, many of the saints in Jerusalem were literally starving to death. Many first-century Christians died in their poverty. Most of the second-century church fathers were poor too.

Knowing this, the wealthy Christian today looks at herself and cries out, "God, it seems my natural talent is to make money. But if I make money, you said it is difficult for me to be saved. What am I supposed to do?"

SHOULD YOU GIVE IT ALL AWAY?

Some rich Christians have answered this question by following the example of the church leader we now refer to as Saint Francis of Assisi. In the year 1208 Francis attended a mass in which the priest read a passage from the gospel of Matthew that changed Francis's life forever. In sending out His disciples, Jesus said,

As you go, preach, saying, "The kingdom of heaven is at hand." Heal the sick, cleanse the lepers, raise the dead, cast out demons. Freely you have received, freely give. Provide neither gold nor silver nor copper in your moneybelts, nor bag for your journey, nor two tunics, nor sandals, nor staffs; for the worker is worthy of his food. (Matt. 10:7–10 NKJV)

Francis took those verses to heart and decided that he would become an evangelist like the early disciples. He left the comforts of a wealthy family and adopted a life of poverty. A few friends and followers joined him and they began a simple ministry—with no large cathedrals, no huge financial budgets, nothing but the clothes on their backs. They traveled the countryside on foot, preaching the gospel and helping anyone who had a need.

Francis boldly took this "new" concept of Christian living to Pope Innocent III, requesting that he might begin a monastic order for others who felt similarly led. The pope was reluctant to allow Francis to start such a group. "My son," he said, "your plan of life seems too hard and rough." But Francis persisted and eventually got permission to start a monastery for those who wished to give up all their worldly goods to serve the poor.

Within eight years Francis's order of monks numbered nearly five thousand men. Francis of Assisi poured out his life, doing good deeds among the hurting and poor people of society. With Mother Teresa-like compassion, Francis ministered among society's worst and least. He died in his midforties of tuberculoid leprosy, but the Franciscan order of monks, with its various brotherhoods, continues to this day as the largest religious order in the Roman Catholic Church.

Don and Sondra Tipton are modern-day Christians who have followed the example of Francis of Assisi, giving up a comfortable lifestyle, selling most of their possessions, and stepping out on faith to serve the poor. In the process they learned how to trust God for large amounts of money and materials to help meet the needs of others.

At the time that Don and Sondra began to hear God speaking to them about using their resources to help others, they were the owners of Park West Polo and Hunt Club in the Beverly Hills area. Besides providing a playground for the rich and famous, their business involved selling horses to parents whose children ride in competitions. It was not unusual for a parent to spend fifty thousand dollars or more, per horse, so their children could compete for a two-dollar ribbon on the wall. The Tiptons also worked for the Gaming Alliance of Nevada, where their primary responsibility was to produce special events to lure more visitors to the gambling tables.

After Don and Sondra committed their lives to Christ, however, they became increasingly disgruntled at their own selfishness and the enormous waste their business promoted. The more they studied Scripture, the more the couple wanted to align their priorities with God's. They became convinced that God wanted them to help feed, clothe, and care for the poor. Don recalls a period of intense inner examination:

My thoughts were only of what I wanted and how to obtain it, as my goals were to fulfill my own needs and desires. I had no concern for the man on the street and no thought for where he would sleep. I made my own destiny (I thought), and he should make his. But in all my arrogance, I couldn't find a way to live with the fact that children were hungry and in pain every night. I couldn't find a way to accept the fact that they were dying at [the rate of] more than 35,000 every day . . .

If I died suddenly at forty from a heart attack caused by rich foods or perhaps from some dumb accident and came before Jesus, what would I say to Him? How would He measure my life? Beside what measuring stick would I stand? I had lived a life of self-indulgence, sometimes doing nice things and being basically a kind man, but I sure wouldn't have wanted to step on one side of the scale and be weighed against the children of poverty, hunger and pain or the man on the street. Had I died at forty, I'm afraid the scale of obedience would have read "tilt."[1]

Don and Sondra became obsessed with an unusual idea: that they should "get a ship, staff it with volunteers, load it with food, clothes, and medicine and deliver it to needy people."[2] An incredible idea? Yes. Audacious faith? Yes, that too, especially since Don did not know the first thing about ships and had never even been to sea, except for a six-dollar ferryboat ride to Catalina Island. He had once owned a Cris Craft Constellation, a forty-foot luxury yacht he used to entertain friends. But he had taken the boat out from dock only once, and then he nearly destroyed both the boat and the dock. Nevertheless, Don realized, "My only real qualification was that I was willing."[3]

And willingness is the only qualification necessary to be used by God. Over the years God has given the Tiptons not one, but five ships, Friend Ships, as they call their ministry, which they have used to take humanitarian aid to the Philippines, Nicaragua, El Salvador, Guatemala, Russia, Albania, Africa, and twenty other nations. In addition, Friend Ships now distributes more than 150,000 meals to needy families in the U.S. every week! Hundreds of thousands of people have come to know Christ as a result of the willing hands and hearts of the Tiptons and their fellow volunteers. To date more than seventy-five million dollars in aid has been distributed through the efforts of a few people who simply wanted to align their priorities with God's.

Should we all follow the examples of Francis of Assisi or Don and Sondra Tipton? Should we sell everything we have, give it to the poor, and invest our time and talents working for the Lord and for the good of humanity? When a rich young ruler came to Jesus and asked Him what he should do to obtain eternal life, Jesus told him to go, sell his possessions, give the proceeds to the poor, and then come follow Him (Matt. 19:16–22; Mark 10:17–22; Luke 18:18–23). Sadly, the young man decided that the cost of discipleship was too high, and he went away grieved. Immediately following that encounter, Jesus initiated the discussion with the disciples concerning how hard it is for a rich person to enter the kingdom of God.

THE REAL ISSUE

It's important to notice, however, that Jesus was answering the rich young ruler's specific question: "What should I do to inherit eternal life?" The question was not, "What should everybody else do?" or even, "What are the basic requirements to enter Your kingdom?" It was a pointed question from a young man, motivated most likely by his own self-interest. "How can I get into heaven?"

Jesus loved the young man enough to put His finger right on the most sensitive issue—his material wealth, his false god of money. That's why Jesus demanded that if the young man were going to follow Him, he would first have to divest himself of his "idols"; he would have to purge himself of his love of money and material things. Jesus basically said, "If *you* wish to be complete, you'll have to decide between that 'stuff' and Me."

We can tell by the young man's response that Jesus was right on target. Having great possessions may not have been a stumbling block for everybody who met Jesus, but it was for this fellow, and he was honest enough to recognize it. He didn't try to snow Jesus, or strike some sort of deal with Him, by offering to give away a large percentage of his property. He realized that Jesus had clearly defined the cost of his discipleship.

Unfortunately, many of us have missed Jesus' main point—that He will tolerate no other gods, no idols, before Him. Instead, we have often implied that the issue was the young man's money and possessions. That is not accurate. It was his *love* of money and what it purchased for him that kept him from following Jesus. Years later, the apostle Paul gave Timothy essentially the same message: "For the love of money is a root of all sorts of evil, and some by longing for it have wandered away from the faith" (1 Tim. 6:10 NASB).

The fact that the young man was rich was not what concerned Jesus. It was his unwillingness to acknowledge Jesus' authority over that area of his life. Tragic mistakes have been made when sincere believers are given the impression that the main issue that concerns Jesus is our finances.

For example, Leo Tolstoy, the famed Russian novelist who wrote such classics as *Anna Karenina* and *War and Peace,* underwent a profound spiritual conversion around 1880, while he was still at the peak of his career. Of noble birth, by the time Tolstoy became a believer, he had added enormous wealth to his already bulging bank account, including thousands of acres of rich Russian farmland. But upon encountering the story of the rich young ruler in Matthew 19, Tolstoy felt he must do exactly what Jesus had commanded the young man to do. Tolstoy sold off his prized farmland and all his possessions, and gave the money to the poor. Unfortunately, his desire to give up his property and live as a peasant disrupted his family and his career.

Worse yet, Tolstoy soon discovered that his spiritual fervor had been manipulated by malicious men for their own financial benefit. Tolstoy had treated the farm hands kindly and fairly; the new landowners oppressed them and took advantage of them. His faith severely shaken, Tolstoy sadly realized that his gift had been perverted. Eventually he was excommunicated by the church for his unorthodox teachings, and his later literary works were banned. Leo Tolstoy, one of the world's most brilliant and talented men, eventually fled his hometown and died of pneumonia at a railroad station.

With the best of intentions Tolstoy had mistakenly taken a specific command of Jesus, given to a specific person for a specific reason, and had turned it into a general spiritual principle that destroyed his life.

How Much Should We Give?

What then should our attitude be toward money? Should we merely continue to use our God-given gifts to make money and then bring 10 percent of everything we have to Christ, through the church? I don't think so. I'm convinced that simply putting money into an offering plate is not all that is involved in making Jesus Lord of our finances.

Please don't misunderstand: I believe you ought to give the first 10 percent of your income or increase to the Lord's work in your local church. That is the "storehouse" referred to in Malachi 3:8–11, out of which the Church, the body of Christ, should be ministering to the community, helping to feed and clothe the poor and otherwise helping needy people around them.

Throughout my years at PTL, no matter how much money we needed or how desperately I implored people to send donations, I always emphasized that their tithe belonged to their local church, not to us. I told people that if they wanted to give to our ministry, it should be an offering over and above the tithe they had already given to their local storehouse. Since my earliest days as a Christian, I have always believed in tithing, and I encourage you, if you are not giving at least 10 percent to the Lord's work in your local area, to set that amount as a goal.

On the other hand, tithing is a great place to start, but it is a lousy place to stop giving. The real issue for many Christians is not whether Jesus is Lord of the first 10 percent. The issue that pricks at most of us is whether He is Lord of the remaining 90 percent of our income or increase. Yes, many of us have given much to the cause of Christ; but after we have given, do we still have too much left over for ourselves?

Many Christians give far less than 10 percent of their income to the work of the Lord. According to a recent survey, Christians whose annual incomes exceed one hundred thousand dollars give only 1.8 percent of their income to their churches or other Christian ministries. No wonder we get so excited when we get to the point in our faith and commitment to Christ that we are able to give a full 10 percent . . . the part Jesus told the Pharisees they ought to do without neglecting the weightier issues of the law. To Jesus, the tithe was a given; surely anyone who loves God would give the bare minimum required.

We make a serious mistake, however, when we focus our attention on only the first 10 percent of our resources. Jesus wants to be Lord of all. No, that's not quite right. When we put it that way, it sounds as though Jesus is some wimpy, milquetoast banker begging you to put your money in his bank. That's not the Jesus of the Bible. Jesus is King of kings and Lord of lords. He *demands* to be Lord of our finances; He demands to be Lord of our time, talents, and treasures.

Tossing 10 percent of my income into the offering plate does not give me the right to do whatever I want with the remaining 90 percent. Does God really help me acquire wealth simply so I can buy a better stereo system, a nicer television, a new car, or a bigger house? I used to believe that, but not anymore. I now believe that when God gives us more, our first consideration should not be how we can improve our lifestyle, but how we can give a higher percentage of our increase toward the Lord's work.

Stan Mitchell, associate pastor of Christ Church in Nashville, provides a revealing insight into the matter of Christian prosperity by acknowledging how he and his wife, Jackie, have had to grapple with this issue. Stan and Jackie noticed that in their seven-year marriage, their income had increased substantially every year, but their percentage of giving toward God's work had remained the same, around 12 to 15 percent of their income.

> We realized that we were making more every year, but we were still giv-ing the same percentage as when we first started out, when we were making thirteen thousand dollars a year and living in a small, cramped, two-bedroom mobile home. Back then we said, "God if you'll just bless us, we will always give our tithes"—and we have kept that promise. But as we looked at our present lifestyle, with new cars and a nice home, we realized that we were out-increasing God nine to one. Sure, God gained on the 10 percent of our increase, but we gained on the 90 percent. And it was a pretty good deal for us.

We sat down and asked God, "Have we missed the point?" We had always made Him Lord of the 10 percent, but we had not made Him Lord of the 100 percent. We had never said, "God, all the money we earn belongs to You." We had the attitude that giving our 10 percent to the Lord's work was like paying dues in God's country club, and the remaining 90 percent belonged to us to do with as we pleased.

The Mitchells realized that God has a right not simply to the first 10 percent of their time, talent, and treasures; He has first right to all that we have.

WORK WELL AND YOU WILL PROSPER

The apostle Paul encouraged believers to excel in our work, not merely to make money. And not merely because our boss or the government requires it, but because everything we do is a reflection of the Lord we serve. "And whatsoever you do, do it heartily, as to the Lord and not to men, knowing that from the Lord you will receive the reward of the inheritance: for you serve the Lord Christ" (Col. 3:23–24 NKJV).

The fact is, when we operate according to God's principles, we do live better, and we do tend to prosper materially, especially in Western countries. When we adopt what I call a Christian work ethic, and we work hard, doing good, quality work "as to the Lord," we make money.

If you are a mechanic who does quality work at a fair price, and you establish a reputation as an ethical businessperson with integrity, your business will prosper. If you run a gas station, make it the best gas station it can be; provide good service in a clean, friendly environment, and you will prosper. If you are an entry-level employee who is not afraid of hard work, and if you have the skills, or the willingness to work at improving your skills, and you work as though Jesus were looking over your shoulder, before long you will be promoted and receive higher pay. If you are a dentist and conduct your business in a Christlike manner, you will have no lack of patients in your waiting room. If you are a lawyer . . . well, we'd better not stretch it! But you get the idea. Doing our work to please Christ inevitably brings personal fulfillment and usually brings financial prosperity, even in the midst of difficult circumstances.

When the economy collapsed following the stock market crash of 1929, many people who had placed their faith in Wall Street and their trust in money and material things literally jumped out of windows to their deaths. Yet in the midst of the worst economic depression our country has ever experienced, with chaos all around them, my parents, grandmother, and other sincere Christians built and paid for a new church in Muskegon, Michigan. How could they do it? My Aunt Maude provided the answer. She wrote in the church minutes from that period, "The people had a mind to work."

Similarly, when interest rates skyrocketed and the U.S. economy plummeted during the 1970s, a group of dedicated believers helped me build a state-of-the-art Christian television studio known as Heritage Village (this was prior to the existence of Heritage USA), in Charlotte, North Carolina. At a time when many people could not afford to put gasoline in their cars, we paid cash for the new TV facility. Why? Because the economy of God is not controlled by the economy of this world. If you "have a mind to work" and honor Him with whatever resources He puts in your hands, God's work will get done, and your needs will be met.

John Wesley, founder of the Methodist Church, recognized this phenomenon. He noticed that when people worked hard, did quality work, as to the Lord, they tended to make a lot of money. Not everyone got rich, of course, but Wesley realized that when people placed their trust in Christ and turned from their formerly sinful behavior patterns, their relationship with Christ often created virtues within them that fostered the accumulation of wealth. Wesley noted,

> Religion [Christianity] must necessarily produce industry and frugality. And if Religion produces frugality and industry, it will produce riches. We ought not to prevent people from being diligent and frugal. We must exhort all Christians to gain all they can; we must exhort all Christians to save all they can and that is in effect growing rich.[4]

Wesley knew well the Scriptures pertaining to money and materialism, and he pondered how he could come to terms with what seemed to be a conflict: that it is hard for a rich person to enter the kingdom of God, yet when a person truly became converted and adopted a Christlike attitude and lifestyle, she tended to prosper financially.

After much contemplation and prayer, Wesley concluded,

There is only one way and no other way under heaven that we can deal with this troublesome issue. If we are to gain all we can, if we are to save all we can, then we must likewise give all we can. Then the more [the people] gain and the more they save, the more they will grow in the grace of God, laying up for themselves treasures in heaven.[5]

CHANGE YOUR ATTITUDE; CHANGE YOUR LIFE

What would happen in your community if Christians began to take seriously the idea that God owns everything, that He has called us to be caretakers of His wealth, and He has allowed us to make more so we might do more for His kingdom? Imagine what might happen if even a few Christians began to say, "Okay, we have enough. We don't need bigger cars. We don't need fancier clothes. We don't need bigger houses. We will be content with what we have, and all that God gives us beyond this point, we will pour back into His work."

What do you suppose might happen if you adopted the godliness-with-contentment attitude of Scripture? Certainly, you would be delivered from worrying about what kind of car you drive, or whether you or your kids are wearing the latest fashion trend, or what neighborhood you live in. Those things are spiritual albatrosses we wear around our necks. And if we are not careful, they can rob us of our spiritual vitality. But beyond that, if even a small percentage of Christians would begin to catch a glimpse of what they could do with what God has entrusted to them, I believe that every ministry in the world could be fully funded.

Many Christians are making lifestyle changes as a way of doing more with their money and material possessions than simply lavishing more affluence on themselves. Not long ago, I heard of a middle-aged couple who was planning to move into a new, million-dollar home. Their business was prospering and it seemed logical that they should move into an upscale neighborhood. But then the Lord began to deal with the couple concerning the reason He had blessed their business financially: it was not simply to buy bigger and better stuff; it was to help finance the work of God.

The couple surprised most of their friends when they announced, "We have decided against purchasing the megabucks home. In fact, we're going to sell the half-million dollar home we now live in, and we are going to move down in scale. At the same time, we are going to expand our business, so we can earn more money, employ more people, and do more for the cause of Christ."

Not everyone can make such a lifestyle change, nor does Jesus demand that everyone do so. Only the Holy Spirit can direct someone to make this kind of decision. Any coercion, whether overt or subtle, designed to make people give more than God commands is reprehensible. Nobody can tell you what you should give to God, so don't allow anyone to put a guilt trip on you by implying that if you were really spiritual, you would give more. The Holy Spirit deals with each of us on an individual basis.

We have all received much more from God than we deserve. In these end times, how important it is that we learn to freely give, as well!

If you are going to be a great giver, it only makes sense that you must have something to give. That's why I believe God wants some people to make money—maybe lots of it—because He wants them to give it for use in His kingdom. He wants to be Lord of everything you are, everything you have.

USING WEALTH WISELY

To illustrate the point of how we can use money or influence to make friends, Jesus told His disciples (with the Pharisees listening close by) an intriguing story about a steward who was about to lose his position for poorly managing his master's money. When the steward received the bad news from his boss, he racked his brain trying to figure out his next move. "What shall I do, since my master is taking the stewardship away from me? I am not strong enough to dig; I am ashamed to beg. I know what I shall do, so that when I am removed from the stewardship, they will receive me into their homes" (Luke 16:3–4 NASB). At that, he summoned each of his masters' debtors and promptly reduced the amounts they owed his master. For instance, to a man who owed one hundred measures of oil, the steward said, "Take your bill, and sit down quickly and write fifty" (v. 6 NASB). The steward did something similar for each debtor, ingratiating himself to a wide segment of the population.

When the master discovered what the unrighteous steward had done, the master did not rebuke him or rail at him for losing more of his money. Instead, the master *praised* him for his shrewd actions! That is particularly interesting when we recall that it is Jesus telling this story. Was Jesus condoning poor work on the part of the steward? Was He ignoring the fact that the steward was giving away money that was not his own? Not hardly, but Jesus wanted to drive home His main point. "And I say to you, make for yourselves friends of the mammon of unrighteousness; that when it fails, they may receive you into the eternal dwellings'" (v. 9 NASB).

Jesus was not saying to make friends of (*ek* in Greek) *money*. He was saying to use your money's influence positively. It is not really your money anyhow; it is your heavenly Master's money. You are merely a steward of His resources. If you really want to use the resources God has given you, then help those poorer than yourself. Use the possessions God has given you to impact eternity, investing in those things which will have value in the world to come.

Notice, too, that Jesus says "when it fails," rather than "if it fails." In other words, you can count on it: *one day soon, money is going to fail you.* Beyond that, one day soon, our entire economic system is going to fail. When it fails, only those things that have been done for Christ will have any real value.

In The Parable of the Unrighteous Steward, Jesus also gave us the answer to why many of us are not more wealthy than we are, even though God wants to bless our lives. Jesus explained,

> He who is faithful in a very little thing is faithful also in much; and he who is unrighteous in a very little thing is unrighteous also in much. If therefore you have not been faithful in the use of unrighteous mammon [riches], who will entrust the true riches to you? (Luke 16:10–11 NASB)

Jesus clearly was implying that if we are unwilling to be faithful to our heavenly Master in the way we use the resources God has given us, how can we possibly expect God to give us more? Instead of using God's gifts and resources for His glory, according to His priorities, many of us have squandered what is not legitimately ours to satisfy our own selfish desires. This must stop.

Ironically, it may be God's mercy and kindness that He does not give us more, because the responsibility and accountability required of the person to whom much is given will be all the greater.

SEEKING TRUE RICHES

The apostle Paul reminded Timothy of this principle when he admonished:

> Instruct those who are rich in this present world not to be conceited or to fix their hope on the uncertainty of riches, but on God, who richly supplies us with all things to enjoy. Instruct them to do good, to be rich in good works, to be generous and ready to share, storing up for themselves the treasure of a good foundation for the future, so that they may take hold of that which is life indeed. (1 Tim. 6:17–19 NASB)

Paul was echoing Jesus, who instructed His disciples to seek after true riches (Luke 16:11), those things that will last forever. To Jesus, true riches have little to do with money or materialism. Scripture equates having a good name, a reputation above reproach, as part of true riches (Prov. 22:1). Investing our treasures in heaven will also result in our having true riches (Matt. 6:19–20). (For a more complete study of true riches, see Appendix A.)

I am convinced that during the times of calamity that are about to come upon the world, some of God's people will receive massive amounts of material goods. I believe that when the tough times come, many of this world's prized possessions will be given to the church and placed in the hands of God's people. But don't set your heart upon them. God is not opposed to our having stuff, but He is very much opposed to stuff having us. Scripture says, "Though your riches increase, do not set your heart on them" (Ps. 62:10 NIV).

Keeping a right perspective toward making money and acquiring material wealth is a heart issue. Jesus told us that if we would abide in Him, we could ask whatever we wanted and it would be done (John 15:7)— *if* we abide in Him and His words abide in us. If He is truly Lord of our lives and His word is in our hearts, we will not ask Him for things to use for our carnal desires.

The apostle Paul encouraged the Philippians, "And my God shall supply all your need according to His riches in glory by Christ Jesus" (Phil. 4:19 NKJV). If you trust Him with everything you have, God will take care of you.

Materialistic Christianity was not the message of the early apostles, nor was it what motivated the great preachers, missionaries, and world-changers down through church history. For instance, Dr. A. W. Tozer, one of the most articulate, self-educated, and effective preachers ever to stand behind a pulpit, may have been prophetic when he wrote:

> It seems that Christian believers have been going through a process of indoctrination and brainwashing, so it has become easy for us to adopt a kind of creed that makes God to be our servant instead of our being God's servant.
>
> Why should a man write and distribute a tract instructing us on "How to Pray so God Will Send You the Money You Need"? Any of us who have experienced a life and ministry of faith can tell how the Lord has met our needs. My wife and I would probably have starved in those early years of ministry if we couldn't have trusted God completely for food and everything else. Of course, we believe that God can send money to His believing children—but it becomes a pretty cheap thing to get excited about the money and fail to give the glory to Him who is the Giver!
>
> So many are busy "using" God. Use God to get a job. Use God to give us safety. Use God to give us peace of mind. Use God to obtain success in business. Use God to provide heaven at last.
>
> Brethren, we ought to learn—and learn it very soon—that it is much better to have God first and have God Himself even if we have only a thin dime than to have all the riches and all the influence in the world and not have God with it![6]

Why is materialistic Christianity so dangerous? Because Jesus is coming back for His bride, the Church, and we are so wrapped up in the things of this world, we are not paying attention to the signs of the times coming to pass before our eyes. I believe Jesus is coming soon, and He is coming for a spotless, pure, holy bride, not one compromised by money and materialism.

Beyond that, the manipulation of money and goods is soon to be revealed as the main method of control imposed upon society by the Antichrist. The god of materialism will soon be revealed as the harlot that robs our affection from God. It is vital that we understand this principle as we see the apocalypse approaching.

PART III

The Coming Apocalypse

8

Get Ready . . . Jesus Is Coming!

The world has not seen the last of Jesus Christ. He came once in human history, imploding into our world as a mere mortal, and He is coming again. Jesus Himself promised that He will return at the end of the age.

More than two hundred Scripture references spoke of His first coming. The Bible accurately predicted that Jesus would be born into the family of Judah; that He would be born to a virgin; that He would be born in Bethlehem; that He and His family would flee to Egypt; that He would heal the sick; that His own people would despise and reject Him; that He would be betrayed by a friend; that He would be sold for thirty pieces of silver; that He would be crucified with sinners; that His side would be pierced; that He would be raised from the dead; and that He would ascend to heaven. Amazingly, every detail of the prophecies concerning His first advent came to pass.

If you are astounded that more than two hundred specific prophecies were fulfilled regarding the first coming of Christ, get ready for a surprise. Over *three hundred* Scripture references point to the Second Coming. But when Jesus Christ returns, He will not come as the Babe in Bethlehem's manger.

The first time He came to Earth, Jesus came as the Man of Sorrows; at His Second Coming, He will appear as Almighty God.

He came first as the Lamb of God; when He returns, He will be the Lion of Judah.

At His incarnation, Jesus came as the Prince of Peace; when He comes again, it will be as King of kings and Lord of lords.

He came the first time to atone for sin. When Jesus Christ returns the second time, He will judge sinners.

The signs of His appearing are all around us; you needn't be a Bible scholar to sense that something unusual is happening on Earth. Newspapers and news magazines practically shout from their pages, "These are getting-ready days!"

Interestingly, it is the scientific community, not Christian theologians, announcing that we are living on the precipice of destruction. Hollywood is heralding the news that the earth is about to encounter something cataclysmic. A few brave prophetic voices are being heard, crying out in the wilderness of our world, warning us that our days are numbered. The earth itself is groaning and creaking, seemingly in anticipation of a major shake-up of the status quo. Ironically, the one group with relatively little to say about Christ's soon return is the evangelical church. Instead, we spend most of our time and energy trying to help people succeed in *this* life, rather than getting them ready for eternity.

Now is the time to get our lives aligned with God's Word, to establish correct priorities, to invest in those things that will last a million years from now, rather than fickle, foolish, transitory material things. Even more important, now is the time for the Church, that group of true believers from every denomination, to begin functioning as the true body of Christ, caring for one another, helping one another as the family of God. Knowledge that we are truly living in what the Bible refers to as "the last days" should also motivate Christians to more actively seek out opportunities to share the gospel with their unsaved friends and family members. In a very real way, the clock is ticking and time is running out.

Have you ever planned for a vacation, dreamed about it, and worked toward it? Finally the time comes, and the night before departure you are busily taking care of last-minute details. That's where we are living right now.

Think of it another way: What would you do if you knew beyond a doubt that you had only one year to live? How would that affect your priority list? On what would you want to spend your time, energy, and money?

The message God gave me while I was in prison burns within my soul: Soon the world will be plunged into chaos—a time of horrendous tribulation, if you will—and Christians will be here to experience at least part of that terror. Do not lose hope; Jesus Christ *will* return, and He will indeed take you to live with Him eternally. However, He will not return before the refining process takes place.

Many people are skeptical concerning Christ's second coming. Even some devout Christians are reluctant to voice a belief in Christ's return for fear they will be considered fanatical. Their fears are not unfounded. Believers looking for the soon return of Christ are frequently dismissed as kooks belonging to the ilk of the Hale-Bopp comet cults, or worse.

You may not believe Jesus Christ is coming again.

That's okay. Really, it is.

He's coming anyway.

Your disbelief will not impact His return one bit; your lack of faith will not keep Him away. It may cost you a life separated from God in eternity, but your unbelief will not affect His coming. Whether you believe or not, however, you need to recognize that the predictions of the Bible will indeed take place; it is only a matter of time.

The Key Questions

What, when, and how is it all going to happen? When will Jesus return? These are some of the questions put to Jesus by His disciples, just a few days prior to His crucifixion. He and His disciples sat privately on the Mount of Olives, overlooking the city of Jerusalem. Gazing across the Kidron Valley, they could clearly see the magnificent beauty of the Jewish temple buildings, built on what was traditionally known as Mount Moriah, the place where, in obedience to God, the Jewish patriarch Abraham had taken his own son Isaac to offer him as a sacrifice. The angel of the Lord stopped Abraham just in the nick of time, but the mountain eventually did become a place of sacrifice as the blood of thousands of lambs spattered the Jewish altars built there in the temple.

The original temple was constructed during the reign of King Solomon, around 960 B.C., on the same site. It had been opulent and ornate beyond belief, but Solomon's temple had long since been razed when Jerusalem fell to Babylon in 586 B.C. A second temple was erected, under the leadership of a fellow named Zerubbabel, when a relatively small group of Jews returned to Jerusalem from their exile in Babylon. Granted, this latest temple area, the panorama that Jesus and the disciples were looking at, paled in comparison to the grandeur of Solomon's temple. But it had recently been beautified by Herod the Great, a project that had taken forty-six years to complete. It was this renovation, no doubt, that so impressed the disciples as they proudly pointed out the temple's various features.

Jesus, however, burst their bubble in a hurry when He said, "Do you not see all these things? Assuredly, I say to you, not one stone shall be left here upon another, that shall not be thrown down" (Matt. 24:2 NKJV). Jesus' prediction that the temple would be destroyed must have shocked His disciples. Nevertheless, His words came to pass in A.D. 70, when the Romans literally tore the structure down stone by stone, and absconded with the priceless gold furnishings.

The disciples' consternation concerning Jesus' comment about the destruction of the temple is what prompted them to ask three rapid-fire questions all rolled into one. They asked Jesus, "Tell us, when will these things be? And what will be the sign of Your coming, and of the end of the age?" (24:3 NKJV).

Jesus' answer is contained in Matthew 24:4—25:46 and is commonly known as the Second Coming Discourse. It is the second longest discourse of Jesus recorded in the Bible; only the Sermon on the Mount (Matthew 5:3—7:27) comprises a longer, uninterrupted address by Jesus. In the course of His talk, Jesus described a wide variety of the "signs of the times," things the disciples should look for before the coming of Christ and the end of the age. As with most apocalyptic statements in the Bible, Jesus' answer had a present-tense fulfillment, which could be applied to the destruction of Jerusalem during the disciples' lifetimes, and a future-tense fulfillment, which we are seeing come to pass before our eyes today, just before Christ returns to Earth again.

SEDUCING SPIRITS AND DEVILISH DOCTRINES

Jesus began His discussion with a warning: "Take heed that no one deceives you" (Matt. 24:4 NKJV). He explained that near the end of the age, many false christs, false messiahs, and false saviors would appear on the public scene. It is interesting that Jesus mentioned this sign three times within a few sentences (24:5, 24:11, 24:24), yet we insist on ignoring His warning.

In my lifetime I have witnessed the rise of such false messiahs as the Maharaj Ji, who claimed to be a savior, with five million followers. Sun Myung Moon, head of "the Moonies," is another who claims to be a savior and has millions of adherents.

Add to these groups the proliferation of spiritual leaders and groups with "messiah complexes," such as Charles Manson, Jim Jones, David Koresh, the Hale-Bopp comet followers, the Baha'i cult, Hare Krishnas, Rastafarians (who worship the former Ethiopian dictator, Haile Selassie), and overt witchcraft and Satan worshipers, and it is obvious that false messiahs, false prophets, and the occult are flourishing. Movies, television programs, and music exalting the devil and demonic activities are common. New Age religions, psychic and paranormal groups, spiritualists, and every weird sort of cult imaginable have become accepted in our society. And all these have burst onto the scene within my lifetime! Moreover, while false prophets are as old as the Scriptures, the majority of cults—those groups that deny that Jesus Christ is God and the only way to heaven—have arisen within the past two hundred years.

You may think it is absurd to worship some of the cult figures and false messiahs being foisted upon the public nowadays, and you are absolutely correct. But understand, when a person turns away from the true Jesus and the true gospel, there is no end to the insanity to which she will stoop in search of a spiritual substitute.

In addition to the blatant false christs, we now have a proliferation of what can only be called the apostate church, churches or groups of worshipers claiming to be Christians, but who have strayed far from biblical doctrine in their search for a more palatable, more accommodating "gospel," a gospel so watered down that it is, in fact, no gospel at all. "Believe what you want to believe" seems to be their only creed.

One sincere, but misguided, person said to me, "I know what the Bible says, but I don't care. I know what I have experienced and that's all that matters." This individual flagrantly disregards the Scriptures, denies the essential doctrines of Christianity, and lives an openly sinful lifestyle; yet he believes that he and his organization have found true salvation.

This is what so deeply disturbs me about some of the proponents of materialistic Christianity. By their twisting and misinterpretation of Scriptures, they have unwittingly set the scene for an acceptance of "another gospel," which will eventually lead to the acceptance of not just another Christ, but an Antichrist, as we shall see in the pages ahead.

The Holy Spirit spoke through the apostle Paul,

> Now the Spirit expressly says that in latter times some will depart from the faith, giving heed to deceiving spirits and doctrines of demons, speaking lies in hypocrisy, having their own conscience seared with a hot iron. (1 Tim. 4:1–2 NKJV)

Nowadays, these "seducing spirits and doctrines of devils" (KJV) are openly received and granted respectability, and are often given more credence than true, biblically-centered Christian groups. Even more frightening, many genuine believers within the Church are unaware or unconcerned that these things are taking place! Jesus said to take heed that you are not deceived.

End-Time Wars and the Threat of Obliteration

A second sign Jesus said would indicate His soon return is the proliferation of "wars and rumors of wars" (Matt. 24:6–7). Skeptics are quick to interject, "But we have always had wars; war has been ingrained in our human experience since the beginning of time." Unfortunately, that is true. Since historical records have been kept, years of war have outnumbered peaceful years thirteen to one. Some sociologists are skeptical that there has ever been a year when the entire world was at peace. War seems to be the norm.

Nevertheless, that does not negate the impact of Jesus' statement. The obvious tenor of this passage is that wars and rumors of wars, nation rising against nation, kingdom against kingdom, will drastically increase. Furthermore, these signs will occur concomitantly with the other phenomena Jesus described, so when you see and hear of wars along with the other signs of the times, all happening about the same time, get ready. When you see all these things converging on one point in human history, we are nearing the end of the age.

Within the past century man has proven his inhumanity by his willingness to destroy his fellow man. As evidence, consider that during the last century of the current millennium, we have experienced two world wars and at least fifteen major "conflicts," such as the Vietnam war, the Korean conflict, and the Desert Storm war with Iraq, not to mention such perennial hot spots as Ireland, Bosnia, and various places in Africa. Wars have increased in number, scope, and in their destructiveness.

Ironically, many people called World War I "the war to end all wars." Nearly 8.5 million people died "to end all wars." Yet hardly twenty years later, in 1939, Adolph Hitler invaded Poland, launching World War II. More than fifty-two million people died in that war, which engulfed the world. At the end of World War II, the leaders of the world agreed with the United Nations' preamble, which declared, "We are the people determined to save succeeding generations from war."

War hero General Douglas MacArthur said, "We have had our last chance. If we do not now devise some greater and more equitable system, Armageddon will be at our door." The general's comment was prophetic. Within three years war broke out again, this time in the Middle East, resulting in the rebirth of Israel as a nation in 1948. Since then, Israel has had to defend its borders by going to war three times, in 1956, 1967, and 1973.

Unquestionably, one of the reasons most Bible scholars believe that Jesus' statements concerning war apply to this age is that human beings now possess the power to obliterate the world by means of nuclear bombs. The first atomic bombs, dropped in 1945 on the Japanese cities of Hiroshima and Nagasaki, produced devastation beyond anything mankind had ever witnessed.

In a city of five hundred thousand people, seventy thousand were killed instantly. Another seventy thousand were severely injured. Many more died in the hours that followed. An area of 4.7 square miles, or over three thousand acres, was completely leveled in downtown Hiroshima. Shock waves moved out from the center of the explosion at speeds of 12.5 miles per minute, over six hundred miles per hour, crumbling twelve-inch walls a mile away. Heat waves of millions of degrees in intensity moved out with the speed of light, melting flesh, stone, and anything else in its path.

And that was a "small" bomb, equivalent to a mere twenty thousand tons of dynamite, only one-fiftieth of a megaton. Now we talk almost casually about 100-megaton nuclear warheads that could wipe out entire cities and states upon impact. During the Cold War era, the former Soviet Union routinely had 100-megaton nuclear warheads aimed at nearly every major industrial or population center in the United States. With the dissolution of the Soviet empire in the 1990s, many of those warheads remain unaccounted for. Military and political leaders worry that the Soviet Union's stockpile of more than thirty thousand nuclear weapons may end up in the hands of emerging nations or terrorists, making those weapons more dangerous now than they ever were under Soviet control. Others in the military and scientific communities fear that China is rapidly emerging as a nuclear threat to the world.

Most of us have grown callous to such information. The potential for global annihilation is so overwhelming, we choose instead to deny its existence. Yet Jesus said we should not be overly alarmed by the proliferation of wars. "See that you are not troubled; for all these things must come to pass, but the end is not yet" (Matt. 24:6 NKJV). Consequently, when we see and hear of wars increasing in frequency and intensity, we should not fear. Although we may detest war and senseless bloodshed, we must recognize that these events are not happening outside the scope of God's knowledge or plan.

SCARCITY OF FOOD

Famine is another disturbing sign of the times Jesus mentions in the Second Coming Discourse (Matt. 24:7). With our modern ability to pinpoint targets, war's bloodletting is often quick and relatively painless compared to famine, which decimates a population, one person at a time, over extended periods of time. Which of us has not grieved over the sight of a child with a distended belly sucking futilely at the collapsed breast of her dehydrated mother? Starvation kills slowly, but just as effectively, as an atomic bomb.

Ironically, in our age of affluence, our world teeters perpetually on the precipice of famine. Some scientists estimate that we are only one bad harvest away from worldwide starvation. Although the United States remains the breadbasket of the world, a drought, heat wave, or changing weather patterns in the U.S. could have devastating effects throughout the global food supply. The El Niño-related floods, tornadoes, and erratic temperatures of 1997 and 1998 ought to cause us to give thought to just how fragile our existence on this planet really is, and how little control over natural disasters we have.

Writing in the book of Revelation, the apostle John foresaw a time when famine and scarcity would be widespread on earth.

> When He opened the third seal, I heard the third living creature say, "Come and see." So I looked, and behold, a black horse, and he who sat on it had a pair of scales in his hand. And I heard a voice in the midst of the four living creatures saying, "A quart of wheat for a denarius, and three quarts of barley for a denarius; and do not harm the oil and the wine." (Rev. 6:5–6 NKJV)

John was predicting a time when food would be so scarce, a day's wages (a denarius, in John's time) could barely buy meager provisions. I have no doubt that we will live to see the reality of that scenario.

Bugs, Vermin, and Viruses

In Luke's account of the Second Coming Discourse, Jesus mentions *pestilences* along with the natural disasters (21:11). This may be the proliferation of new species of bugs and vermin, but it might also include the rise of such killer diseases as AIDS, Ebola, mad-cow disease, and the "chicken flu," which decimated whole flocks of birds in early 1998. One of the ominous concerns on the minds of National Security leaders is the possibility of terrorists smuggling into the U.S. some sort of deadly germ warfare to create a national biohazard, the spread of a virus against which our bodies could not defend.

Consider, for example, what might happen if we had a widespread outbreak of Ebola, a frightening disease discovered in monkeys, in which the animals' flesh literally begins to dissolve, their bodies fall apart, their eyeballs explode out of their heads, and their stomachs burst open . . . all in a matter of hours or days after contracting the disease. No cure exists for Ebola and many similar lethal viruses. More frightening, perhaps, physical contact with an Ebola carrier is not necessary for the disease to spread; it seems to be able to waft through the air itself, infecting those creatures within close proximity. The implications are terrifying.

Again, in the book of Revelation, John sees a day when such death will be widespread:

> When He opened the fourth seal, I heard the voice of the fourth living creature saying, "Come and see." So I looked, and behold, a pale horse. And the name of him who sat on it was Death, and Hades followed with him. And power was given to them over a fourth of the earth, to kill with sword, with hunger, with death, and by the beasts of the earth. (6:7–8 NKJV)

ROCKING, ROLLING, AND REELING

Another sign Jesus told us to watch for is that of earthquakes becoming more prevalent (Matt. 24:7). In his parallel account, Luke said, "And there will be great earthquakes in various places" (21:11 NKJV). Our news media is confirming Jesus' prediction with startling regularity.

I believe the earth itself is groaning (Rom. 8:19–22) in anticipation of the Lord's return. Part of this groaning includes floods, volcanoes, tidal waves, hurricanes, and earthquakes. With the advent of the "information highway," anyone with a computer and an online service can check the daily "groaning reports." I am a computer novice, but in recent months I have become fascinated with the Web site put up by the U.S. Geological Survey, the scientific group whose job it is to track seismological activity. Each time I check the information gathered and reported by the USGS, I am shocked to see the hundreds of small earthquakes taking place in the United States each day. Most of these are minor tremors, barely enough to budge a picture hanging on the wall, but the sheer magnitude of the number of shakings beneath the earth's surface is mind-boggling.

Recently I was scheduled to speak on this subject at a local Bible school, so I decided to print out the USGS report of seismic activity to show the students. To my surprise, the computer printout stretched all the way across the front of the auditorium.

Not only are earthquakes increasing in number, they are increasing in intensity and destructiveness. Part of this can be attributed, of course, to the higher density of our populations living in urban areas, thus resulting in higher casualties and property damage when quakes hit. On the other hand, our ability to predict earthquake activity is greatly improved and has been instrumental in saving countless lives. Yet the destruction caused by earthquakes around the world continues to be staggering. Worse still, I am convinced that we haven't seen anything yet.

Many seismologists are convinced that the Far East, particularly China and Japan, are ripe for a major earthquake. In 1976 China experienced one of the worst quakes in history; more than eight hundred thousand people died. Japan experienced a similar quake in 1993, but because it occurred in a relatively obscure area, few lives were lost and the world ignored it. Another strong quake rocked Japan in 1995, killing more than five thousand people. Seismologists note that Japan may be approaching the end of a cycle, in which it is hit with a massive earthquake approximately every thirty years, the next one due to occur sometime between the years 2000 and 2006. An earthquake of such proportions, coupled with Japan's already teetering economy (currently being propped up by American dollars), could precipitate a global economic collapse as well as the loss of life and property.

In the U.S. we tend to think of earthquakes as a West Coast problem, something the people in California live with on a daily basis, but not a phenomenon affecting the rest of the country. A whole lot of shaking is going on beneath California's surface, but earthquakes are not unique to that part of the country. According to the USGS, the central Mississippi Valley is the most earthquake-prone region east of the Rocky Mountains. Specifically, the New Madrid seismic zone, including areas of Arkansas, Illinois, Indiana, Kentucky, Mississippi, Missouri, and Tennessee, is particularly vulnerable. The USGS estimates that "the probability of a magnitude–6 to –7 earthquake occurring in this seismic zone within the next fifty years is higher than 90 percent. Such an earthquake could hit in the Mississippi Valley at any time."[1]

Interestingly, three of the most powerful quakes ever to shake the U.S. occurred not in Los Angeles, but in and around the town of New Madrid, Missouri, during the winter of 1811–12. The quakes have been logged as magnitude–8 earthquakes by seismologists. To put that in perspective, consider this: the San Francisco earthquake of 1906 was a magnitude 7.8; the 1994 Northridge, California, quake was a magnitude 6.7.

Survivors [of the 1811 New Madrid quakes] reported that the earthquakes caused cracks to open in the earth's surface, the ground to roll in visible waves, and large areas of land to sink or rise . . . Damage was reported as far away as Charleston, South Carolina, and Washington, D.C.[2]

Shaking caused by the New Madrid quakes rang church bells in Boston, one thousand miles away! While most houses within a two-hundred-fifty-mile area were damaged, and some destroyed, relatively few lives were lost due to the small population. Approximately four hundred people lived in New Madrid in 1811. If such a quake should occur today, the devastation would be horrendous. The USGS notes,

In 1811, the central Mississippi Valley was sparsely populated. Today the region is home to millions of people, including those in the cities of St. Louis, Missouri, and Memphis, Tennessee. Adding to the danger, most structures in the region were not built to withstand earthquake shaking, as they have been in California and Japan.[3]

THE PRESSURE OF THE AGES

California, of course, is under the constant threat of a major earthquake. Hundreds of minor tremors shake Southern California every day. Californians have become so accustomed to these minor seismic motions, most of the population does not even flinch when the ground groans beneath their feet. Nevertheless, both scientists and preachers predict the "Big One" is coming.

At the risk of sounding like an alarmist, I feel compelled to report an unusual personal experience that causes me to believe a major earthquake will soon shake Los Angeles to its foundations. In 1997 I traveled to L.A. to appear on the CNN broadcast of *Larry King Live* and to speak at several churches in California. I arrived at night and a chauffeured limousine picked me up. I was thankful for the ride, but a little uneasy about getting into the limo. In the years since I lost PTL, I had become much more comfortable riding in my Jeep.

Nevertheless, the Larry King show had provided the transportation, so I gratefully climbed into the back seat of the stretch limo and settled in for the ride to my hotel. As we drove from the airport toward the bright lights in the heart of L.A., I experienced one of the strangest sensations of my life. It was as though my body became a human Geiger counter; I started resonating with the earth deep below Los Angeles. I began to shake and suddenly, in the Spirit, it was as if I could see down into the earth. I saw huge boulders, bowed upward and grinding against each other, like one fist pushing against another.

The Lord began to speak to my heart and mind as clearly as if He had called me on the limo's car phone. "This is the pressure of the ages," the Lord revealed to me. "And it's about to let go." Trembling, I looked out the car window, just as the limo whisked past the beautiful, statuesque skyscrapers in downtown L.A. It was then that I sensed God speaking to me, words I am reluctant to actually put in print, yet words that have been seared for all eternity into my spirit.

As I stared at the tall buildings, the Lord said to me, "Not one of these buildings will be left standing. There is going to be an earthquake unlike any other earthquake this area has experienced. There will be nothing left."

I shuddered in shock, shaking as if trying to awaken from a bad dream. But this was no dream and I was fully awake. As we drove further away from downtown, the sensation subsided, and the Geiger-counter effect stopped. Looking back, I believe God was impressing upon me once again that I must proclaim this message before it is too late.

Despite the increase in natural disasters, Jesus cautioned us about becoming overly agitated about these things. He said, "But all these things are merely the beginning of birth pangs" (Matt. 24:8 NASB). As any mother knows, the closer the labor pains get, the shorter the interval of time between contractions, the closer it is to the birth of the baby. Jesus was saying that we should regard the prevalence of earthquakes, famines, and other natural disasters similarly. These are warning signs, alerting us that something significant is going to happen soon.

RANDOM ACTS OF VIOLENCE

Jesus went on to warn His disciples that before His return to earth, Christians would fall upon tough times, that they would be delivered up to tribulation, that they would be hated and even killed because of their faith in Christ (Matt. 24:9). Apparently, not every Christian will have the commitment level and moral strength necessary to survive in such a hostile atmosphere. Consequently, many believers will stumble, be offended, and some will even fall away. Others will betray and hate one another (24:10). Still others will be deceived by false prophets. Jesus also predicted that lawlessness will increase and the love of many people will grow cold (24:12). This could mean that they will be lured away from their love for each other, or they will forsake their love for the Lord, or possibly both.

We are seeing all of these things happening today to the nth degree. The sin and moral stench of our society is almost too shocking to categorize anymore. Our newscasts are filled with stories of murder, rape, and rip-offs, children shooting teachers and classmates, "vampire" killings, teachers having sex with students, political corruption, cheating, lawbreaking of every kind.

I used to be shocked at what I saw on my television; today I am shocked that I am not shocked anymore. Our minds have become numb to the onslaught of atrocities; in self-defense, we have allowed ourselves to become callused to the rampant sin around us. Each new report of some horrendous act makes us want to close our eyes and wish it would all just go away . . . and someday soon, it will.

Again, Jesus did not say that our society would be unique in its gross sinfulness. He merely said that when we see all these things happening at the same time, get ready for His return. Nor did He give the impression that it would be easy to live in the time before His coming, that all of God's children would be living like King's Kids. Quite the contrary, Jesus said, "But he who endures to the end shall be saved" (Matt. 24:13 NKJV).

THE GOOD NEWS SPREAD

On the positive side, Jesus gave us one good sign to look for. He said, "And this gospel of the kingdom will be preached in all the world as a witness to all the nations, and then the end will come" (24:14 NKJV). Notice that Jesus did not say that everyone in the world would *believe* the gospel; in fact, He did not even say that every living person would *hear* the gospel. He merely said that His gospel would be *preached* in all the world. With our modern means of communications—television, the Internet, and new communication technologies yet to come—we are the first generation in history to have the potential to see Jesus' words fulfilled.

More important than our mass communications systems, God is pouring out His Spirit in a fresh way all over the world. The past twenty years have seen the greatest period of Spirit-anointed evangelism the world has ever known. Yet I believe God has even greater things in store for us as we reach our world with His Word in these last days. We need to get our eyes off the accumulation of material things and focus on what God is doing by His Spirit. We need to establish our priorities in the light of God's priorities, one of which is certainly the spreading of His Word to the world.

THE KEY TO THE PUZZLE

One of the most significant signs we are to look for is found in Luke's gospel, where Jesus predicted the fall of Jerusalem and the subsequent dispersion of the Jewish people into various nations. Jerusalem was indeed destroyed by the Romans in A.D. 70. But what Jesus said would happen after that time is of particular interest to us today. In describing the calamities the Jewish people would encounter, Jesus said, "And they will fall by the edge of the sword, and be led away captive into all nations. And *Jerusalem will be trampled by Gentiles until the times of the Gentiles are fulfilled*" (21:24 NKJV, emphasis mine). Bible scholars have bandied about various meanings for the Time of the Gentiles, but basically Jesus was telling His disciples (and us) that He would not return until Jerusalem is back in Jewish hands, under Jewish control.

While well-intentioned preachers in past generations attempted to inspire Christians to be ready for the Lord's imminent return, in truth, Jesus' own prophecy had not yet been fulfilled: Jerusalem remained under the control of Gentile nations. The Jewish people were scattered all over the earth. The country of Israel, as we know it today, did not exist.

But on May 14, 1948, David Ben-Gurion declared the independence of the new nation of Israel. Jewish people from around the world began streaming back to Israel, in fulfillment of the prophet Ezekiel's words uttered nearly 2,600 years earlier:

I will open your graves and cause you to come up from your graves, and bring you into the land of Israel . . . Surely I will take the children of Israel from among the nations, wherever they have gone, and will gather them from every side and bring them into their own land; and I will make them one nation in the land, on the mountains of Israel. (37:12, 21–22 NKJV)

The Jewish people had a nation once again, but the city of Jerusalem remained under the control of Israel's Arab neighbors. Then in June 1967, against overwhelming odds, Israel defeated a coalition of Arab nations in six days and reclaimed control of the Old City, including the site where the Jewish temple stood during Jesus' earthly lifetime. Prior to the Six-Day War, this area of Jerusalem had been considered part of Jordan and had been off-limits to Jews during Jordanian occupation. Although now under Jewish control, the ancient temple site remains occupied by the Mosque of Omar, also known as the Dome of the Rock, the third most sacred site in all of Islam. In Muslim lore, it is reputed to be the place from which Muhammad ascended into heaven.

Why is this important? you may be wondering. *What does a Muslim shrine have to do with the second coming of Christ?*

Simply this: the Bible indicates that in the last days, the Jewish temple will be rebuilt on the same site as its precursors, Solomon's temple, and Zerubbabel's temple, the one that stood during the lifetime of Jesus (Dan. 9:27; 11:31–32). Some sort of renewed sacrificial system will be restored at the temple as well. At the halfway point of the seven-year period of time known as the Tribulation (which we will look at more closely in the pages ahead), the Antichrist will desecrate the rebuilt Jewish temple in a most abominable way, and he will declare to the world that he is God (2 Thess. 2:4). Jesus recognized this "abomination of desolation" as a pivotal point in the end-time scenario. "Therefore when you see the 'abomination of desolation,' spoken of by Daniel the prophet, standing in the holy place . . . then let those who are in Judea flee to the mountains." (Matt. 24:15–16 NKJV).

IT'S ALMOST TIME TO GO

Exactly how all these signs of the times will be fulfilled is not our concern. Jesus told us in advance that they will happen, and so far Jesus has a 100 percent batting average when it comes to the fulfillment of prophecy. Many of the predictions He made nearly two thousand years ago have come to pass already, fulfilled to the letter. A few important prophecies have yet to be fulfilled, but by all appearances their potential fulfillment is imminent. It is not a great leap of faith to believe that what He said is yet to happen in the future will also transpire exactly as He has said.

In the meantime, Jesus warned us, "Take heed to yourselves, lest your hearts be weighed down with carousing, drunkenness, and cares of this life, and that Day come on you unexpectedly" (Luke 21:34 NKJV). Furthermore, Jesus told His disciples that as we see the signs of the times coming to pass, we should not despair or go around with a doom-and-gloom attitude. In fact, He encouraged us to have just the opposite outlook. "Now when these things begin to happen, look up and lift up your heads, because your redemption draws near" (Luke 21:28 NKJV).

Jesus gave His disciples an easily understood object lesson concerning the last days:

> Now learn this parable from the fig tree: When its branch has already become tender and puts forth leaves, you know that summer is near. So you also, when you see all these things, know that it is near—at the doors! Assuredly, I say to you, this generation will by no means pass away till all these things take place. Heaven and earth will pass away, but My words will by no means pass away. (Matt. 24:32–35 NKJV)

Notice the words *this generation*. The word for generation can also be translated as race, which would make the meaning "this race of people, humankind, will not pass away until these things happen." But the word *generation* is more often considered to mean a period of time, approximately forty years in duration. Forty years from the reestablishment of the nation of Israel in 1948 would be 1988. If the forty-year period began in 1967, the year the Jewish people reclaimed Jerusalem, it could well mean that we are going to see cataclysmic changes taking place within the next few years.

Jesus warned us against trying to set a date for His return, and those Christians who have ignored His admonition in the past have been sorely embarrassed. On the other hand, Jesus encouraged us to read the signs of the times and to be ready. "Watch therefore, for you do not know what hour your Lord is coming . . . Therefore you also be ready, for the Son of Man is coming at an hour you do not expect" (Matt. 24:42, 44 NKJV).

Jesus could come at any moment . . . or could He?

9

Will We Go Through the Tribulation?

Some dramatic events on God's calendar must take place *before* the Lord returns to earth, and many of these are not going to be pretty. Those Christians who have adopted a materialistic, escapist view of the Christian life may be terribly surprised.

Many of the world crises we are beginning to experience were predicted in the Bible hundreds of years ago. What is shocking, however, is the rapid-fire speed at which these events are now racing ahead. Against all odds, the frameworks of the world's economic, political, and social systems are being shaken and are beginning to crumble.

Before going any further, allow me to make a confession: I do not understand everything the Bible reveals to us concerning the Second Coming. I consider myself a student of the Scriptures, but I must admit, I still have questions about many aspects of eschatology, the study of future things. I do not know when Jesus is coming—it may be in my lifetime or it may not—but I believe He will return to Earth in power and glory, just as He said.

I used to listen in amazement (and sometimes with amusement) to some of the prophecy teachers we hosted at PTL. With their charts and graphs they would dogmatically teach exactly when the events described in the book of Revelation were going to come to pass. "This is going to happen, then *this* will happen, and then will be the Battle of Armageddon . . ." and on and on they would go. I do not mean to imply that these teachers were insincere in their teaching or unlearned in the Scriptures. They were godly Bible teachers who felt strongly that they had exceptional insight or an unusual understanding of a complicated message.

Yet the truth is, we do not know when Jesus Christ is going to return. I can point you to the Scriptures that describe what will happen before His coming; I can (and will in the pages ahead) show you Scriptures that describe His return in power. But to set a date for His return is not my intention. Jesus said, "But of that day and hour no one knows, not even the angels in heaven, nor the Son, but only the Father " (Mark 13:32 NKJV). In one of His last statements to His disciples, after the Resurrection and just before He ascended into heaven, Jesus said, "It is not for you to know times or seasons which the Father has put in His own authority" (Acts 1:7 NKJV). For me to give you a play-by-play description of the events scheduled to take place in the future, events whose timing is known only to our heavenly Father, would be the height of presumption on my part.

On the other hand, I do not subscribe to the popular notion that it is impossible for us to know approximately when to expect our Lord's return. Many Christians are fond of saying, "I am neither pretribulational or posttribulational. I am *pan*tribulational. I just believe it will all pan out in the end."

That's a cute (and nonconfrontational) way to look at the last days, but it flies in the face of Scripture. Jesus definitely gave us a lot of information concerning His return and, as I noted previously, numerous signs to watch for, signs indicating that the time of His return is near.

Sometimes I wish Jesus had been more specific in the information He gave to us. Imagine all the theological arguments He could have prevented if He had only said, "I am coming back at the beginning of the Tribulation period, or the middle, or the end of the Tribulation." Better yet, He could have said, "I am coming back on January 1, 2000, so be ready."

PROCRASTINATORS, BEWARE!

Maybe Jesus did not get more specific so we would live with a constant sense of expectation, looking for His soon return. Clearly that was the message of His story about the ten virgins (Matt. 25:1–13), five of whom were prepared for the bridegroom's coming and five of whom were not. Jesus emphasized the point of the story: "Watch therefore, for you know neither the day nor the hour in which the Son of Man is coming" (25:13 NKJV).

God knows that some of us are terrible procrastinators. We would gladly put off until tomorrow what we should have done yesterday. On the other hand, my mother always prepared well in advance. She had a disciplined manner, and my family members could set their clocks and calendars by Mother's schedule. She washed clothes on Monday; she ironed on Tuesday. She bought groceries on Friday. Her pattern rarely changed. If we planned a picnic, and something happened that we could not go, my mother cried because her plans had changed.

Perhaps as a reaction to Mother's rigidity, I have always been just the opposite. I hate to prepare for trips ahead of time. An hour (or less) before it is time to go, I will be scouring my clothes closet, tossing shirts, socks, and underwear every which way, trying to figure out what I should pack. Similarly, if I am preaching at a church, I wait until the last minute before getting dressed, usually arriving just in time to walk onto the platform.

By not telling us the exact time and date of His coming, perhaps Jesus was being especially gracious to procrastinators like me. If Jesus had given us an exact date for His return, some people would no doubt waste much of their time, talents, and treasures on meaningless or trivial pursuits. They would wait until the last minute to prepare to meet the King of kings face to face.

When it comes to the Second Coming, we will not read an announcement in the newspaper the day before Christ's return. You will not hear an anchorman declare on the evening news, "And tomorrow at five o'clock, Jesus Christ will return to earth in power and glory, with His holy angels. Film at eleven."

Yet if you listen carefully, you will hear prophetic "voices in the wilderness" proclaiming the message that Christ's return is imminent. It is "getting-ready time." This is no dress rehearsal, this is the real thing. Furthermore, we need to fall in love with Jesus now, and not wait until the last minute. If Jesus really is coming soon, how much more important it is that we get to know Him better, and that we center our lives around the things that are important to Him.

Years ago an artist painted a scene in which a young woman was standing on a cliff, looking out to sea, her hand shading her eyes as she eagerly scanned the horizon, watching for the first sign of her husband's returning ship. Her face is filled with love and desire, as though she is recalling exactly what he had promised her concerning his return and when she might expect to see him again. As she looks for his ship, she is already preparing a welcome for him in her heart.

Christians who truly love the Lord Jesus will have a similar attitude as we look for signs of His soon appearing. We should be recalling His every word, studying the Scriptures to help us remember what is important to our loving Lord, scanning the horizon, watching for hints that the time is drawing near, and preparing our hearts in anticipation.

WHAT'S ALL THE FUSS ABOUT THE TRIBULATION?

Believing and expecting the return of Jesus Christ is something most Christians can agree on, but the question that rankles the hearts and minds of many believers—and sometimes even divides Christians into separate camps and denominations—is the issue of whether believers will have to experience some or all of the tough times described in the book of Revelation and other prophetic Scriptures.

Basing their beliefs on information found in the Old Testament book of Daniel and the New Testament book of Revelation, conservative Bible scholars generally concur on the fact that the Great Tribulation will last a total of seven years. During that time the earth will undergo a horrendous time of chaos, including unparalleled earthquakes, floods, famines, pestilences, meteor strikes, and wars. Out of the chaos, rising on a platform of peace and security, will be the Antichrist, a powerful world leader under the direct control of Satan himself. The question is this: will Christians who are alive at that time (which I believe is coming upon us in the near future) escape the Tribulation, or will we have to go through part or all of it? Sincere Christians and intelligent Bible scholars can be found on both sides of the issue, holding to radically different opinions of just when Christ will come and when His church, the body of true believers, will be removed from Earth.

For many years I believed and preached adamantly that Christians would not be here to see the horrors of the Tribulation period. Admittedly, most of my thoughts on the matter were not original; nor were my views arrived at by years of studying the Scriptures and coming to biblically based conclusions. For the most part I simply believed what my mentors had taught, naively accepting their positions as absolute truth. When I went on television and eventually had an audience of millions of people, I continued to teach the things I had heard other sincere men and women of God proclaim—namely, that Jesus was coming back before the seven-year Tribulation, in an event we called the Rapture.

THE PRETRIBULATIONAL RAPTURE . . . WHO WOULDN'T GO?

The word *rapture* comes from the Latin *rapiemur* and means "we shall be caught up." Although the word *rapture* does not appear in the Bible, we based our concept of it on a passage in Paul's first letter to the Thessalonians, in which he encouraged the believers:

> For the Lord Himself will descend from heaven with a shout, with the voice of the archangel, and with the trumpet of God; and the dead in Christ shall rise first. Then we who are alive and remain shall be *caught up together* with them in the clouds to meet the Lord in the air, and thus we shall always be with the Lord. Therefore comfort one another with these words. (4:16–18 NASB, emphasis mine)

This catching away of the saints was to take place secretly, at least as far as unbelievers were concerned. Only believers, it was thought, would be able to witness the appearing of the Lord. Suddenly, Jesus was to appear for us, and in a twinkling of an eye we would be gone, whisked off the ground to meet the Lord in the sky. The dead in Christ, believers who had died prior to His coming, would rise first and together we would all meet Him in the air. From there He would take us to live with Him eternally. Later, Christ would return again, this time in power and glory to judge the world and set up His eternal kingdom. Some Christians who agreed on a pretribulational Rapture had more difficulty agreeing on just how much time would elapse before Christ's final return—some thought it to be after the one thousand years of peace predicted in Revelation 20:3, others thought it might be before that millennium—but all pretrib preachers and teachers were confident of Christ's final victory over Satan and the Lord's return for His people.

Many Christians plastered bumper stickers on their cars with slogans such as, "If Jesus comes, this car will be driverless." Pastors sometimes quipped, "If the Rapture takes place while I am preaching, you'll have to get someone else to finish this sermon." Christians often joked, "Imagine what a mess it's going to be when the Rapture occurs—when millions of people don't show up for work the day after the Rapture because we are all in heaven!" Those with a more morbid outlook fretted over what would happen to planes being piloted by Christians, or buses being driven by Christians, or patients being operated on by Christian doctors at the moment the Rapture takes place. Planes spinning out of control, buses careening off highways, and patients left to die on the operating table were part of the down side to the Rapture.

Although most of my pretribulational mentors were relatively unknown, some of the more recognizable names associated with the pretribulational Rapture position include C. I. Scofield, whose notes in the Scofield Bible influenced many of the preachers of my generation; Hal Lindsey, whose book *The Late Great Planet Earth* did much the same for many laypeople; John F. Walvoord, a Dallas Theological Seminary professor whose book *The Rapture Question* has impacted many who have studied the issue from a more scholarly approach; and Charles C. Ryrie, whose study Bible was one of the best-selling study Bibles in the 1980s.

WHY PROSPERITY AND A PRETRIB RAPTURE GO TOGETHER

For me, belief in the Rapture played right into my prosperity theology. It made for a perfect package: people could get saved by saying a few words, they could live in luxury and excess throughout this lifetime, and then Jesus would return to take them out of the tough times that others were to experience during end-time tribulation. It was pure escapism. My favorite prophetic passage was, "Watch therefore, and pray always that you may be counted worthy to escape all these things that will come to pass, and to stand before the Son of Man" (Luke 21:36 NKJV).

I liked that verse because it gave me an out. Christians did not really have to suffer. They would be taken home to glory before all the bad stuff started happening on earth. I felt it went against God's very nature to allow His family to go through the horrors of the Tribulation. Surely He loves us too much to allow that. "Just keep praying, brother and sister, that you may be counted worthy to escape."

Not only that, but it was easier to raise money if one believed in a pretribulational Rapture. Many sincere Christians who want their lives to count for Christ are easily stimulated to give to ministries when they believe that Jesus Christ could come back at any moment. After all, who wants to send money to a ministry that tells them tough times are coming and you will have to go through them?

In the preface to his book *The Rapture Plot,* author David MacPherson hints at a link between pretrib theology and money. MacPherson describes belief in the Rapture as "Protestant evangelicalism's most popular and most lucrative view of the future."[1] Not surprisingly, most popular prosperity teachers—with a few rare exceptions—hold strongly to a pretribulational view, including belief in a Rapture that will allow believers to escape the calamities to come.

My own thinking on the matter began to change when, in prison, I began a daily, concentrated study of the Scriptures, especially those relating to Jesus Christ. Naturally, I wanted to learn about Christ's return, so I began searching for those passages that described a rapture that precedes the Tribulation.

To my amazement, I couldn't find any. Oh, sure, I found Scriptures that I and other preachers had twisted or had imbued with our own interpretations, but when I allowed the Bible to speak for itself, I came face to face with the fact that my preconceived notions of a pretribulational Rapture were baseless. About that same time, God began to impress upon me that I must warn people concerning the dark days to come.

Over the years since then, I have discovered that I am not alone in my opinion that there is no biblical basis to believe in a pretribulational Rapture. For instance, Dr. George Eldon Ladd, the esteemed former Professor of Exegesis and Theology at Fuller Theological Seminary in Pasadena, California, wrote, "The Scripture nowhere asserts that there is a Rapture which will take place before the Revelation."[2]

Dr. Ladd studied the prophetic Scriptures carefully and wrote numerous books on the Second Coming, including *The Blessed Hope* and *A*

Commentary on the Book of Revelation. In his book *The Last Things,* Ladd contends:

> The only coming of Christ that is spoken of in Matthew 24 is the coming of the glorious Son of Man after the tribulation and the only thing that resembles the Rapture is the gathering of the elect from the four winds [Matt. 24:31]. There is not a hint of a pretribulational return of Christ and Rapture of the church before the Great Tribulation.[3]

THE ORIGIN OF THE PRETRIB VIEW

When I dug into the matter further, I was surprised to discover that many of the ideas associated with the pretribulational Rapture originated not in the Bible, but in an extrabiblical vision experienced by a young Scottish woman named Margaret Macdonald in 1830. The woman sent handwritten copies of her "revelation" to Edward Irving, a controversial minister, who, with his great gifts of oratory and his magnetic personality, was drawing large crowds to his church in London. In his pamphlet, "Why I Believe the Church Will Pass Through the Tribulation," David MacPherson described what happened after Irving got hold of Margaret Macdonald's vision.

> It was from this supposed revelation that the modern doctrine and modern phraseology respecting [the pretribulational rapture] arose; it came not from Scripture, but from that which falsely pretended to be the Spirit of God. Irving accepted this teaching and it was taught at prophetic meetings at Powerscourt House in Ireland, attended by Plymouth Brethren organizer John Darby. Irving's views influenced Darby, C. H. Mackintosh, and C. I. Scofield, whose Bible popularized the new theory. Later, some of the leading Plymouth Brethren scholars, including Benjamin Newton and S. P. Tregelles, rejected this pre-Trib theory. For 1,800 years the Church had believed only in a post-Trib coming which, during persecution, was occasionally thought to be imminent. There is not a shred of historical evidence before 1830 that the Church ever believed in a double coming, or rapture before the Tribulation.[4]

David MacPherson goes on to list some of the elements of Margaret's radical vision, which included splitting

> the second coming of Christ into two phases—first, a pre-Trib rapture; then later, after the Trib, the return of Christ to earth. Her own statement . . . clearly contains most of the major tenets found today in pre-Trib dispensationalism—meeting the Lord in the air, secrecy, suddenness, invisibility, imminency, a pre-Trib separation of believers and unbelievers, distinction between the raptured bride and Trib elect.[5]

How, you may wonder, could a vision experienced by a relatively unknown young woman with no platform or sphere of influence have such an impact? Actually, most people of her time did not know the vision was Margaret Macdonald's. They thought the new truth was something Edward Irving had discovered in the Bible. Keep in mind that Irving was a popular preacher in those days, and his views were quickly adopted. In *The Rapture Plot,* David MacPherson lists four reasons why he believes the young woman was not "credited" with her vision at first: "She was a female in the male-dominated theological world of 1830; she was young; she was uneducated; and she had been a Christian only a year."[6] Interestingly, many of the tenets in the teachings of highly respected prophetic teachers, and other advocates of a pretribulational Rapture, are similar to those first espoused by Margaret Macdonald.

A FALSE HOPE

The more I studied the Scriptures, the more I became convinced that we are living in the last days, and that we will soon begin seeing the fulfillment of the predictions in the prophetic books of the Bible, including the cataclysmic conditions on earth, which will precipitate the rise of the Antichrist.

I also saw a connection between the escapist Rapture and those who espouse a materialistic gospel. I became convinced that we are wasting so much time and energy teaching people how to get rich and how to become self-fulfilled, we have not adequately prepared them for what is to come. Instead of the Church presenting a false hope by preaching the pretribulational Rapture, we should be spending this time informing believers that they will have to go through the Tribulation, or at least some part of it. We should be teaching people to fall in love with Jesus. We should be spending our time, energy, and resources getting spiritually ready for a severe period of persecution and a time of unparalleled upheaval.

To think otherwise, one must totally ignore church history. Brutal persecutions have often been the normal experience for believers. From the earliest years of Christianity, believers were stoned, burned at the stake, dragged through the streets with their feet tied to stampeding animals, and used as human torches. During these persecutions God did not magically remove His people from their tormentors' grasp, but He gave them the grace necessary to go *through* their tortures. What makes us think God should cut us a break and allow us to escape before the onslaught of hell comes on the earth? Have we been more faithful than those early saints? Are we more worthy of an easy ride to heaven than they were?

Going back to Matthew 24, I found that throughout Jesus' listing of the signs of the times, He does not even hint at a pretribulational Rapture. In fact, He laid the emphasis on just the opposite order of events. Jesus described some of the signs that are even now beginning to take place, but the overall tenor of the passage is that even though we will see these things, the end is not yet. Jesus then said,

> For then there will be a great tribulation, such as has not occurred since the beginning of the world until now, nor ever shall. And unless those days had been cut short, no life would have been saved; but for the sake of the elect those days shall be cut short. (vv. 21–22 NASB)

Reading the account naturally, without imposing our own ideas or wishful thinking into it, the order of events seems to take place logically.

> But immediately after the tribulation of those days, the sun will be darkened, and the moon will not give its light, and the stars will fall from the sky, and the powers of the heavens will be shaken, and then the sign of the Son of Man will appear in the sky, and then all the tribes of the earth will mourn, and they will see the Son of Man coming on the clouds of the sky with power and great glory. And He will send forth His angels with a great trumpet and they will gather together His

elect from the four winds, from one end of the sky to the other. (vv. 29–31 NASB).

Notice the order of events. These things happen *after* the Great Tribulation, "and then . . . [we] will see the Son of Man coming." And they certainly do not seem to be done in secret. In fact, the tribes of the world, those who do not know the Lord, will mourn at His coming. In the chapters ahead we will see that they have good reason to mourn.

Will Christians go through the Great Tribulation? I believe we will experience at least some part of it before Jesus Christ returns. When I speak on this subject nowadays, I facetiously tell audiences, "I tried my best to keep us out of the Tribulation. For years I preached that we would escape it. In my studies while in prison, I searched for hours on end, trying to find some way that believers would escape the difficult times about to come on the earth, but I couldn't do it. I am convinced now that we are going through. Hold on tightly to Jesus. It's going to be a wild ride!"

10

The Horses Are Out of the Barn

The book of Revelation is one of the most fascinating, yet least-read, books of the Bible. Many people are afraid to read it. All that talk about beasts, death, and the Antichrist—it sounds more like a horror movie than a Bible story. Other people do not like to read Revelation because they find it hard to understand. "What's going on here?" they ask. "I can't keep it all straight. Somewhere between the seven candlesticks, the seven angels, the seven seals, and the seven bowls and the seven trumpets, I get thoroughly confused and just give up."

Ironically, some church leaders caution their congregations against reading Revelation. When I was a young Bible college student, an elderly professor told me, "Jim, don't even try to preach on the book of Revelation until you are old. You won't be able to understand it."

Granted, the book of Revelation is difficult to understand. Much of it is written in symbolic language that must be interpreted. But the book is meant to be read. God did not give it to us merely to have a twenty-two-chapter buffer at the end of the Bible. He gave us Revelation because He wants us to know in advance what will happen on planet earth in the last days.

Moreover, Revelation is a positive book, not a negative book. It is not the revelation of the Antichrist; it is the Revelation of *Jesus Christ!* And it is not necessary for you to understand everything in the book for your life to be blessed by it. In fact, Revelation is the only book in the Bible that guarantees a blessing for reading it. "Blessed is he who reads and those who hear the words of this prophecy, and keep those things which are written in it; for the time is near" (1:3 NKJV).

The term *revelation* comes from the Greek word *apokalypsis,* from which we get our word *apocalypse,* and means "to take the cover off, to reveal." It is one of three words used in the New Testament to describe our Lord's return, along with *parousia,* which means "coming," "arrival," or "presence"; and *epiphaneia,* which means "manifestation." *Parousia* is the word most often used in the Scriptures in connection with Christ's return.

The apostle John wrote the book of Revelation around A.D. 95, when he was ninety years of age and living in exile on the small, rocky island of Patmos. Revelation was written during a time of intense persecution of Christians by the Roman emperor Domitian. Rome had passed a law requiring the worship of the emperor as God. This, of course, caused the early Christians to recoil. The Christians believed that Jesus is Lord, and they were not about to bow their knee to Caesar. On the other hand, the Romans could not understand what the fuss was all about. The Romans were polytheists, believing in many gods. To them, it was no big deal if the Christians wanted to add their God to the Roman pantheon of gods, so long as one day each year the Christians bowed their knees to the emperor and declared, "Caesar is God."

The Christians said, "No way. We will not worship any other lord but the Lord Jesus Christ."

"Bow, or you will be torn limb from limb," the Romans roared.

"Then let the tearing begin," the Christians answered. "We will not deny that there is only one God and Jesus is His Name."

That was the atmosphere as John, now an elderly man, sat down to write under the command and control of the Holy Spirit. No doubt John was on the island of Patmos as a prisoner. He implies that he was imprisoned because of his faith, "for the word of God and for the testimony of Jesus" (Rev. 1:9 NKJV). Perhaps because of his age, some Roman official had mercy on John and, rather than torturing him or killing him, had allowed him to live out his remaining days in exile at the penal colony on Patmos.

I have come to believe that imprisonments and persecutions are not unusual experiences for God's children. Joseph was unjustly imprisoned,

Daniel found himself joining the Lions' Club against his will, and Paul wrote some of his most powerful letters from prison. Church history is replete with men and women who sincerely loved the Lord yet were tortured, persecuted, or jailed because of their commitment to Christ. People sometimes laugh when I tell them that some of the best Christians I've ever met are in prison, but it's true.

Whether John's captors scrutinized his writings before they were sent to those to whom they were written is a matter of conjecture. We do not know for sure, but it seems likely that the Romans were reading John's mail. Perhaps that is why John makes heavy use of symbolism in his writing, similar to a secret code. John's Jewish readers and the early Christians would understand these symbols, which would be obscure to the Romans. For instance, John uses the term *Babylon* to refer to the city of Rome, a common practice among early Christians because of Rome's oppression. When Christians wanted to talk about Rome without actually using the name, they used Babylon—the Old Testament persecutor of the Jewish people—as a substitute. The apostle Peter did something similar at the close of his letter, when he said, "She who is in Babylon, elect together with you, greets you" (1 Peter 5:13 NKJV).

THE BEGINNING OF THE END

The book of Revelation opens with John announcing that the things God has shown him will "shortly take place" (1:1 NASB). Reading this, some people get confused right from the start. "If John was writing in A.D. 95, and the events he described were meant to happen soon, what relevance does this book have to us?"

But John was not saying that these things would necessarily happen in his lifetime or any time soon. The word translated *shortly* actually means "quickly" in the original Greek. It can also mean, "when started, it will happen suddenly, within a brief space of time." John was saying, "Once these things begin to happen, they will happen quickly." In other words, when the prophecies begin to be fulfilled, they will proceed on an irrevocable, inexorable, unstoppable course, and we will feel as though we are riding a roller coaster that has gone out of control.

I believe we are about to enter that time, and it is going to be terrifying.

What is even more frightening to me is that many Christians will be caught off guard, having been lulled into complacency, assuming that everything is going to get better. Yet the apostle Paul warned,

> But concerning the times and the seasons, brethren, you have no need that I should write to you. For you yourselves know perfectly that the day of the Lord so comes as a thief in the night. For when they say, "Peace and safety!" then sudden destruction comes upon them, as labor pains upon a pregnant woman. And they shall not escape. (1 Thess. 5:1–3 NKJV)

One of the most intriguing visions John records is the account of the Four Horsemen of the Apocalypse (Rev. 6:1–8). These horsemen are not Kentucky Derby winners. In fact, there is nothing sporting about these animals and their riders. What do they represent?

IMPOSTOR ON A WHITE HORSE

The first horse was white in color. John wrote, "And I looked, and behold, a white horse. He who sat on it had a bow; and a crown was given to him, and he went out conquering and to conquer" (6:2 NKJV). Some Christians believe that the rider of this white horse is Christ, moving among His church conquering evil, even in the midst of the Tribulation, and ultimately conquering over all. I view this rider as just the opposite; I believe he is the Antichrist.

This impostor wants to look like Jesus, who also is pictured as a conquering hero on a white horse (Rev. 19:11). Remember, the devil is the great deceiver and the great counterfeiter. He tries to give the impression that he is as powerful as Jesus, but the devil is a defeated foe. The rider of Revelation 6 has no arrows, only a bow. Nevertheless, do not underestimate the power of the devil's agent on earth, the Antichrist. This satanic emissary will rise to power on a platform of peace, prosperity, and miracles. He will not have to use weapons to conquer the world and evoke the worship of man. The Antichrist will not use force; he will use his cunning words. His talk will be slick and enticing; he will promise peace and prosperity to a world that by that time will be ready to hand over the keys of authority to anyone who holds out hope of escaping the chaos that will have begun to plague the earth.

Notice also that the Antichrist does not earn a crown, nor does he inherit a crown; it is not intrinsically his, it is given to him. This crown is not a symbol of royalty but is more the type worn in ancient times by winners of the public games. Indeed, the Antichrist will win over public opinion polls as our world willingly hands him the keys to the kingdoms. And for about three and a half years, the Antichrist will deliver. He will provide peace and security and some measure of happiness.

This is what alarms me so much about the materialistic Christianity that millions of Christians have been taught to accept. The church is unwittingly being prepared to accept the Antichrist. We are being taught to seek happiness rather than joy, to love things more than Jesus. We are being taught to seek after miracles and signs and wonders rather than to develop trust and perseverance. When the Antichrist comes to power, he will offer security for our material things, as well as signs and wonders and miracles.

I believe the Antichrist is alive on Earth today. Somewhere in the world, probably in Western Europe or possibly in the Middle East, is a man more diabolical than any human being who has ever walked the face of the earth. He is more evil than Adolf Hitler; more ruthless than Stalin; more murderous than Mao Tse-tung, Pol Pot, and Idi Amin combined. Within a few years he will rapidly rise to power, and he will dominate future events worldwide, until Jesus Christ comes back to destroy him.

I know it sounds like the plot of a Hollywood movie, but Hollywood could not devise a plot this intricate. If you are a connoisseur of horror movies about the Antichrist, you really ought to read the Book!

THE RED HORSE OF TERROR

The second horseman is about to ride: "Another horse, fiery red, went out. And it was granted to the one who sat on it to take peace from the earth, and that people should kill one another; and there was given to him a great sword" (6:4 NKJV). This is no ordinary sword; this is an assassin's sword, a terrorist's sword. The result will be crime in the streets, people butchering one another. Blood red will be the color of the day.

One does not have to belabor the point in America today. Because of violent crime, in most cities it is unsafe to walk our streets at night, and in many places life feels unsafe even during daylight hours. Senseless drive-by shootings occur frequently, not as acts of revenge or retribution, but often for no reason at all. We have so devalued human life in our society that for many people it is a small thing to kill another person. At first we were shocked when we heard of children and teachers being gunned down on school property; although the tragic killings continue to wrench our stomachs, we are no longer surprised by them.

Even our slang in America reflects the appalling devaluation of human life. Recently I heard a man describe a fellow employee who had lost his temper over some minor issue at work. "He just went postal on me," the man said.

Sadly, "going postal" no longer has anything to do with how the mail gets delivered.

Outside the U.S., terrorist-spawned violence continues to escalate as well. Hardly a day goes by when our senses are not bludgeoned by some new outbreak of terrorism in the Middle East. Despite our best efforts at making and keeping the peace, political, economic, and religious tensions often lead to unrest, violence, and riots. Ethnic cleansing, one group of people trying to exterminate another, continues in various locations around the world, often with terrorist backing.

In the United States we are painfully familiar with terrorist activities: the bombing of the World Trade Center in New York, the bombing of the Federal Building in Oklahoma City, numerous letter bombs by the Unabomber, Ted Kaczynski, and the recent bombings of two U.S. embassies in Africa. In all of these cases, a sobering truth must be faced, namely that a relatively obscure person or group was able to destroy the lives of many. I am convinced that similar senseless killings will increase as we get closer to the coming of Christ.

Our government is rightly concerned about the growing number of nations with nuclear capabilities. Atomic bomb detonations by India and Pakistan in May 1998 reminded us once again that if the technology is out there, someone will use it to create a weapon of mass destruction. With nuclear power spreading to Third World nations, it becomes more and more likely that terrorists will eventually get access to weapons they could only dream about in the past.

Not long ago I was shocked when I heard a message by a man who has a prophetic gift. This man has an incredibly accurate track record—in fact, I have never known him to be incorrect on a single prophecy. For instance, he predicted the Northridge earthquake in the Los Angeles area, and the earthquake took place on the exact day the man predicted. But the message that shocked me did not concern earthquakes.

The man said God had shown him that a terrorist bomb the size of a football will be smuggled into the United States in a suitcase. One of our major cities will be destroyed, this prophet declared.

But the nuclear threat is not the only concern from terrorists. Think, for example, what damage terrorists could do if they could tinker with the nation's water supply. Just a small amount of lethal chemicals in the right place, and millions of people could die. Or think of the awful potential of germ warfare. With all sense of morality flung to the wind, what might happen if a terrorist were able to cast a lethal biohazard into those same winds?

The red horse is out of the barn.

FAMINE AND ECONOMIC COLLAPSE ARE IMMINENT

The third horseman is ready to ride.

> When He opened the third seal, I heard the third living creature say, "Come and see." So I looked, and behold, a black horse, and he who sat on it had a pair of scales in his hand. And I heard a voice in the midst of the four living creatures saying, "A quart of wheat for a denarius . . . and do not harm the oil and the wine." (6:5–6 NKJV)

The rider of the black horse carries with him famine and economic collapse, signified by the weighing scales and the exorbitant prices for food.

It is hard to imagine the impact a major famine might have in the economically developed nations of the world. The closest most of us get to famine is quickly changing the channel when images of starving children appear on our television sets. We have grown all too accustomed to the poignant pictures of shriveled men, women, and even children whose bodies have been affected by famine in Third World countries. I believe that in the days ahead famine will be even more prevalent, and I am not alone in that opinion.

In 1997 and 1998 freak weather conditions brought on by El Niño, declared to be the worst this century by United Nations climate experts and U.S. government scientists alike, provided a graphic object lesson concerning the fragility of our world's food supply. On a one-to-five scale, "this El Niño is at least a five, if not completely off the scale," said Joe Friday, director of research for the National Oceanic and Atmospheric Administration.[1] In the U.S. and Canada, El Niño wreaked havoc in the form of floods, mudslides, tornadoes, and other unusual weather-related phenomena. Heavy rains washed away million-dollar homes in California and flooded towns in Georgia and Alabama. Unusually strong tornadoes struck in locations as diverse as Minneapolis, Minnesota; Nashville, Tennessee; Orlando, Florida; Spencer, South Dakota; and Pittsburgh, Pennsylvania. A five-day ice storm in Canada caused a short-term loss of over one billion dollars and a 2 percent loss in the country's gross domestic product.

But in Africa and Latin America, where living conditions are less developed and food, clothing, medicine, and other forms of humanitarian aid are less available, El Niño's effects put millions of people at risk of starvation. Christine Berthiaume, spokesperson for the UN food agency, World Food Programme, estimated that "27 million people in Africa and some 320,000 people in central America were at risk because of declining food stocks."[2]

In America the most obvious result of El Niño-related weather, besides the millions of dollars expended on disaster relief efforts, has been higher food prices, with some fruits and vegetables rising 50 to 60 percent in price . . . and still going! "Consumers are going to face higher prices for specific vegetables this spring because of interruptions in planting and the possibility of harvesting problems," said Keith Collins, chief United States Department of Agriculture economist.[3] Farmers worried whether they would even be able to plant their next crop. "Some waterlogged vegetable fields are empty—or are flooded with foot-deep runoff—because farmers can't get in to prepare the ground for the next crop."[4]

In the United States we used to keep a surplus of grain to last our people five years or more. Those days are gone. Today investing in grain futures is a lucrative (although risky) business because we now maintain so few food products in storage, less than enough for one year. Should a major drought occur in America, in one growing season our nation could be plunged into famine.

Imagine, if you can, how famine might affect our own nation. Your worst nightmare could soon be a reality. Exacerbating the effects of famine brought on by the galloping of the black horse will also be economic chaos and inflationary prices, which is what is indicated by the phrase "a quart of wheat for a denarius" (Rev. 6:6 NASB). In biblical times, a denarius was equal to a day's wages. The implication is that we could spend a day's wages for a loaf of bread. How could that possibly happen in America? It's quite simple.

I believe our U.S. stock market is on a collision course. Throughout 1998 the market experienced a wild roller-coaster ride, with sweeping upturns and equally as sweeping downturns. Foreign markets are even more volatile. According to *The New York Times,* "If you put a dollar into the Singapore stock market at the end of June [1997], you now have 50 cents. If you put it instead into Malaysia, you've got a quarter."[5] In comparison to the Wall Street crash of 1929, the fall of the Asian markets was far worse. "From the 1929 peak, it took over a year for the Standard & Poor's 500-stock index to lose half its value, and more than two years for it to fall by 75 percent."[6] Sooner or later the market will crash, and when it does, people who have invested their lives in material things will be devastated.

Beyond that, the economic crash will bring out the worst in people. Hungry people with no hope will turn to violent solutions. Witness, for example, the anarchy, burning, looting, rioting, and other mob actions associated with the economic collapse of Indonesia in early 1998. In the capital city of Jakarta, mobs of poor Indonesians rampaged through the streets, looting and burning, carrying bags of rice and armloads of clothing. The nation was paralyzed as protesters demanded the resignation of President Suharto, who had ruled the country with the support of a strong military for thirty-two years. Suharto eventually succumbed to the public's wishes, but not before his country was devastated.

Could such a series of events happen in the USA? I believe a major economic collapse not only can happen, but will happen . . . soon. The coming crash, perhaps triggered by a totally different set of circumstances than the Asian markets, will nonetheless reap similar consequences. Stock markets in countries such as Japan and Russia—whose economy has been struggling to survive since the disintegration of the Soviet Union—are already teetering precariously on the precipice of destruction. I believe that one day soon the economies of a number of nations will tumble in a global tailspin.

WHY WORRY ABOUT Y2K?

Many economists worry that computer problems centered around the year 2000, dubbed Y2K, may contribute to the coming economic chaos. Software creators in the 1970s and 1980s assumed their products would be obsolete by the time the new millennium approached. To save valuable memory space, they programmed their products to recognize only two-digit dates—99, for example, rather than 1999. Consequently, at the stroke of midnight on December 31, 1999, the two-digit dating system in computers will automatically revert to 00, essentially resetting themselves to the year 1900.

While this may not seem to be a big deal for those of us who don't care what date our computer displays, it is a colossal problem. According to a bleak assessment prepared by the U.S. Office of Management and Budget (OMB), "the bug might cause Pentagon weapons to malfunction, the Internal Revenue Service to process taxes improperly, and nuclear-plant security to fail."[7] Beyond that, Y2K is destined to have a profound impact on air-traffic control systems worldwide, most of which depend heavily upon computers. The problem is particularly dangerous in other countries, where computer programmers and repairmen are in short supply.

In addition to national defense mechanisms, the Y2K problem may create chaos in a wide range of everyday equipment run by computers—street lights; public water systems; restaurants; elevators; telephone systems; satellite technology affecting television, radio, and cellular telephones; copiers and fax machines; transportation systems; home and office utilities; the Internet; almost all government programs and agencies; and perhaps most serious of all, our banking and financial centers.

Most of us have been temporarily inconvenienced by a bank's computer system being down. But imagine your frustration if, for instance, you go to your bank on January 3, 2000, and your friendly bank teller informs you that your account records cannot be accessed. You later learn that all your financial records at that institution have been lost completely. Desperate for cash, you call your stock broker to access money in your mutual fund, IRA, or 401K account, only to be told that all records of your life savings have mysteriously disappeared.

WHEN PANIC REIGNS

Worse yet—and to me this is the most disconcerting issue associated with the Y2K problem—many financiers fear there may be a run on the banks due to a loss of confidence in our banks, stock markets, and other financial institutions. Most banks do not actually keep massive amounts of cash on hand; only about 6 percent of the money deposited in banks is available at any one time. The other 94 percent is invested or loaned out to others. What would happen if millions of people choose to drain their bank accounts during the last few weeks of 1999? To a lot of people, especially those who have relatives who lived through the crash of 1929, it just makes sense to get as much of your money in your own hands as possible. Of course, if our entire monetary system falls apart, a wheelbarrow full of thousand-dollar bills will not be worth much more than the wheelbarrow itself.

Lest you think such a scenario is simply the mulling of an overactive imagination, or the plot of the latest science-fiction blockbuster, you should be aware that highly respected computer specialists, economists, and leaders within government and industry now regard the Y2K problem as "a global ticking time bomb." At a June 1998 conference conducted at the Center for Strategic and International Studies (CSIS) in Washington, D.C., Arnaud de Borchgrave, editor at large for *The Washington Times,* reported bluntly, "We know, date certain, that a global computer crisis will occur; only its severity remains to be determined. It is not a question of one thing going wrong but tens of thousands of things going awry."[8]

Bradley D. Belt, director of CSIS, echoed de Borchgrave's dire predictions:

Indeed, most of the world is looking forward to the countdown to January 1, 2000, with great anticipation. Extraordinary millennium parties in exotic locales around the world—the Great Pyramids of Egypt, Bora Bora near the International Date Line, and, of course, Times Square, New York City—have been planned and booked at very high cost for a decade.

A small minority of people, however, those less blissfully ignorant, many of whom are here today [at the CSIS forum], will watch the countdown with great trepidation. They view the event as a cause for great concern rather than joyous celebration. They will be thinking not of fireworks booming and champagne corks popping, but rather computer systems crashing, manufacturing plants grinding to a halt, air-traffic control systems and public utilities failing.

Although the cognoscenti have long been aware of the looming Y2K problem, policymakers have only belatedly recognized the enormous challenges facing us. And the general public at best is only dimly aware of a problem on the horizon.

Some have suggested that the problems are overstated, that the alarmists are simply Chicken Littles. Clearly, there is a certain amount of speculation about Y2K issues. There is really no way to know exactly what will happen . . . but there is much that we do know. Y2K affects everyone at the same time and is global in scope. It's not just a business problem but affects governments and individuals; indeed, it has the potential to touch upon almost every aspect of our daily lives.[9]

Concern about the potentially tumultuous problems that will be caused by Y2K is being heard more frequently in the halls of the United States Congress. The "Paul Revere" who is emphatically sounding the alarm on Y2K issues is Senator Robert Bennett from Utah. A highly successful businessman in the private sector before running for public office, Bennett chairs the Senate Banking Committee's Subcommittee on Financial Services and Technology. He also chairs the U.S. Senate's Special Committee on the Year 2000 Technology Problem.

A grandfatherly, calm, conservative man—not a wild-eyed alarmist at all—Bennett nonetheless expressed profound concerns at the CSIS conference. He listed seven areas his committee plans to address, areas in which Y2K's impact could be devastating and for which contingency plans must be developed:

Number one, utilities, and this means the power grid. Power must be available. Even if every one of your computers is Y2K-compliant [a term used loosely to describe computers in which the problem has been fixed], if you don't have any power to turn them on, it won't do you any good. And water—every water purification plant in this country is run by a computerized system. And if it shuts down, you can imagine the social consequences that will occur in our major cities . . .

Number Two, telecommunications. If the phones don't give you a dial tone, if there's no way to communicate information, the nation also will shut down.

Number Three, transportation. Immediately people think of the FAA, and, of course, that is an agency that's in terrible Y2K trouble. But realize that all railroad traffic is computer controlled, and all of the raw materials that you need for manufacturing in this country goes . . . by rail, as does the coal that fires the power plants. That takes us back up to the power grid, and you now see how connected all of this is . . .

Fourth is the financial system. If you have a system where checks won't clear, or electronic transfers of money won't happen, you have, obviously, a major social problem.

Fifth, general government services, including health care, because 40 percent of the health-care dollar in the United States comes from a government agency, the Health Care Financing Administration. And HCFA's computers are at this point, according to the General Accounting Office, in terrible shape. But you can add any government service you might want, all the way down to the county level. What is going to happen to the social fabric in this country if county officials in Los Angeles or Manhattan or Queens, or any of the other counties or boroughs, cannot deliver welfare checks after the first of January, 2000? Police and fire departments, I lump them in general government services.

Number six, general business activity. If Y2K were to hit this coming weekend, General Motors could not produce a single car in any one of their 157 manufacturing plants.

Number seven—and I place it last only because it is last in terms of time pressure, but by the time this whole thing is finished, it will probably be first in terms of dollar costs—and that is litigation. The first lawsuits under Y2K have already been filed . . .

When people say to me, "Is the world going to come to an end?" I say, "I don't know." I don't know whether this will be a bump in the road—that's the most optimistic assessment of what we've got, a fairly serious bump in the road—or whether this will, in fact, trigger a major worldwide recession with absolutely devastating economic consequences in some parts of the world.[10]

Get Ready for Recession

Indeed, another member of the CSIS panel, Dr. Edward Yardeni, the man named by *The Wall Street Journal* as 1997's top economic forecaster, sees widespread recession as an inevitable result of Y2K. *Barron's* called Yardeni "The Wall Street Wizard," while *Institutional Investor* said he is one of the twenty most important players on the financial web. Clearly, when Edward Yardeni speaks, the financial world listens. And on July 5, 1998, speaking before the National Association of Manufacturers, the economist commanded his listeners' attention when he admitted, "I can no longer say with any confidence that there is enough time to avoid a severe, global Y2K recession."[11] Yardeni predicted that the possibility of a worldwide recession caused by Y2K-related costs and crashes has increased to seventy percent.[12]

How long will the Y2K confusion last? Yardeni, a self-proclaimed economic optimist, is pessimistic over the interruption in the flow of information that will be caused by Y2K. He asks business leaders,

What level of business could you do in your own profession if your computer systems were down for two hours? Hey, that's easy. That happens on a good day. Now you get on your cellular phone and make some calls. Maybe you write a personal note the old-fashioned way, with a pen. That's no big deal.

What if it's down for two days? Two weeks? Two months? Add it up and put in the number that you think we're going to have in terms of time. There's no way it's just going to be two hours. No way it's going to be just two days. It's going to be at least two weeks; two months is kind of reasonable. Could it be six months of major disruptions to our computer systems? Absolutely. Could it be an entire year? Absolutely.[13]

Yardeni also warned of a possible panic by the public because of Y2K problems.

> If we don't let the public in on this problem, then they will panic some time next year [1999]. As it is, no matter what, the public is going to find out about it, because the stock market is going to figure this thing out. And I told you that I think there's a high likelihood of a very severe recession in the year 2000. In 1973–74, the stock market was down 42 percent [during the recession spawned by the Middle East oil crisis].
>
> People out there are not ready for that kind of drop in the stock market . . . They believe that nothing can go wrong. They believe the stock market is going to make their retirement for them. I think the market is going to be down 30 percent next year. How do you like that? And this is coming from an optimist . . . I'm not a doomsayer, and I'm not talking about the end of life on planet Earth. But if we continue to pretend there isn't a problem coming, doomsday scenarios are conceivable, and we have to stop that. We have to make sure there isn't panic. We have to tell the public . . . you're going to have to conduct your business, your life, without some things for a while.[14]

While the immediate problem of the two-digit dating systems is fixable, "the problem is destined to become the most costly, vexing and time-consuming one in the brief history of the information age."[15] To reprogram the myriad existing computer systems—the U.S. military alone has more than one million desktop computers—will be a massive undertaking, and an expensive one. "The Gartner Group, regarded widely as the premier research firm on Year 2000 issues, is standing by its projection of final costs to the federal government alone of $30 billion and as much as $600 billion worldwide."[16]

Peter de Jager, a Canadian who has written prolifically on Y2K for more than seven years and is an advisor to the United Kingdom Year 2000 Task Force, also frames the problem in terms we can all understand—money. "AT&T isn't spending five hundred million dollars because they listened to someone at a podium stating that they have a problem. They are spending that amount of money because they . . . have a problem that's going to cost five hundred million dollars to fix!"[17]

While many people believe that computers will stop at midnight on December 31, 1999, but will be up and running again when everyone goes back to work after the New Year's holiday, de Jager's opinion is much more ominous. He warns, "We are headed for the first turn in the road in this information highway . . . and we forgot to put in a steering wheel."[18]

If you are still unconvinced of the seriousness of the Y2K problem, think back to the last time the power went out in your area. Maybe you were in a grocery store when the lights went out. Or at a gasoline pump that suddenly would not work. Perhaps you were talking on a cordless telephone when it went dead. Now add to that frustration the total absence of phone service, sanitation services, and even food delivery services for a prolonged period of time. Or recall the chaos in May 1998 when a single satellite, Galaxy 4, experienced computer software problems that knocked out cellular phone service and mobile pagers for a day. That is just a fraction of the frustration we may experience as a result of the Y2K problem.

Interestingly, computers have linked mankind together with a common language. Like the people of Old Testament Babel, whose language God scrambled when they attempted to build a tower to the heavens, modern human beings have tried to build a one-world system, a monument to our own intelligence. In doing so, we have created a world that is dependent upon advanced technology, and the "language" that runs that technology is about to be "scrambled" once again.

No one knows for certain exactly what will happen when that fateful moment arrives. But do not dismiss the Y2K warnings from the scientific community as sheer conjecture. They may also be a highly plausible explanation for what the Bible refers to as the black horse of famine and economic chaos.

A FOURTH OF THE WORLD'S PEOPLE . . . GONE!

The fourth horse and rider are about to emerge, following closely behind the second and third horsemen. (Remember, when the events of Revelation begin to unfold, they will happen in rapid succession.)

When He opened the fourth seal, I heard the voice of the fourth living creature saying, "Come and see." So I looked, and behold, a pale horse. And the name of him who sat on it was Death, and Hades followed with him. And power was given to them over a fourth of the earth, to kill with sword, with hunger, with death, and by the beasts of the earth. (6:7 NKJV)

When I first read this verse during my studies in prison, I said, "Come on, now. How could one-fourth of the world's population, approximately one and a half billion people, be wiped out in such a short time by the beasts of the earth?" In the Garden of Eden, God gave men and women dominion over the animal world: "Then God said, 'Let Us make man in Our image, according to Our likeness; let them have dominion over the fish of he sea, over the birds of the air, and over the cattle, over all the earth and over every creeping thing that creeps on the earth'" (Gen. 1:26 NKJV).

Despite Adam and Eve's decision to sin, man's dominion over the animal kingdom has never been rescinded by God. Knowing this, I could not understand how the animals could suddenly become so dangerous to so much of mankind, as Revelation 6:7 states. After all, if a herd of ravenous lions came rampaging down the streets of Chicago, with our many means of immobilizing them, we could minimize their destructive potential in a matter of hours, or days at the worst. If a herd of wild elephants invaded London, we could deal with that equally as well. Yet the Scripture clearly says that the animal kingdom will be a factor in decimating one-fourth of mankind.

As I frequently do when I find something in the Bible I cannot understand, I turned to the original Greek to see if I could glean some insights by studying the individual words in the verse. What I discovered was shocking!

The word translated *death* could also be translated as "plague or pestilence." The Living Bible translates it as "disease." For some time I pondered the connection between diseases and animals. Then I began coming across new information linking the origins of deadly diseases, such as HIV—the virus which leads to the killer AIDS—to monkeys. The statistics on the worldwide spread of AIDS have always been horrifying, but it is becoming increasingly apparent that our government and medical community have been much too optimistic. According to United

Nations figures, the disease is conquering developing nations faster than anyone ever thought possible.

The international edition of *Newsweek* reported, "Each day 16,000 people contract HIV, nearly double the previous estimate of the infection rate. That means that 30.6 million people are now living with the virus. If current transmission rates continue, the number will top 40 million by the end of the century. An estimated 2.3 million of them will have died this year [1997]—up from 1.5 million in 1996. How could the experts have been so wrong?"[19]

How indeed?

The prognosis is even bleaker for parts of Africa:

Though AIDS is spreading in India, China, Southeast Asia and Latin America, it is Africa that accounts for the largest chunk of the epidemiological error. "We are now realizing that the rates of HIV transmission have been grossly underestimated—particularly in sub-Saharan Africa, where the bulk of infections have been concentrated," says Peter Piot, head of UNAIDS. His agency now estimates that 7.4 percent of Africans 15 to 49 are infected. Because voluntary testing is so rare, at least 90 percent don't even know that the virus is lurking in their body fluids, so they spread it unknowingly.[20]

As if the specter of rapidly advancing AIDS were not disheartening enough, truly frightening diseases such as Ebola, mad-cow disease, the Hong Kong "bird flu," and others emanating from the animal kingdom are becoming more prevalent. Other drug-resistant diseases threaten to become epidemics in America. In March 1998, for example, a drug-resistant strain of tuberculosis, a disease that attacks the lungs and is spread as easily as the common cold, struck Nashville, Tennessee.[21] About the same time, health officials in Providence, Rhode Island, were recommending mass vaccinations to prevent the spread of the deadliest strain of bacterial meningitis.[22]

Along with these phenomena in the animal kingdom, plant life is experiencing strange occurrences as well. For instance, in January 1998, *The Christian Science Monitor* reported that a killer weed, a water hyacinth, was threatening the existence of one of the world's most famous freshwater lakes, Lake Victoria in Kenya. According to the *Monitor,*

A foreign weed with an ability to reproduce at extraordinary speeds is baffling authorities, devastating fishing communities, and brutally tampering with the lake's ecosystem. As the water hyacinth expands—choking up ports, sucking up the water's oxygen, and screening out vital sunlight—an apocalyptic vision is taking form in the minds of a few experts: Lake Victoria, the world's second-largest freshwater body, gradually turning into a gigantic puddle of dead, stagnant water.[23]

In his book *And the Waters Turned to Blood,* Rodney Barker paints a frightening picture of huge numbers of fish dying of a freak disease, pfiesteria, that has been linked to unusual deaths among human beings as well. Fishermen who have touched the water contaminated by these fish are particularly susceptible to this disease. They have experienced ulcerated sores on their hands, oozing boils on their bodies, unusual fatigue, and extreme mental disorders. Some people have actually died from a scratch contaminated by pfiesteria.

Add to this the threat of germ warfare, which incorporates animal toxins like anthrax into the nuclear arsenal, and the stage is set for the animal kingdom to play its role in bringing about plagues, pestilences, and other diseases. I now understand how the animals will precipitate the potential deaths of a quarter of our world's population. The devastation on the earth as a result of the horrible famines, pestilences, and wild beasts of Revelation are extremely plausible, not in some science-fiction fantasy, but here and now.

I believe the four horses of Revelation are already out of the barn; they are beginning to ride in our generation. As far as I can tell, we are rapidly moving into Revelation chapter 6 right now. Granted, the events that such a statement portend are discomfiting to us. We are about to endure the rise of the Antichrist, terrorism, horrendous famine and economic collapse, death on a massive scale, plagues, and pestilences our world has never before known.

And please note it well again, I believe these things will happen *before* Jesus Christ returns for the church. The fact that we see signs of the four horsemen galloping through our world today should not fill our hearts with fear, but with excited anticipation that we are indeed the generation that will see the Lord's coming in power and glory.

But before we see Him, we are going to see fire from the sky.

11

Fire from the Sky

J im, there has to be a warning," a friend of mine who has a vibrant
prophetic ministry said to me recently. "Since the church has been
reluctant to speak about the book of Revelation, God is using Hollywood
to warn the world of what is coming."

Although movie productions sometimes mangle the message of the
Bible, Hollywood has indeed shown an unusual interest in apocalyptic
titles. In a curious instance of art imitating life, Paramount Pictures and
Steven Spielberg's DreamWorks production company released the movie
Deep Impact over Mother's Day weekend 1998, just two months after the
world was stunned to learn that a mile-wide asteroid was scheduled to
sweep dangerously close to earth—within thirty thousand miles—on
October 26, 2028.

Intended or not, the movie *Deep Impact* is peppered with biblical
overtones. In the film, the crew of the *Messiah* purposely crashes their
spacecraft into the meteor, willingly giving up their lives to save the
earth. (If movies were shown in heaven, Jesus might say something like,
"Been there, done that.") As the one, true Messiah, Jesus Christ came to
Earth and gave His life willingly on the cross, that the world might be
saved.

Besides the Messiah imagery, the movie also evokes images of Noah's
ark. In *Deep Impact,* the Ark is the name of the location of underground

survival caves, where the winners of earth's ultimate lottery—a computer-selected number granting admission—were saved from destruction. In the celluloid version, although the asteroid did hit and multitudes of lives were lost, the human race survived.

In real life, scientists are not so sure of a happy ending. Indeed, the 1998 threat of a mile-wide asteroid—as large as Manhattan—caused serious consternation for many people. "It scares me. It really does," said Jack G. Hills, an asteroid specialist at the Los Alamos National Laboratory. "An object this big hitting the Earth has the potential of killing many, many people."[1] Fellow astronomer Brian Marsden, of the Harvard-Smithsonian Center for Astrophysics, concurred. "The chance of an actual collision is small, but not entirely out of the question."[2]

In a strange turn of events, less than twenty-four hours after the startling announcement, astronomers at the NASA's Jet Propulsion Laboratory in Pasadena said that the original calculations, done by the Harvard Center in Cambridge, Massachusetts, were wrong. The asteroid was indeed on its way toward Earth, but our planet was in no danger of being struck. Although it may come closer than any other objects that size, the asteroid, tagged by astronomers as 1997 XF11, would miss Earth by six hundred thousand miles.

Paul Chodas of the Jet Propulsion Lab declared confidently, "We don't think there's any chance of a collision."[3] The world breathed a collective sigh of relief, and the report of a potential asteroid impacting the earth was largely written off as another doomsday scare, a cosmic false alarm. Interestingly, a few months later, astronomers were admonished by American government officials to refrain from publicizing future asteroid sightings for fear of alarming the public.[4]

ASTEROIDS IN THE BIBLE?

Whether our government wants us to know about it or not, I believe our planet is going to be hit by an asteroid or a comet. I do not base such a bold assertion on Hollywood movies or scientific evidence; I base my statement on the Word of God.

In his apocalyptic vision, the apostle John saw a sight that would make most of us melt in fright:

I looked when He opened the sixth seal, and behold, there was a great earthquake; and the sun became black as sackcloth of hair, and the moon became like blood. And the stars of heaven fell to the earth, as a fig tree drops its late figs when it is shaken by a mighty wind. Then the sky receded as a scroll when it is rolled up, and every mountain and island was moved out of its place. (Rev. 6:12–14 NKJV)

For centuries most Bible scholars viewed this passage as largely symbolic, assuming that the stars were powerful world leaders who were going to fall from power; the mountains (their kingdoms) would crumble and be moved aside, thus causing a great political shake-up on earth. In the past thirty years, many Bible interpreters have taken a different tack, interpreting the cataclysmic events in John's vision as a scenario that could only be caused by a nuclear blast. That was before information about actual, documented meteor impacts became available. The apostle John, however, was way ahead of us. In the above passage of Scripture, the word John used to describe the "stars of heaven" falling to earth is the Greek word *asteres,* from which we derive our word *asteroid.*

WHAT ARE ASTEROIDS?

Asteroids are stony masses of various sizes, shapes, and materials, which orbit the Sun. At one time astronomers thought asteroids were actually small planets, or fragments of shattered planets, but most modern scientists believe the asteroids are "leftovers" from the formation of our solar system.

Modern astronomers spot about five hundred new asteroids every night. The asteroids are so prevalent that in recent years asteroid-spotting has become something of a game. In 1990, for example, astronomers at Lowell Observatory, in Flagstaff, Arizona, renamed asteroids designated as 4147, 4148, 4149, and 4150 as John, Paul, George, and Ringo, in honor of The Beatles. These asteroids are relatively small and too far away to be seen with the naked eye.

The asteroids that both fascinate us and concern us the most, however, are the larger ones. These "mountains," composed of rock and iron, and ranging in size from slightly more than a half-mile across to monstrous masses more than six hundred miles wide, are careening through our solar system. The largest asteroid discovered to date, known as Ceres, measures a whopping 640 miles in diameter.[5] To put that in perspective, imagine a flying mountain as large as the land mass between Tampa and Nashville!

Most asteroids lie in a belt between the orbits of Mars and Jupiter, but many are in orbits that bring them closer to Earth, and some, such as the Apollo asteroids, even cross the earth's orbit, making collisions possible.[6] These Earth-crossing asteroids are the ones that make astronomers nervous. According to Dr. Bill Botke of Cal Tech, "An asteroid about the size of a house comes between the orbit of the earth and moon once each day. An asteroid about the size of a football field comes between Earth and the moon once each month."[7]

Not Science Fiction Anymore

In 1996 Carl Hergenrother, a graduate student in astronomy, witnessed a close call by a huge Earth-crossing asteroid. "It was real exciting, and even a little scary at first," admits Hergenrother. "When I first saw it, I realized this was heading toward the earth. Then I began thinking, 'Hmm, I wonder if this is going to hit.'" The asteroid that Hergenrother discovered came within four hundred thousand miles of Earth. Had the orbits of the asteroid and Earth crossed just seven hours later, it would have been a direct hit.[8]

Asteroids can and do enter Earth's atmosphere; when they do, they become known as meteors (or meteorites and meteoroids, depending on their size and composition). Meteors seem to have some ice content as well as rock, thus causing the fiery plumes as they near the Sun. Those with more ice content combined with dirt or rock, like a giant dirty snowball in space, are known as comets, and may have long gas-and-dust tails, which can often be seen from Earth without the aid of a telescope.

The terminology can be confusing when discussing these various interplanetary forms. Sometimes scientists use the terms interchangeably, establishing their own set of criteria for each category. To simplify matters for our purposes, since we are primarily interested in the fact that something cataclysmic is soon going to happen to our planet, I will refer to the stony materials orbiting in space as *asteroids* and the ones that approach or strike Earth as *meteors*.

Often meteors can be seen with the naked eye, as what we call shooting stars, which streak across the skyline, or falling stars, which seem to drop out of heaven. Most meteors that enter our atmosphere burn up because of friction long before striking the earth. Others do not even penetrate our atmospheric shield, and simply skip off harmlessly into outer space. Still others explode on contact with Earth's atmosphere, detonating with enormous power, often equivalent to as much as fifty to seventy-five kilotons of TNT.

In 1994 one such meteor hit over the Pacific Ocean above the area of Micronesia. It detonated at about sixty thousand feet above the earth, with the energy of seventy kilotons of TNT, about 3.5 times more powerful than the bombs that destroyed Hiroshima and Nagasaki. The explosion was picked up by U.S. defense satellites and prompted a military alert. Two hundred fifty similar detonations have occurred in the past ten years. To put that in perspective, think of one nuclear explosion occurring somewhere above the earth every two weeks, any one of which could possibly wipe out the human race or a large portion of it.

Thousands of small meteorites, pieces of rock or metal thought to be fragments from asteroids, actually hit Earth's surface every year. Most of these are so small that they do no damage, or they land in the oceans or remote areas and are not recovered.

IMPACT!

In at least 150 cases, however, scientists are convinced that much larger meteors have struck the earth. The largest known meteorite discovered so far is composed of iron, weighs sixty-six tons, and lies in place at Grootfontein, Namibia. Closer to home, Meteor Crater near Flagstaff, Arizona, is about four thousand feet in diameter and about 650 feet deep. It is the most perfectly preserved impact crater on Earth.

Many scientists believe that the extinction of the dinosaurs can be directly linked to a mammoth meteor impacting the earth. The resulting 120-mile-wide crater can be clearly seen today in Mexico's Yucatan Peninsula in the Gulf of Mexico. Scientists believe that an asteroid about six to eight miles wide, roughly the size of Mount Everest, blasted into Earth with an impact exceeding the force of three hundred million (that's 300,000,000!) atomic bombs.

When the fiery mountain hit the earth, it obliterated everything for hundreds of miles and caused an immediate firestorm over much of Central and North America. The firestorm, scientists theorize, destroyed all life in the area. Similar to the mushroom effect of a nuclear bomb, the meteor impact blasted white-hot dust, smoke, and other debris into the air, literally blocking the sun's rays from reaching the earth for nearly a year. During this time a worldwide nuclear winter occurred, violently disrupting the photosynthesis process, and thus wiping out the dinosaur population and many other life forms.

In 1908 a similar but much smaller-scale event occurred in Tunguska, a remote region of Siberia, where a meteor or comet less than two hundred feet wide impacted the earth with the explosive power of a ten-megaton bomb. Many scientists believe the cosmic chunk did not actually strike Earth's soil, but exploded above the surface. Regardless of how it happened, when scientists explored the territory, they could not believe their eyes. For nearly a thousand square miles in the heavily forested area, trees were literally flattened like matchsticks in concentric circles, moving out from the blast. The entire area looked as though it had been the location of a massive nuclear test site. Had such an impact occurred in New York, millions of people in and around the area would have died.

According to Dr. Jasper Wall of the Royal Greenwich Observatory, another major impact took place in Brazil during the 1930s, when three small asteroids exploded about a mile above the jungle, sending a huge fireball to Earth with the force of a thirty-megaton blast, destroying eight hundred square miles of the rain forest. In that event, the sky first turned bloodred, followed by a complete darkening of the sun. Missionaries reported that natives living nearby believed that the sky-god had come to Earth, and that it was the end of the world. To placate the angry sky-god, the natives planned mass suicides, which were only thwarted by the persuasion of missionaries who arrived in the area a few days following the blast.[9]

APOLOGIES TO MRS. O'LEARY'S COW?

The firestorms associated with asteroid and meteor impacts have caused some scientists to take another look at one of the worst catastrophes in

American history, the Chicago Fire of October 8, 1871. Commonly believed to have been started when Mrs. O'Leary's miscreant cow kicked over a lantern, the fire may actually have been ignited by a firestorm connected to a meteor impact. The reason scientists have opened such a Pandora's box of speculation is that at least twelve other reported fires occurred on the same night in a four-state area. The worst of these fires scorched Peshtigo, a small but booming lumber town located on both sides of the Peshtigo River, north of Green Bay, Wisconsin.

The fire in Chicago broke out about 9:00 P.M. By the following afternoon, 250 lives had been lost to the flames and smoke in the Windy City. About one-third of the city's population was homeless, with property damage estimated at two hundred million dollars.

Interestingly, the Peshtigo fire erupted at the same time—almost to the minute—as the fire in Chicago, 240 miles to the north. A prolonged summer drought had turned the Wisconsin woodlands into a tinderbox. Once the fire started, the tiny town of Peshtigo was consumed within one hour, virtually leveled by the flames. More than twelve hundred people of the town's two thousand residents perished in the inferno; 1.25 million acres of surrounding forest land were decimated. The October 14, 1871, edition of the local newspaper, *The Marinette and Peshtigo Eagle*, ran the headline, "A Night in Hell," and described fireballs falling from the sky and forests erupting in flames. Besides the trees that burned, whole forests of maple trees were uprooted and laid flat, similar to freshly mown hay.

Peshtigo historian Robert Couvillian noted that around 8 P.M. on the night of the fire, there was "a lurid glow in the southwestern sky." A sound, similar to thunder, grew increasingly louder.

> [Suddenly] a firestorm blasted [people] off their feet . . . trees were being uprooted, roofs were coming off homes, chimneys were crashing to the ground. Everything was moving horizontally! It was like the heaviest snowstorm you've ever seen, only it contained the burning embers, and the ashes and the red-hot sand and the dirt.[10]

A pamphlet, available at the Peshtigo Fire Museum, describes the conflagration in poignant detail:

On the 8th of October, Peshtigo awakened to find a copper sun in the sky and a village that lay naked and sultry in the deadly still air. In spite of their apprehensions of coming danger, the villagers attended church services as usual in the morning.

The afternoon wore on, hot and still, and smoky enough to make eyes water. When night closed down, a sullen red glow could be seen over the treetops to the southwest. The smoke thickened, and about nine o'clock a low, moaning, far-off roaring of the wind could be heard.

Suddenly the roar became louder and quickly a crashing and deep booming came from the surrounding forest. In less than five minutes there was fire everywhere. The atmosphere quickly grew unbearably warm and the town was enveloped by a rush of air as hot as though it were issuing from a blast furnace. The wind lifted the roofs off houses, toppled chimneys and showered the town with hot sand and live coals. The cries of the men, women, and children were scarcely audible above the rumble of exploding gas and crashing timber. People were numb with terror, seeing nothing but fire overhead and all around them.

There was tragic confusion when the frantic, struggling mass of people tried to escape from the fire. Some were trampled under foot; others rushed to the bridge hoping to find safety on the opposite side and then ran headlong into those coming from that side with the same thought in mind.

Many sought refuge in the Peshtigo River. On their way to the river, they saw men, women, and cattle stagger for a few minutes and then go down burning brightly, like so many pieces of pitch pine.

Refugees in the river tried to avoid the fire rain, which came down, exploding in steam all around them. To add to the horror, the woodenware factory erupted like a volcano and sent a shower of burning wooden tubs and broom handles upon the tortured people in the water . . . While Christian men and women prayed and tried to console their frightened children, the whole village of Peshtigo was wiped out in one hour between nine and ten o'clock.[11]

Reverend Peter Pernin, a survivor of the fire, provided a grim, eyewitness account of the tragedy. The pastor, like many others, survived by jumping into the Peshtigo River. The ordinarily cool, clean water was neither. Reverend Pernin recalled the plight he shared with others seeking refuge from the flames:

> Once in water up to our necks, I thought we would at least be safe from fire, but it was not so. The flames darted over the river as they did over land, the air was full of them, or rather the air itself was on fire. Our heads were in continual danger. It was only by throwing water constantly over them and our faces, and beating the river with our hands that we kept the flames at bay.
>
> The river was so bright, brighter than by day, and the spectacle presented by those heads rising above the level of the water, some covered, some uncovered, the countless hands employed in beating the waves, was singular and painful in the extreme.[12]

The pastor stayed in the water from the time the fire began, around 9:00 P.M., to about 3:30 A.M. At one point during the life-or-death endurance test, a female survivor asked Reverend Pernin, "Do you not think this is the end of the world?"

"I do not think so," Pernin replied. "But if other countries are burned as ours seems to have been, the end of the world, at least for us, must be at hand."[13]

At sunrise the next day, more than twelve hundred people were found dead in the aftermath of the Peshtigo fire. To this day the disaster remains the costliest fire in American history, in terms of human lives lost. Ironically, some people survived by hiding in wells, while others suffocated in similar wells. Clearly, this was not just another forest fire.

Researcher Randall Carlson is convinced that the Peshtigo fire, along with the Chicago fire, was ignited not by the unfortunate kick of a cow, but by a cosmic event, a meteor about one hundred yards wide, exploding about twenty miles in the atmosphere above the affected areas.[14]

WILL IT HAPPEN AGAIN?

I believe such cosmic chaos is going to occur again, only on a much wider scale. Although I have come to this conclusion from a biblical perspective rather than a scientific approach, I have discovered, to my surprise, that many highly respected scientists have been saying the same thing. For instance, Donald W. Cox is a leading authority on space flight. His co-author, James H. Chestek, worked for thirty-five years as an aerospace engineer, where he helped develop a variety of space projects, from inter-planetary probes to the Strategic Defense Initiative. Cox and Chestek are not fatalists. Yet in their book, *Doomsday Asteroid,* they state pointedly:

> We live in a cosmic shooting gallery. Somewhere out in the netherworld of deep space, hurling toward Earth, is a doomsday rock. The question now is not just detecting it, but what can be done to possibly nudge it off course by one means or another before it strikes the earth and anni-hilates a large part—if not all—of humanity.
>
> Such a doomsday asteroid could severely disrupt life on Earth, not only for humanity, but for the other species of plants, fish, birds, and animals. Although no astronomer has yet located the killer object (which will be a mile wide or larger) headed for us, it is inevitable, according to most astronomers, that one will eventually appear. Large Earth-crossing asteroids slam into our home planet every 300,000 to a million years, which means that there is approximately one chance in 6,000 to 20,000 of a cataclysmic impact during the next half-century. In other words, the earth has a much better chance of being struck by a large asteroid than most of us have of winning big in the lottery (the chances in the latter case are usually one in millions).[15]

In the same book, the authors quote Dr. Tom Gehrels, a professor of lunar and planetary science at the University of Arizona and the head of Spacewatch, a team of astronomers that searches the sky for killer aster-oids. Speaking of "the big one," Gehrels says, "Eventually it will hit and be catastrophic. The largest near-Earth one we know of is 10 kilometers in diameter (or about 6.2 miles) wide. If such a thing like that hit, the explo-sion would be a billion times bigger than Hiroshima."[16]

While astronomers worry about "the big one," they also fret about the myriad of smaller Earth-crossing asteroids, and they are quick to point out that they have only begun to locate and track the many asteroids that come close to earth.

While they estimate that perhaps as many as 2,000 asteroids larger than a kilometer (six-tenths of a mile) either cross or come close to Earth's orbit, they have discovered and tracked fewer than 200 of them. "We simply don't know where the other objects are," says JPL astronomer [Eleanor] Helin. "But the ones that have been discovered," she warns, "certainly suggest that we could someday face a surprise encounter with a large, unseen object." The significance of the kilometer size? An impact of anything that large, scientists believe, would cause not just a regional but a global catastrophe.[17]

How much warning will we have to prepare for a meteor strike? Not much, scientists fear. If given a year or more of advance notice, a massive asteroid could be detected and possibly deflected by using nuclear devices to knock it off a collision course with Earth. Unfortunately, with cosmic materials traveling at speeds fifteen times greater than our space shuttle, sometimes as much as fifteen kilometers per second, many "small" meteors give little warning of their approach. For instance, in 1994 a meteor fireball, spotted ten miles above the ground and captured on tape by an amateur video cameraman, streaked across three states in a matter of seconds before it skipped back into outer space. Had it continued in Earth's direction instead, it was large enough to have destroyed an entire city.

Asteroids, while bigger and easier to spot, are sometimes just as elusive. To the late astronomer Gene Shoemaker, it was not a question of *if* the earth will be struck by an asteroid, but *when,* and how destructive will it be? Dr. Shoemaker and his wife, Carolyn, discovered more than thirty comets and hundreds of asteroids during their career. Together with Dr. David Levy, they were the first astronomers to sight the comet which exploded into Jupiter in 1993. In the 1960s and early 1970s, Shoemaker hoped to be a part of the United States' first mission to the moon, but his dream was derailed by a health problem. Nevertheless, he remained part of the U.S. space program and was highly involved in the training of NASA's early lunar astronauts, much of which took place at Meteor Crater in Arizona. Few men in the scientific community were more respected than Gene Shoemaker.

In describing Earth's precarious position amidst the asteroids swirling through space, the impending certainty of an asteroid striking the planet, and the resulting risk of annihilation, Shoemaker said,

It's like being in a hale of bullets going by all the time . . . These things *have* hit the earth in the past; they will hit the earth in the future. It will produce a catastrophe that exceeds all other known natural disasters . . . by a large measure.[18]

THIS IS NO MOVIE!

What will it be like when, as the Bible describes it, "the stars begin to fall" to the earth? Astronomer Jack Hills of Los Alamos National Laboratory described a conservative scenario during the asteroid scare of 1998. "If it hit in the ocean, he predicted, it would cause a tsunami (commonly called a tidal wave) hundreds of feet high, flooding the coastlines of surrounding continents. 'Where cities stood,' he said, 'there would be only mudflats.' A land hit, he calculated, would blast out a crater at least 30 miles across and throw up a blanket of dust and vapor that would blot out the sun 'for weeks, if not months.'"[19]

Understand, even a small meteor, one the size of a basketball, carries with it about thirty thousand tons of nuclear force. Should such a meteor strike a major city anywhere in the world, it would obliterate everything for miles around; the air would be superheated to nine thousand degrees; millions of people would die in an instant. People at ground zero would never know what hit them.

Astronomer David Levy predicts that as a result of an impact, every major fault line could fail, causing earthquakes on an unprecedented scale as the plates below the earth's surface literally buckle. Similar to the tidal waves caused by an impact in the ocean, a land impact would cause tidal waves of *earth*, hundreds of feet tall, to circle the globe at speeds of five hundred miles per hour. The whole planet would shake, quake, and bake. Millions of tons of white-hot earth would be hurled into the sky, then as the dirt falls back to earth it would ignite fires over the entire planet. Anything that could burn would burn. The unusual seismic activity would cause volcanoes to erupt, sending even more smoke, ash, steam, and debris into the already blackened sky.

An ominous dust cloud would encase the earth, blocking out the sun's light, causing the world to be dark even at midday. "This is not a cloud that causes a day to be dull and gray," says Levy. "This is a cloud that would cut off all sunlight, the day would be black, the night would be black, and it would probably last for a year." Photosynthesis would virtually stop. Not even rain would bring refreshment, since the rain coming through the mess in the sky would be laced with nicrice acid. "It would be the mother of all acid rains," says Levy.

> Plant life could not survive. People and animals that eat plants could not survive. Creatures that eat plant-eating creatures could not survive. Death would go right up the food chain . . . The nightmare will include just about every environmental disaster you can think of . . . all happening at once.[20]

What Was That the Bible Said?

With David Levy's horrifying description in mind, let's look again at the description written nearly two thousand years earlier by the apostle John:

> Behold, there was a great earthquake; and the sun became black as sackcloth of hair, and the moon became like blood. And the stars of heaven fell to the earth, as a fig tree drops its late figs when it is shaken by a mighty wind. Then the sky receded as a scroll when it is rolled up, and every mountain and island was moved out of its place. And the kings of the earth, the great men, the rich men, the commanders, the mighty men, every slave and every free man, hid themselves in the caves and in the rocks of the mountains, and said to the mountains and rocks, "Fall on us and hide us from the face of Him who sits on the throne and from the wrath of the Lamb!" (Rev. 6:12–16 NKJV).

For nearly fifty years, like many other Christians, I tacitly agreed with the Bible scholars who attributed the above description to a nuclear exchange between the superpowers of the earth, resulting in worldwide destruction. Certainly, we now possess the awesome capability of obliterating our own planet by means of nuclear bombs, but I no longer subscribe to that notion. In retrospect, I believe it was arrogant to even think that God must bring about the events of His supernatural time of tribulation and judgment through human inventions and institutions. Our God is much bigger than that!

I am now convinced that He will use His own creation, just as He did in Sodom and Gomorrah, to bring punishment on humanity's sinful pride, while providing one last opportunity for men, women, and children all over the world to repent, turn to Him, and plead for mercy and forgiveness. I believe that as we move into the Great Tribulation period, we can expect to see not merely symbolic fulfillments of John's prophecies of stars falling from heaven, but literal asteroids and meteors, which will wreak havoc on the earth.

And it will get worse before it gets better!

After a glimpse into heaven in Revelation 7, the apostle John goes on to describe the total terror that will reign on earth at that time. In chapter 8, he describes more horrors that will take place just prior to the Lord's return. The plagues John describes are amazingly similar to the plagues with which God struck the earth prior to delivering His people from Egyptian slavery (Ex. 7—10). But the coming calamities will encompass far more territory and natural resources and affect far more people.

Doing his best to describe the strange phenomena he sees, John writes:

Then the angel took the censer, filled it with fire from the altar, and threw it to the earth. And there were noises, thunderings, lightnings, and an earthquake. So the seven angels who had the seven trumpets prepared themselves to sound. The first angel sounded: And hail and fire followed, mingled with blood, and they were thrown to the earth. And a third of the trees were burned up, and all green grass was burned up. Then the second angel sounded; And something like a great mountain burning with fire was thrown into the sea, and a third of the sea became blood. And a third of the living creatures in the sea died, and a third of the ships were destroyed. Then the third angel sounded: And a great star fell from heaven, burning like a torch, and it fell on a third of the rivers and on the springs of water. The name of the star is Wormwood. A third of the waters became wormwood, and many men died from the water, because it was made bitter. Then the fourth angel sounded: And a third of the sun was struck, a third of the moon, and a third of the stars, so that a third of them were darkened. A third of the day did not shine, and likewise the night. (Rev. 8:5–12 NKJV).

The devastation John describes will literally wipe out one-third of the earth's vegetation, water supply, sea life, and, perhaps most significant of all, a third of the sun's light. Certainly, this could be the effect of a nuclear holocaust, but it is equally plausible that this could be the result of a massive meteor strike, or a series of meteor impacts. Notice the sound of thunderings (v. 5), hail and fire together, mingled with blood, being thrown to the earth (v. 7). Could this be a comet or a meteor? See also the vegetation being scorched (v. 7), something like a great mountain burning with fire (v. 8). Remember, John did not have a telescope; he never saw an asteroid or a comet, yet he provided an extremely realistic picture of a meteor. Of course, the burning mountain John saw could also have been violent volcanic eruptions caused by a meteor, similar to those described by David Levy.

Imagine being in a ship when the waters begin to boil, or the waves begin to form five-hundred-mile-per-hour tidal waves, as a result of a meteor strike. It is not difficult to assume that a third of the world's great ships and a third of the sea life would be destroyed (v. 9). Certainly water pollution would be at an all time high (vv. 10–11), either because of the debris, or possibly, as Levy theorizes, due to the acidic rain, which will fall on the earth after a major meteor impact. And as we have already noted, the sky will turn dark (v. 12), a bleak scenario universally accepted by scientists who study meteors and the potential they have to block out the sun's rays.

Could a nuclear attack cause such cosmic convulsions? Possibly. Could a large meteor cause such effects? Absolutely.

THE SUN WILL BE BLOTTED OUT

Interestingly, the Old Testament prophets predicted such events thousands of years before the book of Revelation was written. The prophet Joel wrote:

> The earth quakes before them,
> The heavens tremble;
> The sun and moon grow dark,
> And the stars diminish their brightness.
> The LORD gives voice before His army,
> For His camp is very great;
> For strong is the One who executes His word.

> For the day of the LORD is great and very terrible;
> Who can endure it? (2:10–11 NKJV)

The prophet Amos said something similar: "'And it shall come to pass in that day,' says the LORD God, / 'that I will make the sun go down at noon, / and I will darken the earth in broad daylight'" (8:9 NKJV).

Isaiah, perhaps the best-known prophet in the Old Testament, spoke often of future calamities coming upon the earth.

> Behold, the day of the LORD comes,
> Cruel, with both wrath and fierce anger,
> To lay the land desolate;
> And He will destroy its sinners from it.
> For the stars of heaven and their constellations
> Will not give their light;
> The sun will be darkened in its going forth,
> And the moon will not cause its light to shine. (13:9–10 NKJV)

The prophet went on to say, "Therefore I will shake the heavens, / and the earth will move out of her place" (13:13 NKJV).

The prophet Ezekiel concurs: "I will cover the heavens, and make its stars dark; / I will cover the sun with a cloud, / and the moon shall not give her light" (32:7 NKJV).

Clearly, the prophets were foreseeing cataclysmic events, which, in light of the passages in Revelation, and what we know from modern scientific studies, could well come to pass within our lifetime.

Most important, in the Second Coming Discourse Jesus, too, talked about the sun being darkened before His return to earth. After listing some of the signs of the times of which His followers need to be aware, Jesus said,

> Immediately after the tribulation of those days the sun will be darkened, and the moon will not give its light; the stars will fall from heaven, and the powers of the heavens will be shaken. Then the sign of the Son of Man will appear in heaven, and then all the tribes of the earth will mourn, and they will see the Son of Man coming on the clouds of heaven with power and great glory. (Matt. 24:29–30 NKJV)

The parallel accounts in the gospels are equally calamitous. Luke records,

And there will be signs in the sun, in the moon, and in the stars; and on the earth distress of nations, with perplexity, the sea and the waves roaring; men's hearts failing them from fear and the expectation of those things which are coming on the earth; for the powers of the heavens will be shaken. (21:25–26 NKJV)

When Are You Coming, Jesus?

"And *then!*" Jesus said. "Then they will see the Son of Man coming in a cloud with power and great glory. Now when these things begin to happen, look up and lift up your heads, because your redemption draws near" (Luke 21:27–28 NKJV). Notice, Jesus says that the "signs in the sun" will occur *before* His return in power and glory (v. 21).

On the Day of Pentecost the apostle Peter quoted the prophet Joel along these same lines. In his well-known sermon, Peter explained that Jerusalem had just witnessed the outpouring of the Holy Spirit that had been prophesied years earlier.

> And it shall come to pass in the last days, says God,
> That I will pour out of My Spirit on all flesh;
> Your sons and your daughters shall prophesy,
> Your young men shall see visions,
> Your old men shall dream dreams.
> And on My menservants and on My maidservants
> I will pour out My Spirit in those days;
> And they shall prophesy. (Acts 2:17–18 NKJV)

That is where we usually stop reading in this passage; it's where most preachers of my former theological persuasion usually stopped preaching. But Peter did not stop there in his quotation of God's word to the prophet.

> I will show wonders in heaven above
> And signs in the earth beneath:

> Blood and fire and vapor of smoke.
> The sun shall be turned into darkness,
> And the moon into blood,
> Before the coming of the great and awesome
>   day of the LORD.
> And it shall come to pass
> That whoever calls on the name of the LORD
> Shall be saved. (Acts 2:19–21 NKJV)

We have whole denominations built around the events that took place on the Day of Pentecost. Thousands of sermons, songs, seminars, and books have been based on the second chapter of Acts. But in nearly forty years in and around ministry circles, I can count on one hand how many messages I have heard on Acts 2:19–21. Yet I am convinced that these verses (and the others I have mentioned above) provide a key to Christ's return.

As humanity faces its darkest hour, suddenly Jesus Christ will come again, and the whole world will see Him!

12

The Great Event

J ust as all hope seems lost, at the darkest moment in human history, suddenly the skies will be illuminated by a light more brilliant than anything ever before seen on Earth. Jesus Christ, King of kings, Lord of lords,
will roll back the darkness as He returns in power and glory.

What a day that will be! Christ's appearing will be the fulfillment of "the
blessed hope," that long-expected, great event Christians have been waiting for since Jesus ascended to heaven nearly two thousand years ago. But
Christians will not be the only ones who see the Second Coming. Scripture
indicates that the whole world will see Jesus Christ return as King. The
apostle John wrote, "Behold, He is coming with clouds, and every eye will
see Him, even they who pierced Him. And all the tribes of the earth will
mourn because of Him. Even so, Amen" (Rev. 1:7 NKJV).

Some people may say, "Well, I really don't care to see Jesus return. I
might be too busy or have more important things to do that day." Let me
assure you, this is one event nobody will miss. "Every eye will see" Jesus
Christ when He returns, even the people who crucified ("pierced") Him—
a possible reference to the actual people involved in the crucifixion of
Jesus: Pontius Pilate, Herod, Caiaphas, the soldiers who beat Him, and the
throng who cried out, "Crucify Him! Crucify Him." More likely the reference is to the Jewish and Roman people (under whose auspices Jesus was
"pierced"), perhaps representative of both the Jews and the Gentiles who

rejected Jesus as Lord during His earthly ministry. It will be the ultimate payback time, when they see the One whom they despised, rejected, and crucified returning with all power, authority, and judgment.

No doubt this is why some people will wail and mourn when they see Jesus coming. Apparently, the Jewish people will be especially impacted by Christ's return: when they see the Messiah they rejected coming back in glory, the awfulness of their error will devastate them. John's prediction of this mourning harkens back to the Old Testament prophet Zechariah, through whom the Lord said,

> And I will pour on the house of David and on the inhabitants of Jerusalem the Spirit of grace and supplication; then they will look on Me whom they pierced. Yes, they will mourn for Him as one mourns for his only son, and grieve for Him as one grieves for a firstborn. In that day there shall be a great mourning in Jerusalem, like the mourning at Hadad Rimmon in the plain of Megiddo. (12:10–11 NKJV)

Sadly, it will take Armageddon (the last, horrific battle to be fought in the plain of Megiddo) and the coming of the Conquering Christ for some people to realize who Jesus really is.

For years I pondered Revelation 1:7, wondering, *How will everyone in the world see Jesus when He returns?* How could people in Korea see Him at the same time as those in Atlanta, London, or Montevideo? I listened with interest as different Bible teachers postulated complex ideas and some pretty wild theories to explain this unusual phenomenon. Most modern biblical interpreters looked to television as the answer. As a person well aware of television's power to communicate information to the world, for a while at least, that possibility seemed plausible to me. After all, consider the broad reach of international television networks such as CNN. When something "big" happens anywhere in the world, within hours, CNN reporters or their local affiliates are on the scene, broadcasting live, sending out sound and pictures to the world. It only made sense to assume that the major networks would televise Christ's return "live."

I am now convinced, however, that the reason the entire world will see Jesus at His coming has nothing to do with our modern means of communication. It has to do with the incredible, awesome, overpowering presence of Almighty God being manifested at a time when the world is enveloped in darkness. Consider this scenario: The world has been hit by a series of meteor strikes, or possibly one massive impact with global ramifications. The sun has been blotted out for nearly a year by the resultant nuclear-winter dust cloud. It is a time of horrendous terror as the earth endures unprecedented plagues, environmental nightmares, and the many other calamities we discussed in previous chapters. Just when it seems that human beings can endure no longer, Jesus Christ will return, lighting up the sky as the sun. And the whole world will see Him.

To help us understand what is going to happen in the future, we need only look back at the past to see that God has given us several signs of His presence in human history—clouds, a rainbow, the sun, and fire—all of which we will see again at the Second Coming.

GOD IN THE CLOUDS

In the Bible clouds were frequently associated with the Lord's manifestations on earth. For instance, as Moses led the Hebrew people out of Egyptian bondage, they did not just go off in any direction they pleased. "And the LORD went before them by day in a pillar of cloud to lead the way, and by night in a pillar of fire to give them light, so as to go by day and night" (Ex. 13:21 NKJV). The Bible makes it clear that it was God going before the people in a cloud. As I have studied this passage in light of the book of Revelation, I am convinced that this pillar of cloud by day and the pillar of fire by night could well have been a preincarnate (before He was born as a baby in Bethlehem) manifestation of Jesus Christ.

Again, in Exodus 19:9, we find, "And the LORD said to Moses, 'Behold, I come to you in the thick cloud, that the people may hear when I speak with you, and believe you forever'" (NKJV).

When God distributed His Spirit upon the seventy elders chosen to help Moses deal with problems among the Hebrew people, the Lord appeared in a cloud. "Then the LORD came down in the cloud, and spoke to him, and took of the Spirit that was upon him, and placed the same upon the seventy elders; and it happened when the Spirit rested upon them, that they prophesied" (Num. 11:25 NKJV). When the people completed the work on the tabernacle, as God had instructed, once again the

Lord's presence was manifested in a cloud. "Now the LORD appeared at the tabernacle in a pillar of a cloud, and the pillar of cloud stood above the door of the tabernacle" (Deut. 31:15 NKJV).

In the New Testament, clouds are also associated with God's presence. At Jesus' transfiguration, for instance, when Moses and Elijah appeared with Jesus, whose clothing "became shining, exceedingly white, like snow, such as no launderer on earth can whiten them" (Mark 9:3 NKJV), Peter began babbling about building three tabernacles. Suddenly, Peter's bluster was interrupted. "While he was still speaking, behold, a bright cloud overshadowed them; and suddenly a voice came out of the cloud, saying, 'This is My beloved Son, in whom I am well pleased. Hear Him!'" (Matt. 17:4–5 NKJV).

But the clouds are not exclusively present at manifestations of the Father; clouds are also associated with Jesus. After His resurrection and forty days of appearances to His disciples, Jesus ascended into heaven in a cloud (Acts 1:9–11 NKJV). As the disciples stood around looking into the skies, perhaps wondering what was going to happen next, an angel appeared and said, "Men of Galilee, why do you stand gazing up into heaven? This same Jesus, who was taken up from you into heaven, will so come in like manner as you saw Him go into heaven'"(Acts 1:11 NKJV). And Jesus Himself predicted that He would return in the clouds: "Then they will see the Son of Man coming in a cloud with power and great glory" (Luke 21:27 NKJV; also Matt. 24:30). John, in his end-time vision, saw Jesus in the cloud as well. "Then I looked, and behold, a white cloud, and on the cloud sat One like the Son of Man, having on His head a golden crown, and in His hand a sharp sickle" (Rev. 14:14 NKJV).

In late 1996 a Bible conference was held at the former Heritage USA, outside of Charlotte, North Carolina. After a prolonged period of praise and worship, several thousand people witnessed a large cloud hovering over the front of the auditorium as God's presence was manifested in a powerful way.

Not only does the Bible associate clouds with God's presence, we also see God in the rainbow, a symbol that has gotten a bad rap in recent years.

GOD IN THE RAINBOW

Many people associate rainbows with cultic or New Age groups. Not long before my father went home to be with the Lord, I was talking about the rainbow being a sign of God's presence. My ninety-one-year-old father was horrified to hear me say that I thought we should reclaim the rainbow. "Jim," he said with concern in his voice. "The rainbow is a New Age symbol."

In all due respect to my dear, departed father, the rainbow is not a New Age sign. It may have been perverted and prostituted by various groups and cults, but originally the rainbow was a sign of God's promise to us that He would never again destroy the world with water (Gen. 9:9–17). In other words, every time we see a rainbow in the sky (or anywhere else, for that matter), we should be reminded of God's loving mercy toward us. The rainbow is a visible message: "God keeps His promises!"

The rainbow is God's sign, not the devil's. Remember, the devil loves to counterfeit what is real and true. Satan has tried to co-opt the rainbow and turn it into a pagan symbol, just as he has tried to trivialize the cross. Nowadays, the most pagan of rock music stars, and others whose lifestyles are obviously contrary to the Word of God, can be seen wearing crosses. For many people the cross is no longer a sacred symbol, but a symbol of derision. The devil has done something similar with the rainbow, the sign of a precious promise of God.

Yet nowhere in the Bible is a rainbow attributed to anyone but the Lord. In fact, it is often a sign of God's powerful presence, as the prophet Ezekiel witnessed in a vision. The prophet first described the appearance and duties of four living creatures (referred to as cherubim in Ezekiel 10), then he saw the object of the cherubim's worship:

And above the firmament over their heads was the likeness of a throne, in appearance like a sapphire stone; on the likeness of the throne was a likeness with the appearance of a man high above it. Also from the appearance of His waist and upward I saw, as it were, the color of amber with the appearance of fire all around within it; and from the appearance of His waist and downward I saw, as it were, the appearance of fire with brightness all around. Like the appearance of a rainbow in a cloud on a rainy day, so was the appearance of the brightness all around it. This was the appearance of the likeness of the glory of the LORD. (1:26–28 NKJV)

John, too, associated a rainbow with the presence of God in the book of Revelation. "Immediately I was in the Spirit; and behold, a throne set in heaven, and One sat on the throne. And He who sat there was like a jasper and a sardius stone in appearance; and there was a rainbow around the throne, in appearance like an emerald" (4:2–3 NKJV).

A third sign of God's supernatural presence is a bright light.

HIS COUNTENANCE AS THE SUN

We know from Scripture that the presence of God is often enveloped in a bright light (Ps. 4:6, 80:7, 89:15; Dan. 10:6). At the transfiguration of Jesus, as I mentioned, "his face shone like the sun" (Matt. 17:2 NKJV). Similarly, when Saul, the persecutor of Christians, first encountered Jesus Christ, he was blinded by the Lord. In telling his conversion story to the Roman governor, Festus, and the Jewish king, Agrippa, Paul recalled the incident:

> At midday, O king, along the road I saw a light from heaven, brighter than the sun, shining around me and those who journeyed with me. And when we all had fallen to the ground, I heard a voice speaking to me and saying in the Hebrew language, "Saul, Saul, why are you persecuting Me? It is hard for you to kick against the goads." So I said, "Who are you, Lord?" And He said, "I am Jesus, whom you are persecuting." (Acts 26:13–15 NKJV)

Paul was so convinced that the person who spoke to him out of the light was Jesus Christ, he immediately converted, becoming one of the most eloquent and persuasive witnesses of Christ ever to walk the earth.

When the apostle John got his first glimpse of Jesus in heaven, it was not as the gentle, meek friend John had known during Christ's earthly ministry. John reported, "He had in His right hand seven stars, out of His mouth went a sharp two-edged sword, and His countenance was like the sun shining in its strength" (Rev. 1:16 NKJV). Whatever else is associated with Jesus in heaven, we know that He is often seen in an incredibly bright light.

A cloud. A rainbow. A countenance like the sun. And finally feet like brass refined in a furnace. All signs of God's presence.

FEET LIKE BRASS REFINED IN A FURNACE

In describing God's presence, the prophet Daniel wrote, "His body was like beryl, his face like the appearance of lightning, his eyes like torches of fire, his arms and feet like burnished bronze in color, and the sound of his words like the voice of a multitude" (10:6 NKJV). In the Bible, these feet like burnished bronze or brass denote the power to render judgment.

Interestingly, when John describes Jesus in Revelation, he uses similar language. "His feet were like fine brass, as if refined in a furnace, and His voice as the sound of many waters" (1:15 NKJV). Could it be that the pillar of fire that led the Israelites out of Egyptian slavery was the same One whose feet were "like fine brass, as if refined in a furnace"? I believe that Leader was none other than Jesus Christ.

WHAT DOES IT ALL MEAN?

For a number of years I believed and taught that Christians would not have to go through any of the tribulation period described in the book of Revelation. Like many of my contemporaries, I assumed that everything between chapter 4 and the end of chapter 18 was going to be God's pouring out of judgments on a rebellious, sinful world. I believed that we Christians would have been conveniently raptured out of this world before those horrible things began to come upon the earth. I taught that only after the Christians escaped would the awful tribulations come, followed by the final return of Jesus Christ described in Revelation 19, where we see a picture of Christ as Conquering King.

Then I read chapter 10, verse 1.

And read it. And read it again. The more I read it, the more convinced I became that this can only be one person—Jesus Christ. It is not Gabriel, Michael, or some other special angel, as I had been taught and as I later taught thousands of other people. The characteristics John describes can only be rightly attributed to God, not any created being.

Keep in mind what we know about the signs of the presence of Almighty God—He appears often in a cloud, the rainbow, bright light, and fire—and look at what I believe is the point in Scripture where Jesus Christ returns:

I saw still another mighty angel [messenger] coming down from heaven, clothed with a cloud. And a rainbow was on his head, and his face was like the sun, and his feet like pillars of fire. He had a little book open in his hand. And he set his right foot on the sea and his left foot on the land. (10:1–2 NKJV)

I believe with all of my heart that the Person being described here is Jesus Christ. He is coming in the clouds. Only God Almighty has a rainbow on His head. Only His face is like the sun. (Moses reflected a bit of that glory when he came down from Mount Sinai, after receiving the Ten Commandments.) His fiery feet indicate that He is coming to judge the world. (Jesus said in Matthew 28:18, "All authority has been given to Me in heaven and on earth" [NKJV].) And he places one foot on the sea and one foot on the land, to show that He has absolute power and authority over the world.

This is the Jesus that every eye shall see—not the Babe of Bethlehem, not even the Lamb for sinners slain. This Jesus is the regal, awesome Judge of all creation!

For nearly ten years I kept my thoughts on Revelation 10:1 to myself. Finally, as I continued to study, and as I began to speak about what I believed God had shown me in prison and in the years following my release, I felt that I must go public with the message He had given me. I knew it would not be a popular message, and I knew that the prevailing opinions in many Christian circles would be adamantly against my views. Nevertheless, late in 1997 I began to voice my opinion that although the picture of Jesus in Revelation 19 is indeed a portrayal of our King, Revelation 10 is an equally accurate presentation of our victorious Lord. And if we are to understand these Scriptures in any chronological way, it might well be that Jesus will return some time after the tribulation period begins.

I had just spoken on the subject for the first time when I was riding with my daughter, Tammy Sue, and my assistant, Shirley Fulbright. We turned on the radio and to our surprise heard Bible teacher David Jeremiah speaking about Revelation 10. Dr. Jeremiah was one of the Bible teachers I had often listened to on my tiny transistor radio while I had been in prison, and I had greatly benefited from his sound, careful analysis of Scripture. Now, as we listened in the car, I was intensely interested in hearing what he had to say about Revelation 10.

David Jeremiah presented an exposition of the passage and then said, "People won't agree with me, but I believe this can be only one Person: His name is Jesus."

I was thrilled! I had thought that perhaps I was a Lone Ranger in my thinking that Revelation 10:1 refers to Jesus. Not that I minded; I had long since learned that the majority opinion can often be wrong. Still, it was a tremendous encouragement simply to hear that a devout student and teacher of the Word had come to a similar conclusion as my own. In his book *Escape the Coming Night,* Dr. Jeremiah examined the issue again and stated succinctly, "Although the identity of this messenger from heaven seems clear to me, there has been quite a controversy about who He is. I believe this angel is the Angel of Jehovah, the Lord Himself."[1]

The angel, or *messenger,* as the word can also be translated,

> cried with a loud voice, as when a lion roars. When he cried out, seven thunders uttered their voices. Now when the seven thunders uttered their voices, I was about to write; but I heard a voice from heaven saying to me, "Seal up the things which the seven thunders uttered, and do not write them." (10:3–4 NKJV)

This passage is a great enigma to Bible scholars because it is never explained further. Apparently when the Angel cries out like the roar of a lion (see Rev. 5:5), the message resonates throughout the world and is answered by the seven thunders. It is the only part of the Apocalypse that John was not permitted to disclose. The message of the seven thunders remains sealed to this day.

What happens next is one of the true high points of all Scripture.

It's All Over but the Shouting

Have you ever wondered, *Just how long God is going to put up with this sinful world?* The answer is: this long, and no longer. John wrote:

> The angel whom I saw standing on the sea and on the land raised up his hand to heaven and swore by Him who lives forever and ever, who created heaven and the things that are in it, that there should be delay no

longer, but in the days of the sounding of the seventh angel, when he is about to sound, the mystery of God would be finished, as He declared to His servants the prophets. (Rev. 10:5–7 NKJV)

In other words, the messenger stands on the sea and on the land and announces, "Time is over!" Notice, the angel says, "There should be delay no longer" (v. 6). The seventh angel is about to sound the seventh trumpet, and when it sounds, the mystery of the ages will be solved and the Lord's return is at hand.

Ask ten Bible teachers what this mystery is and you may get ten (or more!) different answers. I believe the mystery to which John refers is the same one the apostle Paul spoke of frequently, the mystery of the gospel. Paul wrote, "Now to Him who is able to establish you according to my gospel and the preaching of Jesus Christ, according to the revelation of the mystery kept secret since the world began . . ." (Rom. 16:25 NKJV). He uses the term in a similar way when writing to the Ephesians: "And for me, that utterance may be given to me, that I may open my mouth boldly to make known the mystery of the gospel . . ." (6:19 NKJV).

To the Colossians, Paul was more specific, writing, ". . . the mystery which has been hidden from ages and from generations, but now has been revealed to His saints. To them God willed to make known what are the riches of the glory of this mystery among the Gentiles: which is Christ in you, the hope of glory" (1:26–27 NKJV). It is the preaching of the cross and the opportunity to accept the rich, full salvation Jesus offers that is finished. The only thing left for this world to experience is the wrath of God, but before that wrath is poured out, Jesus says, "That's it. Game over."

With this in mind, Jesus' statement concerning the Great Tribulation is easier for us to understand.

For then there will be great tribulation, such as has not been since the beginning of the world until this time, no, nor ever shall be. And unless those days were shortened, no flesh would be saved; but for the elect's sake those days will be shortened. (Matt. 24:21–22 NKJV)

Time is no more, the gospel is completed; it is time for the Lord to return!

THE RAPTURE CHAPTER

Revelation 11 is what I like to call the real Rapture Chapter. In 11:15 we see the end of life as we have known it and the beginning of a truly new world order: "Then the seventh angel sounded: And there were loud voices in heaven, saying, 'The kingdoms of this world have become the kingdoms of our Lord and of His Christ, and He shall reign forever and ever!'" (NKJV).

When the last trumpet sounds, a number of things will happen almost simultaneously. The apostle Paul wrote about it: "Behold, I tell you a mystery: We shall not all sleep, but we shall all be changed—in a moment, in the twinkling of an eye, at the last trumpet. For the trumpet will sound, the dead will be raised incorruptible, and we shall all be changed" (1 Cor. 15:51–52 NKJV).

Paul was implying that there will be a group of Christians who are alive at the time of the Lord's return; we won't all "sleep," which means we will not all have died. But whether we are alive at Christ's coming, or whether we have already died, we will all be instantaneously changed. In a moment, in a twinkling of an eye, our earthly bodies will be transformed into bodies suitable for an eternity in heaven. I don't know how fast a twinkling of an eye is, but I'm sure that when the seventh angel of Revelation sounds the last trumpet, it will be too fast for anyone to repent and get right with God. There will be no time for that. The trumpet sounds, and instantly, the next thing Christians will know, we will be caught up to meet Jesus.

Paul described that event for the Thessalonians, who were concerned about some of their number who had died. What good would a Second Coming be for them? The apostle answered their question (and many of ours too) with what has become a favorite passage concerning Christ's return. Again, speaking of those who have died as having "fallen asleep," Paul informed us:

> But I do not want you to be ignorant, brethren, concerning those who have fallen asleep, lest you sorrow as others who have no hope. For if we believe that Jesus died and rose again, even so God will bring with Him those who sleep in Jesus. For this we say to you by the word of the Lord, that we who are alive and remain until the coming of the Lord will by no means precede those who are asleep. For the Lord Himself will descend

from heaven with a shout, with the voice of an archangel, and with the trumpet of God. And the dead in Christ will rise first. Then we who are alive and remain shall be caught up together with them in the clouds to meet the Lord in the air. And thus we shall always be with the Lord. Therefore comfort one another with these words. (1 Thess. 4:13–18 NKJV)

Those who believe in a pretribulational rapture do not consider the last trumpet mentioned in 1 Corinthians 15:52 and the trumpet in 1 Thessalonians 4:16 to be the same as that mentioned in Revelation 11:15. But why not? Scripture certainly does not delineate between the trumpets described as the last. Had God wanted to show a clear difference between the trumpets—as He did with the seven trumpets of Revelation—He could have done so. It seems rather presumptuous to read something into the account where there is little room for conjecture. I believe that the last trumpet of 1 Corinthians 15:52, and the trumpet sound of 1 Thessalonians 4:16 are the same as the seventh trumpet sounded in Revelation 11:15— the *last* trumpet mentioned in Revelation. Furthermore, I believe it is the trumpet to which Jesus refers in Matthew. Notice the order of events one more time.

Immediately after the tribulation of those days the sun will be darkened, and the moon will not give its light; the stars will fall from heaven, and the powers of the heavens shall be shaken. Then the sign of the Son of Man will appear in heaven, and then all the tribes of the earth will mourn, and they shall see the Son of Man coming on the clouds of heaven with power and great glory. And He will send His angels with a great sound of a trumpet, and they will gather together His elect from the four winds, from one end of heaven to the other. (24:29–31 NKJV)

For a number of years I taught that Christians should be ready to meet Jesus at any moment—which I still teach today—but I also taught that the Rapture could occur at any moment. That I no longer teach, because I believe the world is on a crash course with the worst trouble ever known. And we Christians, along with nonbelievers, are going to experience some extremely perilous times, possibly as much as three and a half years' worth, maybe more, before Jesus Christ returns.

After that time of tribulation, the wrath of God will be poured out. I do not believe God will subject His faithful children, who have remained steadfast and true through the Tribulation, to remain on earth for that awful time of His wrath. The Tribulation will be a time of testing; the pouring out of God's wrath will be a time of condemnation and judgment. No, I do not believe that Christians will go through God's wrath. Nevertheless, I do believe the Christian church should be preparing people now to go through some portion of the Tribulation, weaning believers away from the things of this world, and teaching Christians how they can endure the difficult times ahead.

JESUS COULD COME FOR YOU

My former teaching that "Jesus could come today" I now regard as a half-truth. For you, Jesus could come today. You could meet with some accident or die of natural causes and be swept into His presence in a heartbeat. But as for Jesus coming back for the Church as a whole, certain events must yet take place before that can happen.

For instance, Paul wrote,

Let no one deceive you by any means; for that Day will not come unless the falling away comes first, and the man of sin is revealed, the son of perdition, who opposes and exalts himself above all that is called God or that is worshiped, so that he sits as God in the temple of God, showing himself that he is God. (2 Thess. 2:3–4 NKJV)

Notice, Jesus will not return until after there has been a great falling away from the truth and the Antichrist has risen to power by promising to bring normalcy to a world whose stability and security is convulsing. Paul continued,

For the mystery of lawlessness is already at work; only He who now restrains will do so until He is taken out of the way. And then the lawless one will be revealed, whom the Lord will consume with the breath of His mouth and destroy with the brightness of His coming. The coming of the lawless one is according to the working of Satan, with all power, signs and lying wonders, and with all unrighteous deception among those who perish, because they did not receive the love of the truth, that they might be saved. (2 Thess. 2:7–10 NKJV)

Paul is implying that the Holy Spirit now restrains the Antichrist from catapulting to power, but one day soon that holy hindrance will be removed, and the Antichrist will be revealed to the world. At that time the world will be clamoring for peace, but this false messiah will bring just the opposite. "For when they say, 'Peace and safety!' then sudden destruction comes upon them, as labor pains upon a pregnant woman. And they shall not escape" (1 Thess. 5:3 NKJV).

If your hope is in this world, get ready for the ride of your life. The material systems of this world, the harlot of Revelation, are about to be destroyed!

13

The Day the Money Goes Away

On October 4, 1997, more than 1.4 million men gathered on the Mall in Washington, D.C., for what was described by Promise Keepers, the Christian men's organization sponsoring the event, as a "sacred assembly." Men traveled from across the country to spend six hours together in prayerful repentance for their individual sins and for the sins of our nation.

I was unable to attend the event, but since several television networks were covering the sacred assembly live, I tried to follow it on television. Excitedly, I switched back and forth from one news service to another, getting as much coverage of the event as possible. It was an awesome sight to see so many men, from such a wide diversity of backgrounds, gathered together for one main purpose, to repent and beg God's mercy for our nation.

As I watched men of different races and cultures kneel on the ground and cry out to God in repentance, and as I listened to the messages and prayers coming from the stage, the Spirit of the Lord spoke to my heart and mind. He said, "You may think this is just another religious event, an event that man has manipulated to bring this group together, but it is not. There is no way the church could get more than a million men together if I did not want it to happen."

I continued switching channels, listening to the commentary. Much of the banter was between women, most of whom were radical feminists, criticizing what the Promise Keepers were doing in Washington. They accused the men of being politically motivated, of having an agenda to set women back to the 1950s, and all sorts of other distortions. The reporters and their interviewees totally missed the point of why the men had gathered.

One network showed a white man and a black man kneeling, arms around each other, on their faces before Almighty God, repenting to Him and to each other. But as I listened to the mindless drivel masked as commentary, the debate remained focused on the supposed political agenda of the men.

I sensed the Spirit of God confirming to my heart, "This is the last quiet warning. America has failed the last test."

Imagine if we could put a description of the Promise Keepers' sacred assembly in Old Testament language. It might read something like this: "And God caused one million four hundred thousand men to come into the city, into the seat of power, within sight of the king's palace, and the multitude of men bowed on their faces and repented before Almighty God!"

If we were to read something like that in the Old Testament, we would assume God was trying to say something important to that nation. But America missed it. Our nation was too busy debating the merits of the men, or the motives of the organizers, and we missed what I believe was God's last "quiet" call to our nation to repent. His next call will be much more violent, a "judgment" call. God *will* get our attention. It would have been much better for us to have humbled ourselves and fallen on the Rock, Jesus Christ, than to have the Rock fall on us!

THE CHURCH HAS MISSED IT TOO

Sadly, the church has done little better than the media at discerning what God is doing in these last days. God has given us a sure word of prophecy in the book of Revelation and, for the most part, we have ignored it. In many churches we are still teaching people how to succeed, how to get rich, how to make use of their talents—not for the Lord, but for themselves.

One of the most telling pictures of our culture could be seen when Princess Diana of England and Mother Teresa of Calcutta died during the same week. As tragic as Diana's death was, the outpouring of grief was astonishing. More flowers were placed in her honor than at any other funeral in history.

The world wept at Diana's passing. She was a living fairy tale, one of the finest-dressed women in the world, the woman that other women looked at with envy. She was not supposed to die. Princesses are supposed to live happily ever after . . . and when our idols die, it forces us to face our mortality, and it shakes us. No wonder the world mourned.

How ironic that during that same week a diminutive Catholic nun, Mother Teresa, went to be with the Lord. Certainly, many people grieved over the loss of the saintly woman, but not nearly so much as those who grieved over Princess Diana. One rather acerbic talk show host posed the question, "Who had a greater impact, Princess Diana or Mother Teresa?"

Even the razor-tongued personality was surprised when most of his audience declared that Princess Diana's life was ultimately more influential. "After all, look at all the important causes she championed," one member of the audience after another claimed, as though Mother Teresa's cradling of disease-ridden homeless people in her arms, allowing them the opportunity to live, or to die, with dignity was not a cause worth mentioning.

What does that say about our society? We weep for a woman who lived in immorality and who lived a life of material luxury, yet we ignore the woman who poured her life out for others in the name of Jesus.

Unfortunately, that pattern of "worship" will lead many people into the clutches of the mother of all harlots. The "great harlot" of Revelation 17 can be defined as "one who leads people away from God and the worship of Him, or all that takes God's place in our lives." Although it grieves me to say so, I believe the modern church is now dancing with the harlot, largely living in whoredom, compromising with the world.

Not a Pretty Woman

According to Revelation, the great harlot is a system—the system of false religion centered around money—and a city, known in Scripture as Babylon. John introduces us to her:

> Then one of the seven angels who had the seven bowls came and talked with me, saying to me, "Come, I will show you the judgment of the

great harlot who sits on many waters, with whom the kings of the earth committed fornication, and the inhabitants of the earth were made drunk with the wine of her fornication." (17:1–2 NKJV)

During His earthly ministry Jesus underscored the seriousness of the offense of Christians who compromise their souls for money. Jesus warned, "No man can serve two masters: for either he will hate the one and love the other, or else he will be loyal to the one and despise the other. You cannot serve God and mammon" (Matt. 6:24 NKJV). The word *mammon* is often translated merely as "money," but the word means more than just dollars and cents. It includes "any designation of material value," wealth personified, and avarice deified. In the original Greek, *mammon* is "a comprehensive word for all kinds of possessions, earnings, and gain," in other words, riches. By trying to serve both God and material things, many people are going to lose both.

If the Scripture is true (and we know that it is!) when it says that the love of money is the root of all evil, it only makes sense that the great harlot of Revelation should have much to do with fostering just such an attitude. And indeed she does!

This is why the teaching and preaching of materialism is the most abominable thing that has happened within Christianity in the past three decades. In many places, and in many ways, the church is doing a much better job of paving the way for the rise of the Antichrist than we are in preparing for the return of Jesus Christ. Instead of teaching people how to "think and grow rich," we should be encouraging one another to "pursue righteousness, godliness, faith, love, patience, [and] gentleness" (1 Tim. 6:11 NKJV).

In Scripture the most frequent imagery used to describe spiritual compromise on the part of God's people is that of a harlot, a whore, or an adulterer. Strong language, to be sure, so we should understand that God takes the matter of compromise with the world very seriously. James, the brother of Jesus, wrote, "You adulteresses, do you not know that friendship with the world is hostility toward God? Therefore whoever wishes to be a friend of the world makes himself an enemy of God" (4:4 NASB). James was warning Christians who were prone to compromise with the world system. To be a friend of the world system automatically places one in opposition to God. It is tantamount to committing spiritual adultery.

That is what the apostle John is talking about in Revelation 17 when he described people who have committed fornication with the great harlot. The fact that the great harlot "sits on many waters" (v. 1 NKJV) means that she has a relationship with, and an influence over, a large number of people (v. 15). A great multitude of people will have bought into her way of living.

John went on to paint the picture of this repugnant "woman" sitting on a strange creature that looks as though it is a mechanical prop in a B movie:

> And I saw a woman sitting on a scarlet beast which was full of names of blasphemy, having seven heads and ten horns. The woman was arrayed in purple and scarlet, and adorned with gold and precious stones and pearls, having in her hand a golden cup full of abominations and the filthiness of her fornication. (17:3–4 NKJV)

The woman's gaudy apparel implies that while she is despicable, she is also enormously wealthy. Notice, too, that she is holding a golden cup, beautiful on the outside, but filled with all sorts of awful things. Much about materialistic Christianity looks good on the outside, but inside it is rotten and foul.

John continues in verse five with his description of this diabolical woman, noting the unusual names she has written on her forehead:

MYSTERY,

BABYLON THE GREAT,

THE MOTHER OF HARLOTS

AND OF THE

ABOMINATIONS OF THE EARTH. (NKJV)

Worse yet, John said, the woman is "drunk with the blood of the saints and with the blood of the martyrs of Jesus" (Rev. 17:6 NKJV). This woman is drunk, but not on alcohol; she is drunk on the blood of Christians who have died for their faith. In verses 7 through 18, the angel who is showing John this scene explains in further detail how it is to be interpreted. The harlot is associated with a system of false religion, leading people away from the true gospel and a relationship with Jesus. Moreover, the harlot is headquartered in a specific city, Babylon, which most Bible scholars consider to be Rome.

Eventually, the beast on which the woman is sitting will rise up and turn on the woman. "And the ten horns which you saw on the beast, these will hate the harlot, make her desolate and naked, eat her flesh and burn her with fire" (17:16 NKJV). The beast represents the empire led by the Antichrist and under the control of Satan. The beast and the harlot will work together for some period of time preceding the coming of Christ. But this marriage of convenience, in which both parties use each other for their own purposes, will end in a violent "divorce." When the Antichrist decides he no longer needs the religious-economic system provided by the harlot, he will dump her and set himself up to be worshiped, while imposing his own economic system to control everything that is bought or sold.

DANGEROUS GUESSING GAMES

For years Bible commentators have concentrated on the physical aspects of this most intriguing chapter, attempting to connect the Antichrist with a particular personality, or to prove that the city in which the harlot resides is Rome, or to link the whore of Babylon with the Roman Catholic Church. I am convinced that such speculations are dangerous and counterproductive. In fact, we really don't know for sure.

More important, I believe there is a parallel interpretation of this passage that we have missed because we have focused our attention on the geopolitical aspects of the message, while neglecting the spiritual principle involved. Simply stated: the harlot is not a particular church; it is the economic system of this world.

In chapter 18 of Revelation, another angel with great authority (so much so, in fact, that some commentators have hinted it may be Jesus) continues to take John on a guided tour of "Babylon," further explaining the world's compromising collusion with the wicked woman, and the sudden destruction that will befall this spiritual-economic system. "And he cried out with a mighty voice, saying, 'Fallen, fallen is Babylon the great! And she has become a dwelling place of demons and a prison of every unclean spirit, and a prison of every unclean and hateful bird'" (v. 2 NASB). Regardless of who this messenger is, there is no mistaking the message. The party is over for Babylon. Judgment will fall on both the false, occultic, religious system and the economic system as well. Whether it means that the city itself will be destroyed is a matter of speculation.

Her sins, however, are horrendous. "For all the nations have drunk of the wine of the wrath of her fornication, the kings of the earth have committed fornication with her, and the merchants of the earth have become rich through the abundance of her luxury" (18:3 NKJV). The word *merchants* comes from the Greek word *emporos,* which can be translated as "wholesale tradesmen," people in business. In other words, the business people of the world have become rich through their relationship with the harlot. She is further described in 18:7 as having "glorified herself and lived luxuriously," which means to live for luxury and pleasure, to be insolent because of wealth.

SUDDEN DESTRUCTION

Wealthy as the system may be, it will all come crashing down in an amazingly short period of time. "Therefore her plagues will come in one day—death and mourning and famine. And she will be utterly burned with fire, for strong is the Lord God who judges her" (18:8 NKJV).

Those people who have compromised themselves with the harlot and placed their confidence in her system—possibly even selling their souls, literally—will watch her destruction with abject horror.

> The kings of the earth who committed fornication and lived luxuriously with her will weep and lament for her, when they see the smoke of her burning, standing at a distance for fear of her torment, saying, "Alas, alas, that great city Babylon, that mighty city! For in one hour your judgment has come." And the merchants of the earth will weep and mourn over her, for no one buys their merchandise anymore: merchandise of gold and silver, precious stones and pearls, fine linen and purple, silk and scarlet, every kind of citron wood, every kind of object of ivory, every kind of object of most precious wood, bronze, iron, and marble; and cinnamon and incense, fragrant oil and frankincense, wine and oil, fine flour and wheat, cattle and sheep, horses and chariots, and bodies and souls of men. (18:9–13 NKJV)

The startling ruin of the scarlet woman will unnerve the merchants who dealt with her, as they see all their dreams go up in smoke. Businessmen and women all over the world will weep loudly at Babylon's fall. Everything they have spent their lives trying to achieve will be gone, almost instantly.

> The fruit that your soul longed for has gone from you, and all the things which are rich and splendid have gone from you, and you shall find them no more at all. The merchants of these things, who became rich by her, will stand at a distance for fear of her torment, weeping and wailing, and saying, "Alas, alas, that great city that was clothed in fine linen, purple, and scarlet, and adorned with gold and precious stones and pearls! For in one hour such great riches came to nothing." Every shipmaster, all who travel by ship, sailors, and as many as trade on the sea, stood at a distance and cried out when they saw the smoke of her burning, saying, "What is like this great city?" They threw dust on their heads and cried out, weeping and wailing, and saying, "Alas, alas, that great city, in which all who had ships on the sea became rich by her wealth! For in one hour she is made desolate." (18:14–19 NKJV)

An interesting possibility is raised by Revelation 18:21.

> Then a mighty angel took up a stone like a great millstone and threw is into the sea, saying, "Thus with violence the great city Babylon shall be thrown down and shall not be found anymore." (NKJV)

Could this sudden, awful destruction that takes place in one hour be the result of a meteor strike? We cannot say for sure, but certainly the possibility must be considered.

The passage goes on to describe the total destruction of this bastion of worldly pleasure. But while it may have once been known for its bright lights, music, art, and merchandising, all commerce and entertainment will cease (18:22–24). In a lightning-fast manner, God will avenge the blood of His apostles, prophets, and saints, many of whom were persecuted by the harlot and the Antichrist.

John summed up the demise of the harlot system by saying, "For your merchants were the great men of the earth, for by your sorcery all the nations were deceived" (18:23 NKJV).

Interestingly, he uses the term *sorcery* to describe the insidious influence the "great men" have had. The word in the Greek is *pharmakeia,* the same root from which we get our word *pharmacy.* It is also used in the Greek to denote drugs, poisons, or magic spells.

I am convinced that one day soon the powerbrokers of Wall Street who control our world's systems—who have worked their magic spells on the world for so long—will suddenly come to nothing.

ANOTHER BABYLON?

I believe the awful destruction we read of in Revelation 18 could just as easily be poured out on New York City as it could Rome or any other center of commerce. What is the root of all sorts of evil? The love of money. What has taken the hearts of so many people from God? The love of money. Many people work two or three jobs, trying to get enough money to buy more trinkets or live in a style to which they have grown accustomed. Multitudes of men and women sacrifice their families and their faith in their insatiable quest to possess more and more material things.

We are in love with money, and we worship at the altar of materialism. Imagine if someday our society were unearthed and archaeologists discovered huge, palatial structures. "Oh, those must have been the temples to their gods," the archaeologists might say with awe.

No, those are our shopping malls.

Yet, in a way, we do worship at those temples. We express our worship with our checkbooks, cash, and credit cards, as we bow to the gods of pleasure, materialism, and money. We have allowed our hearts to be consumed by lust for material things, and in the process, we have aligned ourselves with the whore of Babylon. The whore is the love of money. The great harlot is materialism . . . and it will be destroyed in one hour.

God help us to fall in love with Jesus!

14

Surviving the Coming Apocalypse

If even a small percentage of the calamities we have examined within these pages comes to pass, it will be enough to shake the world to its core. Undoubtedly, these events will shake many Christians to their spiritual foundations as well.

As I share this message at churches and conferences around the country, many people express deep concerns. I hear a recurring theme: "Jim, is there any hope? Is there any place of safety in these last days?"

In every instance I answer unequivocally, "Yes! There is hope. As we band together and become the body of Christ in reality, not merely in name, we can make it through the difficult times ahead."

The *body of Christ* is a term tossed around tritely these days. Often it is used as a euphemism for Christians of all sorts, a tag including just about anybody who has ever gone to church in his or her lifetime. This is not an appropriate application of the term. While the body of Christ is an inclusive group, not all religious people are part of it. Membership means much more than merely sitting through a church service once in a while. To be part of the body, one must have a genuine faith in Jesus Christ. The body of Christ is a community of true believers from every background, culture, and Christian denomination.

Being part of the church universal does not depend on membership in a particular church or denomination. Some people who are part of the body of Christ do not hold membership in any religious organization. On the other hand, there may be people who have gone through all sorts of religious rituals and ceremonies, signed membership cards, been baptized, catechized, and received every certificate of authentication the church can bestow. But without a vibrant relationship with Jesus Christ, such a person is not a part of the body. It is the difference between being in the church *building* and being in the *Church;* being a member of an *organization,* compared to being a part of the living *organism,* the body of Christ.

The body is supposed to care for all of its members. Some parts of the body may require more attention, other parts may seem worthy of higher honor, but as the apostle Paul reminds us, all parts of the body are valuable:

> But now indeed there are many members, yet one body. And the eye cannot say to the hand, "I have no need of you"; nor again the head to the feet, "I have no need of you." No, much rather, those members of the body which seem to be weaker are necessary. And those members of the body which we think to be less honorable, on these we bestow greater honor . . . But God composed the body, having given greater honor to that part which lacks it, that there should be no schism in the body, but that the members should have the same care for one another. And if one member suffers, all the members suffer with it; or if one member is honored, all the members rejoice with it. (1 Cor. 12:20–23, 24–26 NKJV)

According to Paul, the intrinsic value of every individual and the mutual caring for one another are basic principles for a healthy body-life. These concepts will be absolutely crucial for survival as the apocalypse approaches.

An Unlikely Model

The greatest practical example of the body of Christ I have ever seen was not at Heritage USA. Nor was it in a local church. As strange as it may seem, the closest model of a New Testament church that I have experienced was in a federal prison.

During the last year of my incarceration, prison authorities transferred me from a medium-security prison in Rochester, Minnesota, to a minimum-security prison in Jesup, Georgia, a small town about 240 miles south of Atlanta. What could easily have been accomplished by a two-hour flight took nearly two weeks of travel by plane and bus as I was shuffled across the country and made to endure the ordeal the prison population describes sarcastically as "diesel therapy."

When I arrived at Jesup I was physically and emotionally exhausted. I felt as though I had aged twenty years in two weeks' time. Despite my haggard condition, however, I immediately recognized that Jesup was a different sort of prison than anything I had experienced previously. For one thing, the moment I walked through the doors, I was greeted by a group of inmates with outstretched hands and open, friendly faces—neither of which are standard fare in prison.

The leader of the welcoming party was a big, friendly fellow named Larry Wright. "We've brought you a few things you might need until your own items arrive," Larry said, as he handed me a bag of toiletries, shower shoes, stamps, and a small New Testament. "We're part of the Christian brothers here at Jesup," Larry explained, as the other "greeters" nodded and smiled enthusiastically, "and we're available to help you any way we can."

I later discovered that every man entering Jesup was greeted in a similar manner. Over the next few months Larry and the brothers held true to their word, not just toward me, but to every man who was processed into that prison. The Christians at Jesup put their faith into action, first by meeting practical needs—toiletries, stamps, shower shoes, things that were tangible expressions of the love of Christ—and then by offering spiritual assistance. As a result, inmates who didn't know Chronicles from a concordance, men who could have cared less about the Bible, were impacted with Christ's concern for them.

Once a man was settled and rested, the Christian brothers at Jesup began to minister to him. For example, after a few days, tired as I was, the men encouraged me to get out of my bunk and into a chapel service. When I balked, one of the brothers, a wiry little bulldog named Chuck, prodded me. "Are you backslidden? How are you supposed to be spiritually encouraged if you neglect the fellowship of believers?"

Chuck was right and I knew it. I needed the fellowship of other believers;

I needed the Word of God in my life; and I needed to be giving, not just receiving, spiritual encouragement.

In Jesup prison, God began to show me what true ministry is all about: not acquiring material things or building a great work for God, but believers functioning as the body of Christ—people caring for one another, teaching the Word, studying the Bible together, and applying it to our lives on a daily basis. As a result, every week more men—some of them so-called hardened criminals—came to trust Jesus Christ as their Savior and Lord. Evangelism was not the result of special chapel services announced as revival meetings, or the efforts of famous guest speakers and singers; evangelism was the natural outgrowth of a functioning body of believers relating to each other and to the non-Christians around them.

As non-Christians observed the body of Christ in action, they developed an insatiable hunger for that kind of camaraderie, concern, and compassion. Nonbelievers sought out a relationship with Jesus Christ because they had seen His love in the lives of His followers. Evangelism is relatively easy when the world sees the real gospel lived out daily in real-life situations.

Unfortunately, in most churches I have attended in my lifetime, we avoid getting real as much as possible. The first thing most of us do when we enter the church is to tell a lie.

Think about it. You step inside the doorway and Brother or Sister So-and-So slaps you on the back. "Hey, buddy. How are you doing?"

"Fine," you answer rather sheepishly, knowing that you have just avoided being real. Other people deflect the question with another question. "I'm doing great; how about you?" For many Christians the answer often takes on a more spiritual tone. "Oh, I'm blessed, hallelujah!"

We certainly don't want to dump our heavy load of burdens on every person who greets us. Every church seems to have a few chronic whiners who want to unload on anyone who will listen. You don't even want to ask some people how they are doing for fear they will tell you!

On the other hand, many Christians are hurting deeply. They are *not* doing fine. Their faith has been stretched, torn, and sometimes shattered, and it is only because they are painfully aware that there are so few brothers and sisters who really care how they are doing that they answer glibly, "I'm fine." And the heavy load weighs even heavier on their heart.

I have gotten into a habit of being more persistent. If I ask how a brother or sister is doing and I sense that he or she is troubled about something, often I will stop, look the person right in the eyes, and ask, "Are you really okay? Is there anything we can pray about together right now?"

Sure, that sort of relationship takes time. Yes, it demands that we be sensitive to the true needs of our fellow believers. But we are supposed to be the body of Christ! We are supposed to care for one another. The apostle Paul instructed us, "Bear one another's burdens, and thus fulfill the law of Christ" (Gal. 6:2 NASB). If the "law of Christ" is love, we should show our love for Christ by bearing each other's burdens, genuinely caring for one another.

What does it mean to bear someone else's burdens? To some people it seems to mean, "You dump on me and I'll dump on you. Then we can both go away feeling worse than we were before." That is not bearing burdens; that is a mutual pity party.

To bear one another's burdens means that if your brother or sister has a need, you do whatever you can to help meet that need or ease that load. When the multitudes asked John the Baptist what they should do to show they had repented, he did not tell them to enroll in a self-help program. He said, "Let the man who has two tunics share with him who has none; and let him who has food do likewise" (Luke 3:11 NASB). Practically speaking, bearing one another's burdens may involve the sharing of food, clothing, housing, money, providing childcare for a single parent, loaning your car to a brother or sister, or a variety of other tangible things that express Christ's love. It also involves spiritual and emotional support. Sometimes the best gift you can give to another person is a listening ear, not merely sympathizing with them but empathizing with them, taking that burden upon yourself.

At Jesup we shared our deepest pains, questions, and concerns, as well as our greatest joys. We spent time together, talking and praying with each other. We ate together, we worked together, and we played together (if working out in prison can be called playing). We had plenty of spiritually uplifting services at Jesup, including long hours of Bible study, Prison Fellowship meetings, Christian videos, chapel services, and other events— and all those things were wonderfully helpful—but the main characteristic of the church at Jesup was that the guys cared for each other in genuine, godly, practical ways.

When one of the fellows received a "Dear John" letter from his wife or girlfriend—a common experience in prison—and wanted to curl up on his bunk and die from the feelings of hurt, rejection, despair, and hopelessness, the Christian brothers would not allow him to do so. They pulled him out of his bunk and said, "Come on; we're going out to walk the track, and you're coming too. You're not going to stay here and wallow in self-pity. We are your brothers, and we are going to take care of you, even when you don't care enough to take care of yourself."

On the other hand, when something good happened to one of the guys, we all rejoiced together, just as the apostle Paul instructed. The believers in Jesup prison did not live in isolation. We carried each other's burdens and cheered each other on when someone was struggling toward the light at the end of the tunnel. It was the closest thing I have ever experienced to the sort of caring that Paul describes as the body of Christ in 1 Corinthians 12.

Now More Than Ever

More than ever, we need a fresh understanding of the way members of the body of Christ are to love and care for one another. Moreover, if you are going to survive the coming apocalypse, it will be imperative that you be a part of a fellowship of believers that actually incorporates Paul's teaching about the body of Christ into their daily lives—in other words, they don't just talk about it, they do it! As Paul told the Philippians, "Let each of you look out not only for his own interests, but also for the interests of others" (2:4 NKJV). Helping each other, cheering each other on, ministering to each other's needs, praying with and believing with each other—the need for all of these aspects of caring for one another will be heightened as the apocalypse approaches. This sort of Christian community will be absolutely crucial for physical, emotional, and possibly even spiritual, survival as we enter the Tribulation.

Understand, the church of Jesus Christ will not be immune to the awful things coming upon the earth. As Arthur Katterjohn, a Wheaton College professor who has taught numerous courses on the subject of the Great Tribulation, says,

The tribulation, as the name implies, will not be a happy time for God's people. Hunger, economic pressure, imprisonment, death, and worldwide oppression will characterize these final days on earth. Loyalty to Jesus will face its most strenuous test, and perseverance will require more resolute courage, more brother-helping brotherliness, and more sheer resistance of evil than ever a generation of Christian believers has needed. The Master's comfort will surely be evident to those who go through it, and His requirement of discipleship—"take up your cross daily"—will be the hourly challenge of faithful disciples across the globe.[1]

Christians will need each other as we have never needed one another before. Our own self-sufficiency will suffer a meltdown in the face of the compounding calamities coming upon the earth. No one person will have all the knowledge and skills necessary to deal with the various aspects of the Tribulation. In the past our society has relished self-sufficiency; we have honored and attempted to emulate the self-made man or woman, the person who says, "I can make it on my own. I don't need anyone else to help take care of me." Sadly, those attitudes have often infected Christian hearts and minds as well.

While attitudes of self-sufficiency and self-importance have never been appropriate for Christians, in the face of the coming apocalypse, anything other than a mutually dependent spirit of cooperation between members of the body of Christ will be counterproductive at best, and possibly downright sinful. Remember the Old Testament account of Achan, who took for himself some of the spoils from the battle of Jericho. Achan's sin dragged the name of the Lord through the dirt, caused the defeat of the Israelite army, and cost his life as well as the lives of his family. Achan's selfishness impacted the entire body. If we are to survive the apocalypse, any attitudes that hint at selfishness must be repented of immediately.

REFINED AS GOLD

Unquestionably, the Tribulation will be a refining time for Christians. When the heat is turned up on last-days Christians, the dross in our lives will be stripped away, just as gold is refined by fire, until the Master Refiner sees His reflection in us. No, that process will not be fun. Yet we should not despair. We know the pressure is coming, so we should not be surprised when we experience it; we can even rejoice in the midst of those trials.

Writing to encourage first-century believers who were beginning to endure persecutions for their faith, the apostle Peter reminded them,

> In this you greatly rejoice, even though now for a little while, if necessary, you have been distressed by various trials, that the proof of your faith, being more precious than gold which is perishable, even though tested by fire, may be found to result in praise and glory and honor at the revelation of Jesus Christ. (1 Peter 1:6–7 NASB)

In the same manner, the last-days Church, the body of Christ, will come through the time of trials and testings refined as pure gold. The Church, that group of true believers from every tongue, tribe, and denomination, will not be destroyed by the Antichrist or anyone else. We have Jesus' word on it. He said, "I will build my church; and the gates of hell shall not prevail against it" (Matt. 16:18 KJV). That word has never been rescinded.

In the meantime, life on earth will seem almost intolerable at times. It will not be easy, but take heart. You can make it—

> Because God from the beginning chose you for salvation through sanctification by the Spirit and belief in the truth, to which He called you by our gospel, for the obtaining of the glory of our Lord Jesus Christ. Therefore, brethren, stand fast and hold the traditions which you were taught. (2 Thess. 2:13–15 NKJV)

The Community of Christ

The community of believers—the Church, the body of Christ—is the modern-day ark, the only safe place to be in the midst of the coming storms. I do not mean that we should all move into the local church sanctuary (although that wouldn't be such a bad idea). Better still, the members of the body of Christ need to be encouraging one another, helping one another, building each other up in tangible ways. The writer to the Hebrews put it this way:

Let us hold fast the profession of our faith without wavering; (for he is faithful that promised;) and let us consider one another to provoke unto love and to good works: not forsaking the assembling of ourselves together, as the manner of some is; but exhorting one another: and so much the more, as ye see the day approaching. (10:23–25 KJV)

The New Testament church did not merely meet for a few hours on Sunday morning. They exhorted one another daily. They spent time with each other; they cared for each other; they didn't just get together to sing, preach, teach, and pray, and then live the rest of their lives independently of each other. "So continuing daily with one accord in the temple, and breaking bread from house to house, they ate their food with gladness and simplicity of heart" (Acts 2:46 NKJV). As we see the day of the Lord approaching, we should be spending more time with each other, encouraging one another, helping to meet each other's needs, and working together for the glory of God.

During the dark days of the Great Depression, following the 1929 stock market crash, my parents' home church provided a shining example of the body of Christ in action. Similar to the early church described in the book of Acts, the people in the congregation took care of each other. If someone in the church needed a pipe on the kitchen sink fixed, a plumber within the community of believers fixed it for free. If someone needed some carpentry done, a carpenter from the church volunteered his or her services. Not one person in their church body missed a single meal. The church members planted gardens together and shared whatever food they could grow. Contrast that to the world at large, where people were standing in bread lines or selling apples on the street to make enough money just to buy milk or eggs.

DAYS OF OPPORTUNITY

This end-time period may well be one of the most glorious times in history for the Church. Besides the joy of working together to help meet each other's practical needs, we may see more genuine miracles take place than at any time since the earthly ministry of Jesus, or the ministry of the Church in the book of Acts. A friend of mine, a highly respected prophet, told me of a vision he had. He saw a group of people praying for each other, and thousands of people were being healed. Interestingly, the people who were praying over the sick and infirm were themselves faceless.

"Lord, what does this mean?" the prophet asked.

God spoke to his heart and mind, saying, "When my people do not care who gets the credit, I will restore healing to My church."

I am convinced that during the coming days of peril, when "all hell breaks loose," hospitals may be overcrowded, doctors may be worked to a frazzle, the resources of insurance companies will be exhausted, but the Lord's people will not go unattended. God is going to expand divine healing within His church—real physical healings, not spiritual shenanigans—as He provides wonderful miracles for His people. I believe other practical gifts of the Spirit will be enhanced as well.

It is imperative that you become an active part of the body of Christ *now*. Get connected with the body in every way possible. Many churches have established cell groups, small groups that meet for Bible study, prayer, and fellowship in members' homes. In the small-group context it is much easier to know and care for one another. If you are not involved in such a group, I encourage you to find one and boldly plunge in. You may feel awkward at first, or reluctant to open up, but as you become convinced of the members' unconditional love and concern for you, your confidence level will rise. Ideally, you will find that you can be vulnerable within your group, honestly expressing your needs without fear of embarrassment or condemnation; conversely, you can be a vessel through whom the Lord works to help meet the needs of others. I believe groups of this kind will become even more important during the dark days ahead. In fact, my next book will explore the concept of community and its tremendous importance to the church.

We must learn how to bear one another's burdens now, while the load is relatively light. If we are reluctant to help each other now, how will we ever be willing to care for bruised, broken, and banged-up believers when persecution comes? The Scripture is quite clear about this point. John writes:

By this we know love, because He laid down His life for us. And we also ought to lay down our lives for the brethren. But whoever has this world's goods, and sees his brother in need, and shuts up his heart from him, how does the love of God abide in him? My little children, let us not love in word or in tongue, but in deed and in truth. (1 John 3:16–18 NKJV)

WON'T WE GRATE AGAINST EACH OTHER?

Living and working in such close proximity to each other in the body of Christ lends itself to occasional scrapes and misunderstandings.

In my younger years I enjoyed studying how gems are polished. It's an interesting procedure. To the uninitiated eye the stones seem to be nothing more than pieces of gravel. But when put into a metal container and jostled either electronically or by hand-turned rollers, all that is not gemstone gets knocked off in the process. The friction caused by the grating against one another actually transforms the unpolished stones into works of great beauty.

God does something similar to us by allowing us to be thrust together with other members of the body of Christ in pressure-packed situations. More often than not, we might feel as though we are driving the wrong direction on a bumper-car ride. We carom off one person and bounce into the next. Just about the time we regain our equilibrium long enough to look up, *wham!* Somebody slams into us head-on.

Sure, we sometimes rub each other the wrong way, but if we are committed to the Lord, and if we love each other, God will use those situations to transform us into works of rare quality, each one intrinsically valuable, and polished to individual beauty.

DO SOMETHING NOW!

Now is the time to begin allowing that refining process to take place. I cannot emphasize it too much: you need to be actively involved in your local church, functioning within the body of Christ, and using the gifts and talents the Lord has given you to help edify others. There are no Lone Rangers in the Kingdom of God.

Begin to function within the body now; please don't wait until the calamities overtake us. Life will be chaotic enough at that point; you won't have time to try and figure out where you fit within the church. Moreover, it is not inconceivable that when the trials and tribulations come, many selfish people will flock to the church, looking to leech off the body. While this may be a marvelous opportunity for ministry to some, remember Jesus' parable of the ten virgins. Five of them were wise enough to maintain their supply of oil for the long haul and five were not. While the five foolish virgins were out searching for more oil, "the bridegroom came, and those who were ready went in with him to the wedding feast; and the door was shut. And later the other virgins also came, saying, 'Lord, lord, open up for us.' But he answered and said, 'Truly I say to you, I do not know you'" (Matt. 25:10–12 NASB).

Throughout the Bible, we know that God honors preparation on the part of His people. Scripture says, "A sensible man watches for problems ahead and prepares to meet them. The simpleton never looks, and suffers the consequences" (Prov. 27:12 TLB). I encourage pastors and other spiritual leaders to begin organizing now for some sort of crisis management among their congregations.

Most cities, counties, and states have crisis-management plans in place to help deal with limited natural disasters such as floods, tornadoes, earthquakes, hurricanes, and other emergencies. The government has deemed such plans necessary on the assumption that sooner or later they will have to act on them. But as the nightmares of the book of Revelation become daily realities, no government agency—local, state, or federal—will have the ability to take care of so many hurting people. It is imperative that the church prepare to fill that void. Yet many Christians who have heard the Bible preached and can see the signs of the times coming to pass continue to conduct their lives oblivious to the truth. It is as though they do not want to admit what is coming upon the earth for fear that they will be branded as religious kooks.

Nevertheless, we need to be wise. It just makes good sense to begin storing some food and water to be used in case of emergencies. Now is the time to become aware of some basic survival strategies for you and your family.

Let's Get Practical

Owning a piece of land, especially enough land on which you could grow food if necessary, might be a wise investment. Clearly, our world's monetary systems will be in jeopardy under an economic system controlled by the

Antichrist. When that happens, Grandma sitting in her rocking chair, out on the farm, will be in a much better position than the most successful Wall Street stockbroker sitting at his computer terminal.

In late 1997 I was visiting in the home of a wealthy family in the Atlanta area. As I looked around their beautiful home, valued in the millions of dollars, I sensed an unusual urging of the Holy Spirit. At first I thought I must be imagining things, but the longer I hesitated, the stronger the urging became. Finally, I opened my mouth and spoke to my gracious hosts. "I'm not in the habit of doing this," I began, "and I hope you won't be offended, but I honestly feel that the Holy Spirit is telling me to encourage you to sell your house and move out to the country. Please forgive me if I am out of line, but I feel that I must tell you what God has spoken to me."

The husband looked at the wife, who was staring back at him. Then both of them smiled broadly as the husband said, "Jim, we're not offended at all. God has already spoken that message to our hearts and we are putting our house up for sale. We believe God wants us to purchase some land in the country, away from the city, so we can stockpile food, water, and other resources to help the body of Christ when the difficult times come."

You may not be able to move to the country, but, as many civilians did during World War II, you might be able to grow a Victory Garden. Read a book on growing vegetables if you don't know anything about farming or having a garden. Food will be a better commodity than gold, not simply for consumption but for trading. People cannot eat gold. As the Tribulation continues, seed will become increasingly difficult to obtain, so buy non-hybrid seed that will produce more seeds for follow-up crops.

When I was a young boy, our society was much more agrarian than it is today. More people had ready access to farmland and homegrown vegetables. Today things are just the opposite. The majority of the world's population lives in the cities or suburbs, with farmland a shrinking part of the landscape. For most of us, it is not possible to have a farm or even a large garden. But use any plot of ground you can to grow food. If possible, build a small greenhouse, which will prolong your growing season. A temporary greenhouse can be built inexpensively right now, using plastic sheeting, in your back yard or even on the top of your roof. Again, advance preparation is essential. If you wait until an emergency, you may not be able to get the supplies you need.

Consider growing your crops in a kibbutz-style cooperative with other members of the body of Christ. By working together we can help feed a lot more people, while continuing to build a stockpile of grains and beans and other nonperishable staples. Any surplus of vegetables can be used for bartering.

Whether you choose to work directly with your church in planting and harvesting food, it would be a good idea to grow a little extra, beyond what you think you will need, just to be better able to help the body of Christ and your neighbors. If everyone will do a little extra to help others, there may be no serious food shortages. We must face reality, however, and know that one-third of the earth's population will be severely impacted by these calamities. More than two billion people will die, despite our best efforts to help them.

The important thing about all survivalist actions is that you start them now, before there is a crisis. If you wait until the famine, earthquake, Y2K crisis, or a meteor impact, or once the general public realizes what is coming, basic foodstuffs may be unobtainable at any price. Dried grains, beans, powdered milk, and other nonperishables will vanish from the grocery store shelves within hours.

These days, I encourage churches to consider how they will care for their people when the really tough times come. I believe it is unconscionable to pour multiple millions of dollars into building huge megachurches without planning how we can help people with the basic needs of life when the plagues of Revelation begin. Of course, the rationalization for such spending on the part of many ministries is their sincere belief that the church will be raptured out of the world before the Tribulation begins, so therefore the money could be better spent now. To the holders of such an opinion, I have one simple question: What if I am right and you are wrong?

I believe that every pastor, elder, or church board member has a moral obligation to consider how the local body of Christ can best meet the needs of its people when the disasters begin to strike. One church, for example, has a food stockpile program; for sixty dollars a member can purchase enough rice or grain or corn to feed one person for an entire year. Some of the items may not be real tasty, but they will help keep people alive.

Many Christian churches view such programs as unnecessary or extremist. But in the Old Testament, God instructed Joseph to prepare for the famine that was to come. What if Joseph had said, "Lord, that's silly. Look how prosperous this country is. The economy is going great. People are fat and happy. Surely we don't need to stockpile food." Had Joseph ignored God's Word, not only would he have perished, but his entire family, and his nation, would have been wiped out as well.

I believe God is looking for some Josephs in these last days.

Because of my strong statements warning Christians not to fall in love with money, some people have gotten the impression that I am opposed to Christians having vast sums of money. That is patently false. I am opposed to Christians hoarding the blessings of God for their own use, to the exclusion of the body of Christ.

Recently I talked with a wealthy businessman about how he was using his money. During our conversation I said, "God did not bless you just so you could be a millionaire to spend your money on yourself and your family. God has blessed you so you could help meet the needs of the body of Christ in the last days." He readily agreed. I believe this man represents just one of many Joseph-type ministries that will rise to the fore in the body of Christ in the days ahead.

WHY ME, LORD?

You may be wondering why your heavenly Father would allow you to go through the Tribulation. Is God some sort of cosmic sadist who wants to see how much pain and suffering His children can stand? Of course not.

Many nights in prison I lay awake in my cell, wondering why God would allow me to go through such humiliation. Sure, I had made some mistakes, done some things wrong, but didn't God love me? Wasn't I His child? Could He not have disciplined me and brought me out of the mess I was in, rather than allow me to be thrown into a pit? I can now see that part of the reason I had to go through my prison experience was to change my heart, mind, and theology, to prepare me to receive the message of this book. But even at that, could God not have arranged the details of my life in such a way that I could have heard His voice without having to go to prison? Apparently not.

Why would God allow His special, chosen people, the Israelites, to suffer through years and years of bitter slavery in Egypt? Yes, they had disobeyed Him, but could He not have delivered them from their bondage sooner, or better yet, allowed them to avoid it altogether? Of course He could have . . . but He didn't.

Perhaps the ultimate "why" question is this: Why would God allow His own Son to suffer such pain and public humiliation, paying for sins He never committed, by dying on a cross?

There is only one answer to all of our "whys": God has a plan.

In the days ahead we will need to remember that; we will need to remind each other of that truth repeatedly. *God has a plan.* These things are not happening by accident; they are not happening outside the scope of His control. Even when we are surrounded by darkness, God still has a plan. In every crucible of life, God has a plan.

Part of the reason we will experience the Tribulation is so we can become the kind of bride fit for a King. Jesus is not coming back for a filthy, sinful bride. He is coming for a spotless, holy people. The apostle Paul explained that Christ's purpose in giving Himself up to the cross was so "that He might present her to Himself a glorious church, not having spot or wrinkle or any such thing, but that she should be holy and without blemish" (Eph. 5:27 NKJV). For some of us, the Tribulation will be part of the process the Holy Spirit uses to get us ready for life in heaven.

I am not suggesting that unbelievers can be saved simply by surviving the coming apocalypse; nor am I implying that believers will be sanctified solely by enduring the Tribulation. God's plan has not changed. We are saved, sanctified, and one day we will be glorified, by faith in Jesus Christ alone, not by our works. On the other hand, the Tribulation may well be the testing ground God uses to bring many people into alignment with His plan for their lives.

The Danger of Being Lukewarm

Will some people not make it? Sad to say, the intense pressures of the tribulation period may cause some people to turn their backs on Jesus. Many others who have been straddling the fence will discover that they must make up their minds concerning whom they are going to serve. Many so-called Christians will find that it is much easier simply to go along with the Antichrist than it is to commit themselves completely to Jesus and to risk being persecuted for their faith.

Others who have followed Jesus for fun, frolic, and whatever else they could get out of Him, will discover for the first time the true cost of discipleship. Still others who have believed a prosperity gospel will suddenly be confronted with how spiritually bankrupt they really are. Although it grieves me to say it, I am convinced that we have many lukewarm people in our churches today—people who have a form of godliness, who can keep up appearances as religious people, but who do not have a genuine relationship with Jesus Christ. To this group, Jesus speaks a firm word:

> So then, because you are lukewarm, and neither cold nor hot, I will vomit you out of My mouth. Because you say, "I am rich, have become wealthy, and have need of nothing"—and do not know that you are wretched, miserable, poor, blind, and naked—I counsel you to buy from Me gold refined in the fire, that you may be rich; and white garments, that you may be clothed, that the shame of your nakedness may not be revealed; and anoint your eyes with eye salve, that you may see. As many as I love, I rebuke and chasten. Therefore be zealous and repent. (Rev. 3:16–19 NKJV)

The good news is that even with this firm word of rebuke, Jesus still offers hope to those who will open their hearts to Him. He said,

> Behold, I stand at the door and knock. If anyone hears My voice and opens the door, I will come in to him and dine with him, and he with Me. To him who overcomes I will grant to sit with Me on my throne, as I also overcame and sat down with My Father on His throne. (Rev. 3:20–21 NKJV)

God may use the tribulation period to shake some people out of their lukewarm condition, to help them see the life-and-death seriousness of a radical commitment to Christ.

How Then Should We Live?

Only by establishing a firm relationship with God will you have any hope of surviving the coming apocalypse. The Scripture says,

> God is our refuge and strength,
> A very present help in trouble.
> Therefore we will not fear,
> Even though the earth be removed,
> And though the mountains be carried into the midst of the sea;
> Though its waters roar and be troubled,
> Though the mountains shake with its swelling. (Ps. 46:1–3 NKJV)

God will take care of His people during the difficult days to come. He will make a way for you to go through whatever is required. His grace will be sufficient for you.

On the other hand, it would be naive to think that believers will not die during the Tribulation. Many, in fact, will be martyred for their faith. But if your faith and hope are in Christ, death cannot hurt you. As the apostle Paul wrote,

> "O Death, where is your sting?
> O Hades, where is your victory?"
> The sting of death is sin, and the strength of sin is the law. But thanks be to God, who gives us the victory through our Lord Jesus Christ. Therefore, my beloved brethren, be steadfast, immovable, always abounding in the work of the Lord, knowing that your labor is not in vain in the Lord (1 Cor. 15:55–58 NKJV).

For those who are living in the last days, I offer three simple keys to survival: (1) fall in love with Jesus; (2) get into the Word of God; and (3) become vibrantly involved with the body of Christ.

Throughout this book I have emphasized the importance of the first two keys. Fall in love with Jesus, not money or material things. Don't be deceived, running to and fro, looking for those who can astonish you with some new spiritual insight or mesmerize you by performing great miracles. Scripture tells us that in the last days representatives of the devil will also have great powers and will even perform mighty miracles. But they are "spirits of demons, performing signs" (Rev. 16:14 NKJV). In these last days, you dare not allow yourself to be distracted from your first love; keep your focus on Jesus.

Do you want to survive the coming apocalypse? Fall in love with Jesus, study His Word, and obey what He tells you to do. It is the Word of God that gives me comfort. If I am still alive when the economy crashes or a meteor hits the earth, I will be telling everyone I can, "Don't despair. This is exactly what God said would happen. He told us in advance. Here it is; I'll show you right here in the Bible. Sure, things are difficult right now, but don't be discouraged. Jesus is coming soon! Look up, our redemption draws near!"

More than ever before, I believe last-days Christians need to be studying God's Word. We need to know what He says, and what He does not say. The only way we will get to know Jesus better is through His Word. While other books are helpful, only the Word of God is sharper than a two-edged sword. Only the Word can provide the daily replenishment of your spiritual resources. Certainly, spending time in prayer is vital as well, but if we do not know the Word of God, our prayers are likely to be skewed by our experiences. The Word of God will keep us on target, whether we feel we are experiencing God's presence or not.

It is vital that we focus our eyes on Jesus and on His Word, rather than the world. Keep in mind the apostle John's exhortation: "Do not love the world or the things in the world" (1 John 2:15 NKJV). Our priorities must be to fall in love with Jesus, study and obey His Word, and do the will of God.

For me, doing the will of God and worshiping the Lord means doing what Jesus would do. I am convinced that Jesus would not simply preach the gospel; He would feed the hungry, clothe the naked, heal the hurting, and restore those who have been broken, battered, and beaten by this world. In the mid-1970s through the 1980s, following that conviction led me to build Heritage USA. In 1998 following that same conviction led me to the ghetto of Los Angeles, to work at the Dream Center.

IN THE GHETTO

The Dream Center was formerly known as Queen of Angels Hospital in the heart of old Los Angeles, just off the Hollywood Freeway. Once a thriving hospital with the unusual distinction of having birthed nearly three-quarters of the children born in the city, the 400,000-square-foot hospital had been closed for years and had dropped in price from sixteen million dollars to 3.9 million dollars. One day my friend Matthew Barnett (the twenty-one-year-old son of Tommy Barnett, pastor of First Assembly of God Church in Phoenix, Arizona) drove by and noticed the property for sale. Matthew's heart beats with a passion to help hurting people, so, against enormous odds, in 1995 he and his father's congregation, with the help of churches all over America, purchased and reopened the huge complex as a "spiritual hospital" for the inner city.

With fourteen hundred rooms and the potential housing of five thousand guests in the nine-building complex, the Dream Center opens its doors every day to the homeless, drug addicts, prostitutes, AIDS victims, gang members, unwed mothers, and a wide assortment of other hurting people, including burned-out or fallen pastors who need a place to be restored and renewed. Those seeking help at the Dream Center receive food, shelter, and most important, the gospel of Jesus Christ that can set them free. It is a place where the body of Christ is actively helping people on a daily basis to dream their dreams once again.

Many of my friends have questioned my wisdom in moving to Los Angeles, knowing what I do about the impending disasters that will hit the city. "Jim, of all places, why would you move there?" they ask in astonishment.

My only answer is, "I'm doing what God has called me to do." I must confess that at times I feel like Jonah. I'd rather be somewhere else. But then I think, *What better place could I be to preach a message of repentance than in a modern-day Nineveh?* How long I will remain in Los Angeles, only God knows. For now, I am where He wants me to be, doing my best to bring a cool drink of water in His name to those who desperately need it.

In Matthew 25 Jesus described the judgment He will render upon His return to earth. Interestingly, the basis on which the rewards or punishments will be meted out is not how much money we made, how long we prayed, sang, danced, or preached. On that day, Jesus said, He will separate the sheep from the goats according to a far different standard.

> Then the King will say to those on His right hand, "Come, you blessed of My Father, inherit the kingdom prepared for you from the foundation of the world: for I was hungry and you gave Me food; I was thirsty

and you gave Me drink; I was a stranger and you took Me in; I was naked and you clothed Me; I was sick and you visited Me; I was in prison and you came to Me." (vv. 34–36 NKJV)

Strangely enough, in this account, the righteous people whom the Lord is rewarding were almost surprised at the King's compliments. Barely aware they were doing things so high on the King's priority list, they were just doing what many might consider to be mundane acts of kindness. Yet the King of kings said, "I say to you, inasmuch as you did it to one of the least of these My brethren, you did it to Me" (v. 40 NKJV).

What an incredible concept! Jesus rewards every act of kindness done in His name, not simply because in doing so we help to alleviate the hurts of humanity, but because it is as though we are doing it to Him.

Yet if many will be unexpectedly honored on that day of judgment, Jesus makes it equally clear that many will be horribly surprised at the verdict rendered on their lack of concern for helpless, hurting people.

Then He will also say to those on the left hand, "Depart from Me, you cursed, into the everlasting fire prepared for the devil and his angels: for I was hungry and you gave Me no food; I was thirsty and you gave Me no drink; I was a stranger and you did not take Me in, naked and you did not clothe Me, sick and in prison and you did not visit Me." (vv. 41–43 NKJV)

Once again the King's assessment will elicit shocked protest; but from the unrighteous the uproar will take a different tone. "Lord, when?" they will want to know. "When did we see You hungry or thirsty or a stranger or naked or sick or in prison, and did not minister to You?" (v. 44 NKJV).

The King's answer will echo throughout eternity. "'Inasmuch as you did not do it to one of the least of these, you did not do it to Me.' And these will go away into everlasting punishment, but the righteous into eternal life" (vv. 45–46 NKJV).

Clearly, we are going to be judged on the basis of what we did or did not do to help those in need. If we love God, we will do the works that are on His heart. No, you will not be able to meet the needs of every tired, sick, hungry, or hurting person in the world. You may not even be able to scratch the surface in your own city. But each of us has a sphere of influence—your neighborhood, your apartment complex, or your church—and in these exciting last days we should be preparing to minister to the people within that sphere. Wherever you have the power to provide Christlike assistance in the days ahead, you must be ready to do so.

In the days ahead you may be stripped of everything you have ever held dear. You may lose your money, your home, your material possessions, your career, your spouse or other family members. Perhaps that process has already begun in your life. Please do not be dismayed or discouraged. If you are like many of us, we don't get our priorities straightened out until we go through such a stripping.

I know. I have been through the stripping myself, losing everything I ever held dear. Yet I can say from the bottom of my heart that it has been worth it, because I have come to know Jesus Christ in a way I might never have experienced Him had He not arrested me in my own foolishness. I have been through the valley of the shadow of death, and I can testify that the Savior will never leave you nor forsake you, no matter how dark or difficult your future looks.

The psalmist said, "Yea, though I walk through the valley of the shadow of death, / I will fear no evil; / For You are with me; / Your rod and Your staff, they comfort me" (23:4 NKJV). The phrase "valley of the shadow of death" refers to a deep, thick darkness, terror, and calamity. Yet as we go through this darkness, we will fear no evil. When the sun is blocked out and the earth turns dark, we will not fear because God is with us.

Even then, He will prepare a table for us in the presence of our enemies (Ps. 23:5). God will take care of us through the coming apocalypse and beyond. And we will dwell in the house of the Lord forever!

Appendix A

My Daily Walk
by Jim Bakker

Just prior to my release from prison on July 1, 1994, I decided to write down some of the things I had learned during my nearly five-year incarceration, and some of the fresh commitments I had made. I believe these commitments will be necessary as we move into the difficult days ahead.

I encourage you to adopt these principles, based on the Scriptures—or better yet, write out your own. As always, the Word of God must be our guide, no matter what comes our way.

1. I will humble myself and walk daily in humility before my God.
   1 Peter 5:5, Matt. 23:12, 2 Chron. 7:14, James 4:1–10, Isa. 57:15, Matt. 18:3–4, 1 Sam. 15:17, Prov. 6:16–17, Prov. 16:5–8, 2 Chron. 32:24–26, 2 Sam. 15:30, 2 Chron. 34:27, Num. 12:3, Phil. 2:1–8, Eph. 4:1–3

2. I will seek God today and every day and do nothing without consulting Him.
   1 Chron. 10:13–14, Phil. 4:4–7, 2 Chron. 26:5, Matt. 6:33, John 16:13–15, Acts 6:4, Ps. 118:8–9, 1 Cor. 2:9–16, 1 Thess. 5:17, Rev. 8:3–4, 2 Sam. 21:1, 1 Sam. 23:1–4, James 1:5–6, 1 Tim. 2:8, Heb. 4:14–16, 2 Sam. 5:19–25, James 5:16, 2 Sam. 2:1–2

3. I will read, study, and meditate on God's Word today and every day, and I will implement it in my life.

    Ps. 1:1–3, Ps. 119, 2 Tim. 2:15, Rom. 10:17, Ps. 119:133, Deut. 17:18–20, Ps. 119:11, John 8:32, John 1:1–3, 2 Chron. 34:30, 1 Tim. 4:13–16, Rev. 1:3, 2 Tim. 3:14–17, 1 John 2:3–6

4. I will have no other gods or idols, nor will I place anything before my God.

    Gal. 5:1, Phil. 4:8, 1 Tim. 4:1–2, 1 John 2:15–19, 1 John 5:21, Ex. 20:3, 1 Cor. 10:1–14, 1 Cor. 3:16–17, Deut. 5:7, 1 Cor. 15:33–34, Gal. 1:6–9, Gal. 4:7–9, 2 Chron. 33, Heb. 12:1–2, 2 Chron. 34:1–4, Deut. 6:14

5. I will love, trust, praise, and worship my God with all my heart today and every day.

    1 Tim. 4:10, Matt. 22:37, 2 Sam. 15:32, John 9:31, Rom. 10:8–10, 1 Thess. 5:18, Heb. 13:15, 1 Peter 2:9, Ps. 37:1–9, Job 13:15, Isa. 12:2, 2 Sam. 22:1–7, Ps. 52:8, 2 Sam. 7:22, 2 Sam. 12:20

6. I will daily show mercy, forgiving all, and I will love my neighbor as myself.

    Gal. 5:13–14, Matt. 5:7, Matt. 22:39, Matt. 5:44, Matt. 6:14–15, Matt. 9:9–13, Matt. 18:35, Matt. 25:32–46, John 13:34–35, 1 John 3:10–24, 1 John 4:7–21, Gal. 6:1–10, Eph. 4:32, 2 Sam. 22:26, 1 Peter 3:8–12, Job 42:10

7. I will abide in Christ and allow His Word to abide in me, and I will keep His commandments.

    Phil. 4:13, John 15, Col. 1:26–28, 2 John 9, John 6:51–58, John 8:31, John 14:1–24, 1 Tim. 6:14, 1 John 2:3, 1 Cor. 12:26–27, 2 Cor. 6:14–18, Eph. 3:17, 1 John 2:22–29, 1 John 4:4

8. I will crucify my flesh and die to it daily, fleeing temptation and sin.

    Rom. 6, Rom. 7:18–25, Rom. 8:1–15, Gal. 5, 1 Tim. 6:1–12, 1 Cor. 6:15–20, 1 Cor. 10:14, Rom. 13:14, 1 Cor. 15:31, Matt. 16:24–26, 1 Cor. 9:27, 2 Cor. 7:1, John 12:24–26, Gal. 2:19–21, 2 Cor. 12:1–10, 2 Tim. 2:22, Col. 3:1–4, 1 Peter 2:11, 2 Peter 2:9–22

9. I will accept the trial of my faith as more precious than gold, knowing that whom God loves He chastises.

Acts 14:22, 1 Peter 1:7, Heb. 12:6–8, Col. 1:24, John 16:33, Rev. 3:17–19, Rom. 8:16–18, 2 Cor. 4:7–11, James 1:2–3, 2 Tim. 2:10–13, 2 Cor. 6:1–10, 2 Tim. 3:12, James 5:10–11

10. I will always confess that Jesus Christ is Lord, my Master, Owner, and Possessor.
Heb. 9:11–28, Phil. 2:11, Rev. 17:14, John 3:16–18, Rom. 1:16, Rom. 10:9, 1 John 4:15, 1 Cor. 2:2, 1 Cor. 12:3, Phil. 3:7–10, 2 Tim. 1:12, Heb. 13:8, 1 John 5:1–14

11. I will keep my heart right toward God, confessing my sins and never lying to the Holy Spirit.
Eph. 4:30, 1 Kings 2:3, Matt. 12:31–37, Acts 5:1–6, Matt. 22:37, 2 Cor. 4:2, 2 Cor. 7:10–11, 2 Cor. 10:3–5, Heb. 10:22, James 5:8, 1 Sam. 12:20, 1 Sam. 16:7, Heb. 3:7–15, 1 Sam. 13:14, 2 Sam. 24:10

12. I will live by the total counsel of God's Word.
Matt. 4:4, Phil. 2:16, Ps. 119:133, Acts 4:31, Heb. 4:12, Acts 17:11, Eph. 6:10–20, Col. 3:16, James 1:22, Ps. 119, 2 Chron. 24:20, 1 Cor. 2:13, 1 Cor. 4:2, 2 Tim. 3:16, 2 Tim. 4:3–4, 2 Pet. 1:1–10

13. I will not judge others, nor lean to my own understanding or trust the arm of flesh.
1 Peter 1:22–25, Matt. 7:1, Prov. 3:5, Rom. 2:1, Rom. 12:1–2 and 19–21, 2 Chron. 32:8, Rom. 14:12–13, James 4:11–17, Rom. 7:18, Jer. 48:7, Jer. 17:5, Ps. 146:3, John 7:24, Ps. 44:6, Ps. 49:6–7, Ezek. 33:13

14. I will demonstrate love, joy, peace, longsuffering, gentleness, goodness, faith, meekness, and temperance.
Gal. 5:22–25, Matt. 7:16–27, 1 Cor. 13, Eph. 4:1–2, Heb. 11, Col. 3:12–15, Matt. 3:10, Matt. 13:18–23, Col. 1:10–11, 1 Tim. 1:16, Eph. 5:8–12, Heb. 12:14, Neh. 8:10, 1 Peter 4:8, James 3:17–18, 2 Peter 1:8

15. I will keep my eyes on heaven, the mark of the prize of the high calling in Christ Jesus.
Phil. 3:14, 1 John 3:3, 2 Cor. 5:2–8, 2 Peter 3:12, Phil. 1:23, Luke 12:33, Heb. 11:10–16, Matt. 6, Matt. 25:13, 1 Thess. 4:16–18, Eccl. 9:11–12, 1 Cor. 9:27, 2 Tim. 4:7–8, Heb. 12:1

Appendix B

Scripture References
for Further Study

All Scripture quotations in this appendix are
from the King James Version of the Bible.

Prosperity and Riches

Deut. 23:6
Thou shalt not seek their peace nor their prosperity all thy days for ever.

1 Sam. 25:6
And thus shall ye say to him that liveth in prosperity, Peace be both to thee, and peace be to thine house, and peace be unto all that thou hast.

1 Kings 10:7
Howbeit I believed not the words, until I came, and mine eyes had seen it: and, behold, the half was not told me: thy wisdom and prosperity exceedeth the fame which I heard.

Job 15:21
A dreadful sound is in his ears: in prosperity the destroyer shall come upon him.

Job 36:11
If they obey and serve him, they shall spend their days in prosperity, and their years in pleasures.

Ps. 30:6
And in my prosperity I said, I shall never be moved.

Ps. 35:27
Let them shout for joy, and be glad, that favor my righteous cause: yea, let them say continually, Let the LORD be magnified, which hath pleasure in the prosperity of his servant.

Ps. 73:3
For I was envious at the foolish, when I saw the prosperity of the wicked.

Ps. 118:25
Save now, I beseech thee, O LORD: O LORD, I beseech thee, send now prosperity.

Ps. 122:7
Peace be within thy walls, and prosperity within thy palaces.

Prov. 1:32
For the turning away of the simple shall slay them, and the prosperity of fools shall destroy them.

Eccl. 7:14
In the day of prosperity be joyful, but in the day of adversity consider: God also hath set the one over against the other, to the end that man should find nothing after him.

Jer. 22:21
I spake unto thee in thy prosperity; but thou saidst, I will not hear. This hath been thy manner from thy youth, that thou obeyedst not my voice.

Jer. 33:9
And it shall be to me a name of joy, a praise and an honor before all the nations of the earth, which shall hear all the good that I do unto them: and they shall fear and tremble for all the goodness and for all the prosperity that I procure unto it.

Lam. 3:17
And thou hast removed my soul far off from peace: I forgat prosperity.

Zech. 1:17
Cry yet, saying, Thus saith the LORD of hosts; My cities through prosperity shall yet be spread abroad; and the LORD shall yet comfort Zion, and shall yet choose Jerusalem.

Zech. 7:7

Should ye not hear the words which the LORD hath cried by the former prophets, when Jerusalem was inhabited and in prosperity, and the cities thereof round about her, when men inhabited the south and the plain?

Matt. 13:22

He also that received seed among the thorns is he that heareth the word; and the care of this world, and the deceitfulness of riches, choke the word, and he becometh unfruitful.

Matt. 19:23–24

Then said Jesus unto his disciples, Verily I say unto you, that a rich man shall hardly enter into the kingdom of heaven. And again I say unto you, it is easier for a camel to go through the eye of a needle, than for a rich man to enter into the kingdom of God.

Matt. 27:57

When the even was come, there came a rich man of Arimathaea, named Joseph, who also himself was Jesus' disciple.

Mark. 4:19

And the cares of this world, and the deceitfulness of riches, and the lusts of other things entering in, choke the word, and it becometh unfruitful.

Mark 10:23–25

And Jesus looked round about, and saith unto his disciples, How hardly shall they that have riches enter into the kingdom of God! And the disciples were astonished at his words. But Jesus answereth again, and saith unto them, Children, how hard is it for them that trust in riches to enter into the kingdom of God! It is easier for a camel to go through the eye of a needle, than for a rich man to enter into the kingdom of God.

Mark 12:41, 44

And Jesus sat over against the treasury, and beheld how the people cast money into the treasury: and many that were rich cast in much . . . For all they did cast in of their abundance; but she of her want did cast in all that she had, even all her living.

Luke 1:53

He hath filled the hungry with good things; and the rich he hath sent empty away.

Luke 6:24

But woe unto you that are rich! for ye have received your consolation.

Luke 8:14

And that which fell among thorns are they, which, when they have heard, go forth, and are choked with cares and riches and pleasures of this life, and bring no fruit to perfection.

Luke 12:16, 21

And he spake a parable unto them, saying, The ground of a certain rich man brought forth plentifully . . . So is he that layeth up treasure for himself, and is not rich toward God.

Luke 14:12

Then said he also to him that bade him, When thou makest a dinner or a supper, call not thy friends, nor thy brethren, neither thy kinsmen, nor thy rich neighbours; lest they also bid thee again, and a recompence be made thee.

Luke 16:1, 11

And he said also unto his disciples, There was a certain rich man, which had a steward; and the same was accused unto him that he had wasted his goods . . . If therefore ye have not been faithful in the unrighteous mammon, who will commit to your trust the true riches?

Luke 16:19, 21–22

There was a certain rich man, which was clothed in purple and fine linen, and fared sumptuously every day . . . And desiring to be fed with the crumbs which fell from the rich man's table: moreover the dogs came and licked his sores. And it came to pass, that the beggar died, and was carried by the angels into Abraham's bosom: the rich man also died, and was buried.

Luke 18:23–25

And when he heard this, he was very sorrowful: for he was very rich. And when Jesus saw that he was very sorrowful, he said, How hardly shall they that have riches enter into the kingdom of God! For it easier for a camel to go through a needle's eye, than for a rich man to enter into the kingdom of God.

Luke 19:2

And, behold, there was a man named Zaccheus, which was the chief among the publicans, and he was rich.

Luke 21:1

And he looked up, and saw the rich men casting their gifts into the treasury.

Rom. 2:4

Or despisest thou the riches of his goodness and forbearance and longsuffering; not knowing that the goodness of God leadeth thee to repentance?

Rom. 9:23

. . . and that he might make known the riches of his glory on the vessels of mercy, which he had afore prepared unto glory.

Rom. 10:12

For there is no difference between the Jew and the Greek: for the same Lord over all is rich unto all that call upon him.

Rom. 11:12

Now if the fall of them be the riches of the world, and the diminishing of them the riches of the Gentiles; how much more their fullness?

Rom. 11:33

O the depth of the riches both of the wisdom and knowledge of God! how unsearchable are his judgments, and his ways past finding out!

1 Cor. 4:8

Now ye are full, now ye are rich, ye have reigned as kings without us: and I would to God ye did reign, that we also might reign with you.

2 Cor. 6:10

. . . as sorrowful, yet alway rejoicing; as poor, yet making many rich; as having nothing, and yet possessing all things.

2 Cor. 8:2

. . . how that in a great trial of affliction the abundance of their joy and their deep poverty abounded unto the riches of their liberality.

2 Cor. 8:9

For ye know the grace of our Lord Jesus Christ, that, though he was rich, yet for your sakes he became poor, that ye through his poverty might be rich.

Eph. 1:7

. . . in whom we have redemption through his blood, the forgiveness of sins, according to the riches of his grace.

Eph. 1:18
. . . the eyes of your understanding being enlightened; that ye may know what is the hope of his calling, and what the riches of the glory of his inheritance in the saints.

Eph. 2:4
But God, who is rich in mercy, for his great love wherewith he loved us.

Eph. 2:7
. . . that in the ages to come he might show the exceeding riches of his grace in his kindness toward us through Christ Jesus.

Eph. 3:8
Unto me who am less than the least of all saints, is this grace given, that I should preach among the Gentiles the unsearchable riches of Christ.

Eph. 3:16
. . . that he would grant you, according to the riches of his glory, to be strengthened with might by his Spirit in the inner man.

Phil. 4:19
But my God shall supply all your need according to his riches in glory by Christ Jesus.

Col. 1:27
. . . to whom God would make known what is the riches of the glory of this mystery among the Gentiles; which is Christ in you, the hope of glory.

Col. 2:2
. . . that their hearts might be comforted, being knit together in love, and unto all riches of the full assurance of understanding, to the acknowledgement of the mystery of God, and of the Father, and of Christ.

1 Tim. 6:9
But they that will be rich fall into temptation and a snare, and into many foolish and hurtful lusts, which drown men in destruction and perdition.

1 Tim. 6:17–18
Charge them that are rich in this world, that they be not high-minded, nor trust in uncertain riches, but in the living God, who giveth us richly all things to enjoy; that they do good, that they be rich in good works, ready to distribute, willing to communicate.

Heb. 11:26

. . . esteeming the reproach of Christ greater riches than the treasures in Egypt: for he had respect unto the recompense of the reward.

James 1:10–11

. . . but the rich, in that he is made low: because as the flower of the grass he shall pass away. For the sun is no sooner risen with a burning heat, but it withereth the grass, and the flower thereof falleth, and the grace of the fashion of it perisheth: so also shall the rich man fade away in his ways.

James 2:5–6

Hearken, my beloved brethren, Hath not God chosen the poor of this world rich in faith, and heirs of the kingdom which he hath promised to them that love him? But ye have despised the poor. Do not rich men oppress you, and draw you before the judgment seats?

James 5:1–3

Go to now, ye rich men, weep and howl for your miseries that shall come upon you. Your riches are corrupted, and your garments are moth-eaten. Your gold and silver is cankered; and the rust of them shall be a witness against you, and shall eat your flesh as it were fire. Ye have heaped treasure together for the last days.

Rev. 2:9

I know thy works, and tribulation, and poverty, (but thou art rich) and I know the blasphemy of them which say they are Jews, and are not, but are the synagogue of Satan.

Rev. 3:17–18

Because thou sayest, I am rich, and increased with goods, and have need of nothing; and knowest not that thou art wretched, and miserable, and poor, and blind, and naked: I counsel thee to buy of me gold tried in the fire, that thou mayest be rich; and white raiment, that thou mayest be clothed, and that the shame of thy nakedness do not appear; and anoint thine eyes with eyesalve, that thou mayest see.

Rev. 5:12

. . . saying with a loud voice, Worthy is the Lamb that was slain to receive power, and riches, and wisdom, and strength, and honor, and glory, and blessing.

Rev. 6:15
And the kings of the earth, and the great men, and the rich men, and the chief captains, and the mighty men, and every bondman, and every free man, hid themselves in the dens and in the rocks of the mountains.

Rev. 13:16
And he causeth all, both small and great, rich and poor, free and bond, to receive a mark in their right hand, or in their foreheads.

Rev. 18:3
For all nations have drunk of the wine of the wrath of her fornication, and the kings of the earth have committed fornication with her, and the merchants of the earth are waxed rich through the abundance of her delicacies.

Rev. 18:15, 17, 19
The merchants of these things, which were made rich by her, shall stand afar off for the fear of her torment, weeping and wailing . . . For in one hour so great riches is come to nought. And every shipmaster, and all the company in ships, and sailors, and as many as trade by sea, stood afar off . . . And they cast dust on their heads, and cried, weeping and wailing, saying, Alas, alas, that great city, wherein were made rich all that had ships in the sea by reason of her costliness! for in one hour is he made desolate.

THE DANGERS OF PROSPERITY

Deut. 8:10–18
When thou hast eaten and art full, then thou shalt bless the LORD thy God for the good land which he hath given thee. Beware that thou forget not the LORD thy God, in not keeping his commandments, and his judgments, and his statutes, which I command thee this day: lest when thou hast eaten and art full, and hast built goodly houses, and dwelt therein; and when thy herds and thy flocks multiply, and thy silver and thy gold is multiplied, and all that thou hast is multiplied; then thine heart be lifted up, and thou forget the LORD thy God, which brought thee forth out of the land of Egypt, from the house of bondage; who led thee through that great and terrible wilderness, wherein were fiery serpents, and scorpions, and drought, where there was no water; who brought thee forth water out of the rock of flint; who fed thee in the wilderness

with manna, which thy fathers knew not, that he might humble thee, and that he might prove thee, to do thee good at thy latter end; and thou say in thine heart, My power and the might of mine hand hath gotten me this wealth. But thou shalt remember the LORD thy God: for it is he that giveth thee power to get wealth, that he may establish his covenant which he sware unto thy fathers, as it is this day.

Deut. 31:20

For when I shall have brought them into the land which I sware unto their fathers, that floweth with milk and honey; and they shall have eaten and filled themselves, and waxen fat; then will they turn unto other gods, and serve them, and provoke me, and break my covenant.

Deut. 32:15

But Jeshurun waxed fat, and kicked:
thou art waxen fat, thou art grown thick,
thou art covered with fatness;
then he forsook God which made him,
and lightly esteemed the Rock of his salvation.

2 Chron. 12:1

And it came to pass, when Rehoboam had established the kingdom, and had strengthened himself, he forsook the law of the LORD, and all Israel with him.

2 Chron. 26:16

But when he was strong, his heart was lifted up to his destruction: for he transgressed against the LORD his God, and went into the temple of the LORD to burn incense upon the altar of incense.

2 Chron. 32:25

But Hezekiah rendered not again according to the benefit done unto him; for his heart was lifted up: therefore there was wrath upon him, and upon Judah and Jerusalem.

Jer. 5:7

How shall I pardon thee for this? thy children have forsaken me, and sworn by them that are no gods: when I had fed them to the full, they then committed adultery, and assembled themselves by troops in the harlots' houses.

Hos. 4:7

As they were increased, so they sinned against me: therefore will I change their glory into shame.

Hos. 13:6

According to their pasture, so were they filled; they were filled, and their heart was exalted; therefore have they forgotten me.

Sowing and Reaping

2 Kings 19:29

And this shall be a sign unto thee, Ye shall eat this year such things as grow of themselves, and in the second year that which springeth of the same; and in the third year sow ye, and reap, and plant vineyards, and eat the fruits thereof.

Job 4:8

Even as I have seen, they that plow iniquity, and sow wickedness, reap the same.

Job 31:8

. . . then let me sow, and let another eat; yea, let my offspring be rooted out.

Ps. 107:37

. . . and sow the fields, and plant vineyards, which may yield fruits of increase.

Ps. 126:5

They that sow in tears shall reap in joy.

Prov. 11:18

The wicked worketh a deceitful work: but to him that soweth righteousness shall be a sure reward.

Prov. 16:28

A froward man soweth strife: and a whisperer separateth chief friends.

Prov. 22:8

He that soweth iniquity shall reap vanity: and the rod of his anger shall fail.

Eccl. 11:4, 6

He that observeth the wind shall not sow; and he that regardeth the clouds shall not reap . . . In the morning sow thy seed, and in the evening withhold not thine hand: for thou knowest not whether they shall prosper, either this or that, or whether they both shall be alike good.

Isa. 28:24

Doth the plowman plow all day to sow? doth he open and break the clods of his ground?

Isa. 30:23

Then shall he give the rain of thy seed, that thou shalt sow the ground withal; and bread of the increase of the earth, and it shall be fat and plenteous: in that day shall thy cattle feed in large pastures.

Isa. 32:20

Blessed are ye that sow beside all waters, that send forth thither the feet of the ox and the ass.

Isa. 37:30

And this shall be a sign unto thee, Ye shall eat this year such as groweth of itself; and the second year that which springeth of the same: and in the third year sow ye, and reap, and plant vineyards, and eat the fruit thereof.

Jer. 4:3

For thus saith the LORD to the men of Judah and Jerusalem, Break up your fallow ground, and sow not among thorns.

Jer. 31:27

Behold, the days come, saith the LORD, that I will sow the house of Israel and the house of Judah with the seed of man, and with the seed of beast.

Jer. 35:7

Neither shall ye build house, nor sow seed, nor plant vineyard, nor have any: but all your days ye shall dwell in tents; that ye may live many days in the land where ye be strangers.

Hos. 2:23

And I will sow her unto me in the earth; and I will have mercy upon her that had not obtained mercy; and I will say to them which were not my people, Thou art my people; and they shall say, Thou art my God.

Hos. 10:12

Sow to yourselves in righteousness, reap in mercy; break up your fallow ground: for it is time to seek the LORD, till he come and rain righteousness upon you.

Amos 9:13
Behold, the days come, saith the LORD, that the plowman shall overtake the reaper, and the treader of grapes him that soweth seed; and the mountains shall drop sweet wine, and all the hills shall melt.

Mic. 6:15
Thou shalt sow, but thou shalt not reap; thou shalt tread the olives, but thou shalt not anoint thee with oil; and sweet wine, but shalt not drink wine.

Zech. 10:9
And I will sow them among the people: and they shall remember me in far countries; and they shall live with their children, and turn again.

Matt. 6:26
Behold the fowls of the air: for they sow not, neither do they reap, nor gather into barns; yet your heavenly Father feedeth them. Are ye not much better than they?

Matt. 13:3, 24–25, 27, 37
And he spake many things unto them in parables, saying, Behold, a sower went forth to sow . . . Another parable put he forth unto them, saying, The kingdom of heaven is likened unto a man which sowed good seed in his field; but while men slept, his enemy came and sowed tares among the wheat, and went his way . . . So the servants of the householder came and said unto him, Sir, didst not thou sow good seed in thy field? from whence then hath it tares? . . . He answered and said until them, He that soweth the good seed is the Son of man.

Mark 4:3, 14
Hearken; Behold, there went out a sower to sow . . . The sower soweth the word.

Luke 8:5
A sower went out to sow his seed: and as he sowed, some fell by the way side; and it was trodden down, and the fowls of the air devoured it.

Luke 12:24
Consider the ravens: for they neither sow nor reap; which neither have storehouse nor barn; and God feedeth them: how much more are ye better than the fowls?

Luke 19:21–22

. . . for I feared thee, because thou art an austere man: thou takest up that thou layedst not down, and reapest that thou didst not sow. And he saith unto him, Out of thine own mouth will I judge thee, thou wicked servant. Thou knewest that I was an austere man, taking up that I laid not down, and reaping that I did not sow.

John 4:36–37

And he that reapeth receiveth wages, and gathereth fruit unto life eternal: that both he that soweth and he that reapeth may rejoice together. And herein is that saying true, One soweth, and another reapeth.

2 Cor. 9:6

But this I say, He which soweth sparingly shall reap also sparingly; and he which soweth bountifully shall reap also bountifully.

Gal. 6:7–8

Be not deceived; God is not mocked: for whatsoever a man soweth, that shall he also reap. For he that soweth to his flesh shall of the flesh reap corruption; but he that soweth to the Spirit shall of the Spirit reap life everlasting.

EARTHQUAKES

Isa. 29:6

Thou shalt be visited of the LORD of hosts with thunder, and with earthquake, and great noise, with storm and tempest, and the flame of devouring fire.

Joel 2:9–11

They shall run to and fro in the city; they shall run upon the wall, they shall climb up upon the houses; they shall enter in at the windows like a thief. The earth shall quake before them; the heavens shall tremble: the sun and the moon shall be dark, and the stars shall withdraw their shining: and the LORD shall utter his voice before his army: for his camp is very great: for he is strong that executeth his word: for the day of the LORD is great and very terrible; and who can abide it?

Nah. 1:2–8

God is jealous, and the LORD revengeth; the LORD revengeth, and is furious; the LORD will take vengeance on his adversaries, and he reserveth wrath for his enemies.

The LORD is slow to anger, and great in power, and will not at all acquit the wicked: the LORD hath his way in the whirlwind and in the storm, and the clouds are the dust of his feet. He rebuketh the sea, and maketh it dry, and drieth up all the rivers: Bashan languisheth, and Carmel, and the flower of Lebanon languisheth. The mountains quake at him, and the hills melt, and the earth is burned at his presence, yea, the world, and all that dwell therein. Who can stand before his indignation and who can abide in the fierceness of his anger? his fury is poured out like fire, and the rocks are thrown down by him. The LORD is good, a stronghold in the day of trouble; and he knoweth them that trust in him. But with an overrunning flood he will make an utter end of the place thereof, and darkness shall pursue his enemies.

Matt. 24:7–8
For nation shall rise against nation, and kingdom against kingdom: and there shall be famines, and pestilences, and earthquakes, in divers places. All these are the beginning of sorrows.

Mark 13:8
For nation shall rise against nation, and kingdom against kingdom: and there shall be earthquakes in divers places, and there shall be famines and troubles: these are the beginnings of sorrows.

Luke 21:11
And great earthquakes shall be in divers places, and famines, and pestilences; and fearful sights and great signs shall there be from heaven.

Luke 21:26–28
. . . men's hearts failing them for fear, and for looking after those things which are coming on the earth: for the powers of heaven shall be shaken. And then shall they see the Son of man coming in a cloud with power and great glory. And when these things begin to come to pass, then look up, and lift up your heads; for your redemption draweth nigh.

Rev. 6:12–17
And I beheld when he had opened the sixth seal, and, lo, there was a great earthquake; and the sun became black as sackcloth of hair, and the moon became as blood; and the stars of heaven fell unto the earth, even as a fig tree casteth her untimely figs, when she is shaken of a mighty wind. And the heaven departed as

a scroll when it is rolled together; and every mountain and island were moved out of their places. And the kings of the earth, and the great men, and the rich men, and the chief captains, and the mighty men, and every bondman, and every free man, hid themselves in the dens and in the rocks of the mountains; and said to the mountains and rocks, Fall on us, and hide us from the face of him that sitteth on the throne, and from the wrath of the Lamb: for the great day of his wrath is come; and who shall be able to stand?

Rev. 8:1–5
And when he had opened the seventh seal, there was silence in heaven about the space of half an hour. And I saw the seven angels which stood before God; and to them were given seven trumpets. And another angel came and stood at the altar, having a golden censer; and there was given unto him much incense, that he should offer it with the prayers of all saints upon the golden altar which was before the throne. And the smoke of the incense, which came with the prayers of the saints, ascended up before God out of the angel's hand. And the angel took the censer, and filled it with fire of the altar, and cast it into the earth: and there were voices, and thunderings, and lightnings, and an earthquake.

Rev. 11:13
And the same hour was there a great earthquake, and the tenth part of the city fell, and in the earthquake were slain of men seven thousand: and the remnant were affrighted, and gave glory to the God of heaven.

Rev. 11:19
And the temple of God was opened in heaven, and there was seen in his temple the ark of his testament: and there were lightnings, and voices, and thunderings, and an earthquake, and great hail.

Rev. 16:18–21
And there were voices, and thunders, and lightnings; and there was a great earthquake, such as was not since men were upon the earth, so mighty an earthquake, and so great. And the great city was divided into three parts, and the cities of the nations fell: and great Babylon came in remembrance before God, to give unto her the cup of the wine of the fierceness of his wrath. And every island fled away, and the mountains were not found. And there fell upon men a great hail out of heaven, every stone about the weight of a talent: and men blasphemed God because of the plague of the hail; for the plague thereof was exceeding great.

STARS, METEORS, AND ASTEROIDS

Isa. 34:2–4

For the indignation of the LORD is upon all nations, and his fury upon all their armies: he hath utterly destroyed them, he hath delivered them to the slaughter. Their slain also shall be cast out, and their stink shall come up out of their carcasses, and the mountains shall be melted with their blood. And all the host of heaven shall be dissolved, and the heavens shall be rolled together as a scroll: and all their host shall fall down, as the leaf falleth off from the vine, and as a falling fig from the fig tree.

Amos 5:7–8

Ye who turn judgment to wormwood, and leave off righteousness in the earth, seek him that maketh the seven stars and Orion, and turneth the shadow of death into the morning, and maketh the day dark with night: that calleth for the waters of the sea, and poureth them out upon the face of the earth: The LORD is his name.

Matt. 24:29–30

Immediately after the tribulation of those days shall the sun be darkened, and the moon shall not give her light, and the stars shall fall from heaven, and the powers of the heavens shall be shaken: and then shall appear the sign of the Son of man in heaven: and then shall all the tribes of the earth mourn, and they shall see the Son of man coming in the clouds of heaven with power and great glory.

Mark 13:25–26

. . . and the stars of heaven shall fall, and the powers that are in heaven shall be shaken, and then shall they see the Son of man coming in the clouds with great power and glory.

Luke 21:25–28

And there shall be signs in the sun, and in the moon, and in the stars; and upon the earth distress of nations, with perplexity; the sea and the waves roaring . . . for the powers of heaven shall be shaken. And then shall they see the Son of man coming in a cloud with power and great glory. And when these things begin to come to pass, then look up, and lift up your heads; for your redemption draweth nigh.

Acts 19:35

And when the townclerk had appeased the people, he said, Ye men of Ephesus, what man is there that knoweth not how that the city of the Ephesians is a worshiper of the great goddess Diana, and of the image which fell down from Jupiter?

Rev. 6:13–14

. . . and the stars of heaven fell unto the earth, even as a fig tree casteth her untimely figs, when she is shaken of a mighty wind. And the heaven departed as a scroll when it is rolled together; and every mountain and island were moved out of their places.

Rev. 8:6–12

And the seven angels which had the seven trumpets prepared themselves to sound. The first angel sounded, and there followed hail and fire mingled with blood, and they were cast upon the earth: and the third part of trees was burnt up, and all green grass was burnt up. And the second angel sounded, and as it were a great mountain burning with fire was cast into the sea: and the third part of the sea became blood; and the third part of the creatures which were in the sea, and had life, died; and the third part of the ships were destroyed. And the third angel sounded, and there fell a great star from heaven, burning as it were a lamp, and it fell upon the third part of the rivers, and upon the fountains of waters; and the name of the star is called Wormwood: and the third part of the waters became wormwood; and many men died of the waters, because they were made bitter. And the fourth angel sounded, and the third part of the sun was smitten, and the third part of the moon, and the third part of the stars; so as the third part of them was darkened, and the day shone not for a third part of it, and the night likewise.

Sun and Moon to Be Darkened

Isa. 13:6–10

Howl ye; for the day of the LORD is at hand; it shall come as a destruction from the Almighty. Therefore shall all hands be faint, and every man's heart shall melt: and they shall be afraid: pangs and sorrows shall take hold of them; they shall be in pain as a woman that travaileth: they shall be amazed one at another; their faces shall be as flames. Behold, the day of the LORD cometh, cruel both with wrath and fierce anger, to lay the land desolate: and he shall destroy the sinners thereof out of it. For the stars of heaven and the constellations thereof shall not give their light: the sun shall be darkened in his going forth, and the moon shall not cause her light to shine . . . Therefore I will shake the heavens, and the earth shall remove out of her place, in the wrath of the LORD of hosts, and in the day of his fierce anger.

Isa. 24:18–20, 23

And it shall come to pass, that he who fleeth from the noise of the fear shall fall into the pit; and he that cometh up out of the midst of the pit shall be taken in the snare: for the windows from on high are open, and the foundations of the earth do shake. The earth is utterly broken down, the earth is clean dissolved, the earth is moved exceedingly. The earth shall reel to and fro like a drunkard, and shall be removed like a cottage; and the transgression thereof shall be heavy upon it; and it shall fall, and not rise again . . . Then the moon shall be confounded, and the sun ashamed, when the LORD of hosts shall reign in mount Zion, and in Jerusalem, and before his ancients gloriously.

Isa. 50:2–3

Wherefore, when I came, was there no man? when I called, was there none to answer? Is my hand shortened at all, that it cannot redeem? or have I no power to deliver? behold, at my rebuke I dry up the sea, I make the rivers a wilderness: their fish stinketh, because there is no water, and dieth for thirst. I clothe the heavens with blackness, and I make sackcloth their covering.

Ezek. 32:3–15

Thus saith the Lord GOD; I will therefore spread out my net over thee with a company of many people; and they shall bring thee up in my net. Then will I leave thee upon the land, I will cast thee forth upon the open field, and will cause all the fowls of the heaven to remain upon thee, and I will fill the beasts of the whole earth with thee. And I will lay thy flesh upon the mountains, and fill the valleys with thy height. I will also water with thy blood the land wherein thou swimmest, even to the mountains; and the rivers shall be full of thee. And when I shall put thee out, I will cover the heaven, and make the stars thereof dark; I will cover the sun with a cloud, and the moon shall not give her light. All the bright lights of heaven will I make dark over thee, and set darkness upon thy land, saith the Lord GOD. I will also vex the hearts of many people, when I shall bring thy destruction among the nations, into the countries which thou hast not known. Yea, I will make many people amazed at thee, and their kings shall be horribly afraid for thee, when I shall brandish my sword before them; and they shall tremble at every moment, every man for his own life, in the day of thy fall. For thus saith the Lord GOD; The sword of the king of Babylon shall come upon thee. By the swords of the mighty will I cause thy multitude to fall, the terrible of the nations, all of them: and they shall spoil the pomp of Egypt, and all the multitude thereof shall be destroyed. I will destroy also all the beasts thereof from beside the great waters; neither shall the foot of man trouble them any more, nor the hoofs of beasts trouble them. Then will I make their waters deep, and cause their rivers to run like oil, saith the Lord GOD. When I shall make the land of Egypt desolate, and the country shall be destitute of that whereof it was full, when I shall smite all them that dwell therein, then shall they know that I am the LORD.

Joel 2:1–5, 10–11

Blow ye the trumpet in Zion, and sound an alarm in my holy mountain: let all the inhabitants of the land tremble: for the day of the LORD cometh, for it is nigh at hand; a day of darkness and of gloominess, a day of clouds and of thick darkness, as the morning spread upon the mountains: a great people and a strong; there hath not been ever the like, neither shall be any more after it, even to the years of many generations. A fire devoureth before them; and behind them a flame burneth: the land is as the garden of Eden before them, and behind them a desolate wilderness; yea, and nothing shall escape them. The appearance of them is as the appearance of horses; and as horsemen, so shall they run. Like the noise of chariots on the tops of mountains shall they leap, like the noise of a flame of fire that devoureth the stubble, as a strong people set in battle array . . . The earth shall quake before them; the heavens shall tremble: the sun and the moon shall be dark, and the stars shall withdraw their shining: and the LORD shall utter his voice before his army: for his camp is very great: for he is strong that executeth his word: for the day of the LORD is great and very terrible; and who can abide it?

Joel 2:28, 30–31

And it shall come to pass afterward, that I will pour out my spirit upon all flesh . . . And I will show wonders in the heavens and in the earth, blood, and fire, and pillars of smoke. The sun shall be turned into darkness, and the moon into blood, before the great and the terrible day of the LORD come.

Joel 3:13–16

Put ye in the sickle, for the harvest is ripe: come, get you down; for the press is full, the fats overflow; for their wickedness is great. Multitudes, multitudes in the valley of decision: for the day of the LORD is near in the valley of decision. The sun and the moon shall be darkened, and the stars shall withdraw their shining. The LORD also shall roar out of Zion, and utter his voice from Jerusalem; and the heavens and the earth shall shake: but the LORD will be the hope of his people, and the strength of the children of Israel.

Amos 5:16–20

Therefore the LORD, the God of hosts, the Lord, saith thus; Wailing shall be in all streets; and they shall say in all the highways, Alas! alas! and they shall call the husbandman to mourning, and such as are skilful of lamentation to wailing. And in all vineyards shall be wailing: for I will pass through thee, saith the LORD. Woe unto you that desire the day of the LORD! to what end is it for you? the day of the LORD is darkness, and not light. As if a man did flee from a lion, and a bear met him; or went into the house, and leaned his hand on the wall, and a serpent bit him. Shall not the day of the LORD be darkness, and not light? even very dark, and no brightness in it?

Amos 8:8–10

Shall not the land tremble for this, and every one mourn that dwelleth therein? and it shall rise up wholly as a flood; and it shall be cast out and drowned, as by the flood of Egypt. And it shall come to pass in that day, saith the Lord GOD, that I will cause the sun to go down at noon, and I will darken the earth in the clear day: and I will turn your feasts into mourning, and all your songs into lamentation; and I will bring up sackcloth upon all loins, and baldness upon every head; and I will make it as the mourning of an only son, and the end thereof as a bitter day.

Zeph. 1:1–3, 7–11, 14–18

The word of the LORD which came unto Zephaniah the son of Cushi . . . I will utterly consume all things from off the land, saith the LORD. I will consume man and beast; I will consume the fowls of the heaven, and the fishes of the sea, and the stumbling blocks with the wicked; and I will cut off man from off the land, saith the LORD . . . Hold thy peace at the presence of the Lord GOD: for the day of the LORD is at hand: for the LORD hath prepared a sacrifice, he hath bid his guests. And it shall come to pass in the day of the LORD's sacrifice, that I will punish the princes, and the king's children, and all such as are clothed with strange apparel. In the same day also will I punish all those that leap on the threshold, which fill their masters' houses with violence and deceit. And it shall come to pass in that day, saith the LORD, that there shall be the noise of a cry from the fish gate, and a howling from the second, and a great crashing from the hills. Howl, ye inhabitants of Maktesh, for all the merchant people are cut down; all they that bear silver are cut off . . . The great day of the LORD is near, it is near, and hasteth greatly, even the voice of the day of the LORD: the mighty man shall cry there bitterly. That day is a day of wrath, a day of trouble and distress, a day of wasteness and desolation, a day of darkness and gloominess, a day of clouds and thick darkness, a day of the trumpet and alarm against the fenced cities, and against the high towers. And I will bring distress upon men, that they shall walk like blind men, because they have sinned against the LORD: and their blood shall be poured out as dust, and their flesh as the dung. Neither their silver nor their gold shall be ale to deliver them in the day of the LORD's wrath; but the whole land shall be devoured by the fire of his jealousy: for he shall make even a speedy riddance of all them that dwell in the land.

Matt. 24:21–22, 27, 29–33

For then shall be great tribulation, such as was not since the beginning of the world to this time, no, nor ever shall be. And except those days should be shortened, there should no flesh be saved: but for the elect's sake those days shall be shortened . . . For as lightning cometh out of the east, and shineth even unto the west; so shall also the coming of the Son of man be . . . Immediately after the tribulation of those days shall the sun be darkened, and the moon shall not give her light, and the stars shall fall from heaven, and the powers of the heavens shall be shaken: and then shall appear the sign of the Son of man in heaven: and then shall all the tribes of the earth mourn, and they shall see the Son of man coming in the clouds of heaven with power and great glory. And he shall send his angels with a great sound of a trumpet, and they shall gather together his elect from the four winds, from one end of heaven to the other. Now learn a parable of the fig tree; When his branch is yet tender, and putteth forth leaves, ye know that summer is nigh: so likewise ye, when ye shall see all these things, know that it is near, even at the doors.

Mark 13:19–20, 24–29

For in those days shall be affliction, such as was not from the beginning of the creation which God created unto this time, neither shall be. And except that the Lord had shortened those days, no flesh should be saved: but for the elect's sake, whom he hath chosen, he hath shortened the days . . . But in those days, after that tribulation, the sun shall be darkened, and the moon shall not give her light, and the stars of heaven shall fall, and the powers that are in heaven shall be shaken. And then shall they see the Son of man coming in the clouds with great power and glory. And then shall he send his angels, and shall gather together his elect from the four winds, from the uttermost part of the earth to the uttermost part of heaven.

Luke 21:20–26

And when ye shall see Jerusalem compassed with armies, then know that the desolation thereof is nigh. Then let them which are in Judea flee to the mountains; and let them which are in the midst of it depart out; and let not them that are in the countries enter thereinto. For these be the days of vengeance, that all things which are written may be fulfilled. But woe unto them that are with child, and to them that give suck, in those days! for there shall be great distress in the land, and wrath upon this people. And they shall fall by the edge of the sword, and shall be led away captive into all nations: and Jerusalem shall be trodden down of the Gentiles, until the times of the Gentiles be fulfilled. And there shall be signs in the sun, and in the moon, and in the stars; and upon the earth distress of nations, with perplexity; the sea and the waves roaring; men's hearts failing them for fear, and for looking after those things which are coming on the earth: for the powers of heaven shall be shaken.

Rev. 6:12–13

And I beheld when he had opened the sixth seal, and, lo, there was a great earthquake; and the sun became black as sackcloth of hair, and the moon became as blood; and the stars of heaven fell unto the earth, even as a fig tree casteth her untimely figs, when she is shaken of a mighty wind.

Rev. 8:12–13

And the fourth angel sounded, and the third part of the sun was smitten, and the third part of the moon, and the third part of the stars; so as the third part of them was darkened, and the day shone not for a third part of it, and the night likewise. And I beheld, and heard an angel flying through the midst of heaven, saying with a loud voice, Woe, woe, woe, to the inhabiters of the earth by reason of the other voices of the trumpet of the three angels, which are yet to sound!

Rev. 9:1–6

And the fifth angel sounded, and I saw a star fall from heaven unto the earth: and to him was given the key of the bottomless pit. And he opened the bottomless pit; and there arose a smoke out of the pit, as the smoke of a great furnace; and the sun and the air were darkened by reason of the smoke of the pit. And there came out of the smoke locusts upon the earth: and unto them was given power, as the scorpions of the earth have power. And it was commanded them that they should not hurt the grass of the earth, neither any green thing, neither any tree; but only those men which have not the seal of God in their foreheads. And to them it was given that they should not kill them, but that they should be tormented five months: and their torment was as the torment of a scorpion, when he striketh a man. And in those days shall men seek death, and shall not find it; and shall desire to die, and death shall flee from them.

Rev. 16:8–10

And the fourth angel poured out his vial upon the sun; and power was given unto him to scorch men with fire. And men were scorched with great heat, and blasphemed the name of God, which hath power over these plagues: and they repented not to give him glory. And the fifth angel poured out his vial upon the seat of the beast; and his kingdom was full of darkness; and they gnawed their tongues for pain.

Patience While Waiting for the Lord's Return

Eccl. 7:8

Better is the end of a thing than the beginning thereof: and the patient in spirit is better than the proud in spirit.

Luke 21:10–19

Then said he unto them, Nation shall rise against nation, and kingdom against kingdom: and great earthquakes shall be in divers places, and famines, and pestilences; and fearful sights and great signs shall there be from heaven. But before all these, they shall lay their hands on you, and persecute you, delivering you up to the synagogues, and into prisons, being brought before kings and rulers for my name's sake. And it shall turn to you for a testimony. Settle it therefore in your hearts, not to meditate before what ye shall answer: for I will give you a mouth and wisdom, which all your adversaries shall not be able to gainsay nor resist. And ye shall be betrayed both by parents, and brethren, and kinfolks, and friends; and some of you shall they cause to be put to death. And ye shall be hated of all men for my name's sake. But there shall not a hair of your head perish. In your patience possess ye your souls.

Rom. 2:6–8

. . . who will render to every man according to his deeds: to them who by patient continuance in well doing seek for glory and honor and immortality, eternal life: but unto them that are contentious, and do not obey the truth, but obey unrighteousness, indignation and wrath . . .

Rom. 5:3

And not only so, but we glory in tribulations also: knowing that tribulation worketh patience . . .

Rom. 12:12

Rejoicing in hope; patient in tribulation; continuing instant in prayer . . .

1 Thess. 5:14

Now we exhort you, brethren, warn them that are unruly, comfort the feeble-minded, support the weak, be patient toward all men.

2 Thess. 3:5

And the Lord direct your hearts into the love of God, and into the patient waiting for Christ.

1 Tim. 3:2–3

A bishop then must be blameless, the husband of one wife, vigilant, sober, of good behavior, given to hospitality, apt to teach; not given to wine, no striker, not greedy of filthy lucre; but patient, not a brawler, not covetous . . .

1 Tim. 6:10–14

For the love of money is the root of all evil: which while some coveted after, they have erred from the faith, and pierced themselves through with many sorrows. But thou, O man of God, flee these things; and follow after righteousness, godliness, faith, love, patience, meekness. Fight the good fight of faith, lay hold on eternal life, whereunto thou art also called, and hast professed a good profession before many witnesses. I give thee charge in the sight of God, who quickeneth all things, and before Christ Jesus, who before Pontius Pilate witnessed a good confession; that thou keep this commandment without spot, unrebukable, until the appearing of our Lord Jesus Christ . . .

2 Tim. 2:24

And the servant of the Lord must not strive; but be gentle unto all men, apt to teach, patient . . .

James 5:7–11

Be patient therefore, brethren, unto the coming of the Lord. Behold, the husbandman waiteth for the precious fruit of the earth, and hath long patience for it, until he receive the early and latter rain. Be ye also patient; stablish your hearts: for the coming of the Lord draweth nigh. Grudge not one against another, brethren, lest ye be condemned: behold, the judge standeth before the door. Take, my brethren, the prophets, who have spoken in the name of the Lord, for an example of suffering affliction, and of patience. Behold, we count them happy which endure. Ye have heard of the patience of Job, and have seen the end of the Lord; that the Lord is very pitiful, and of tender mercy.

Rev. 1:9

I John, who also am your brother, and companion in tribulation, and in the kingdom and patience of Jesus Christ, was in the isle that is called Patmos, for the word of God, and for the testimony of Jesus Christ.

Rev. 2:19

I know thy works, and charity, and service, and faith, and thy patience, and thy works; and the last to be more than the first.

Rev. 3:10

Because thou hast kept the word of my patience, I also will keep thee from the hour of temptation, which shall come upon all the world, to try them that dwell upon the earth.

Rev. 13:10

He that leadeth into captivity shall go into captivity: he that killeth with the sword must be killed with the sword. Here is the patience and the faith of the saints.

Rev. 14:9–13

And the third angel followed them, saying with a loud voice, If any man worship the beast and his image, and receive his mark in his forehead, or in his hand, the same shall drink of the wine of the wrath of God, which is poured out without mixture into the cup of his indignation; and he shall be tormented with fire and brimstone in the presence of the holy angels, and the presence of the Lamb: and the smoke of their torment ascendeth up for ever and ever: and they have no rest day nor night, who worship the beast and his image, and whosoever receiveth the mark of his name. Here is the patience of the saints: here are they that keep the commandments of God, and the faith of Jesus. And I heard a voice from heaven saying unto me, Write, Blessed are the dead which die in the Lord from henceforth: Yea, saith the Spirit, that they may rest from their labors; and their works do follow them.

Notes

Chapter 1

1. "Volcanoes stir concerns about L.A. water supply," *USA Today,* 16 December 1997, 10-A.
2. Ibid.
3. "Moscow Record Coldest Day," *New York Times Service, Herald Tribune,* 19 December 1997 6-A.
4. Malcolm W. Brown, "The Hunt For Meteor Is On in Greenland," *New York Times Service, Herald Tribune,* Singapore, 20–21 December 1997, Weekend Edition, 1-A.
5. Ibid.
6. *Fire From the Sky,* Turner Original Productions/Warner Brothers, 1997.

Chapter 3

1. Jim Bakker, *Eight Keys to Success* (Charlotte, NC: Heritage Village Missionary Church, 1980), 29–30.
2. Jim Bakker, *You Can Make It* (Charlotte, NC: PTL Enterprises, 1983), 37.
3. George Ricker Berry, Ph.D., *Greek-English Lexicon to the New Testament* (Grand Rapids, MI: Zondervan Publishing House, 1958; 1974 ed.), 43.
4. William Barclay, *The Letters of John and Jude* (Philadelphia, PA: The Westminster Press, 1958; 1960 ed.), 172. See also: Robert Jamieson, A. R. Fausset, and David Brown, *Commentary on the Whole Bible* (Grand Rapids, MI: Zondervan Publishing House, 1961), 1514.

Chapter 4

1. Florence Bulle, *God Wants You Rich and Other Enticing Doctrines* (Minneapolis, MN: Bethany House Publishers, 1983), 30.
2. William W. Klein, Craig L. Blomberg, Robert L. Hubbard Jr., *Introduction to Biblical Interpretation* (Dallas: Word Publishing, 1993), 387.
3. Ibid.
4. Ibid., 388.

5. Ibid., 389.
6. Ibid.
7. Ibid.
8. Ibid., 390.

Chapter 6
1. Joe Sharkey, *Above Suspicion* (New York: Simon & Schuster, 1993), 137.

Chapter 7
1. Don Tipton, *Jesus & Company* (Hemet, CA: Via Verde Publishing, 1996), 22–23.
2. Ibid., 25.
3. Ibid., 27.
4. *Wesley's 52 Standard Sermons,* compiled by Rev. N. Burwash (Salem, OH: Convention Book Store, H. E. Schmul; 1967), 498–499.
5. Ibid.
6. A. W. Tozer, *I Talk Back to the Devil* (Harrisburg, PA: Christian Publications, Inc., 1972), 30–31.

Chapter 8
1. U.S. Geological Survey Fact Sheet 168–95 (U.S. Geological Survey, Center for Earthquake Research and Information, University of Memphis; Memphis, TN 38152).
2. Ibid.
3. Ibid.

Chapter 9
1. David MacPherson, *The Rapture Plot* (Simpsonville, SC: Millennium III Publishers, 1995), viii.
2. George Eldon Ladd, *The Last Things* (Grand Rapids, MI: William B. Eerdmans Publishing Company, 1978), 54.
3. Ibid., 66.
4. David MacPherson, "Why I Believe the Church Will Pass Through the Tribulation," Heart of America Bible Society pamphlet.
5. Ibid.
6. MacPherson, *The Rapture Plot,* 7.

Chapter 10
1. John Ritter, "El Niño 'off the scale,'" *USA Today,* 26 February 1998, 1-A.

2. Reuters News Service, "It's Not Over for Africa and Latin America," 16 December 1997, 10.
3. Joe Bigham, "El Niño boosts veggie, fruit prices 50 to 60 percent," Associated Press, *Peninsula Clarion,* Anchorage, Alaska, 1 March 1998, C-4.
4. Ibid.
5. Floyd Norris, "In Asia, Stocks Melt Faster than in '29," *The New York Times,* 12 January 1998, 1.
6. Ibid.
7. "Air-traffic control in U.S. vulnerable to Year 2000 bug", *USA Today,* 3 May 1998, 6-A.
8. Videotape, "Year 2000 Computer Problems," Center for Strategic & International Studies, Washington, DC; June 2, 1998; C-Span Archives at Purdue University; © 1998 Purdue Research Foundation.
9. Ibid.
10. Ibid.
11. Mike Wendland, © 1998, Mike Wendland Communications, LLC; www.awesomepages.com; 1.
12. Ibid.
13. Videotape, "Year 2000 Computer Problems."
14. Ibid.
15. Ibid.
16. Ibid.
17. Ibid.
18. Ibid.
19. Alan Zarembo, "Hope and Despair," *Newsweek,* international edition, 8 December 1997, 41.
20. Ibid., 41, 42.
21. Beth Warren, "Drug-Resistant TB Strikes Nashville," *The Tennessean,* 20 March 1998, 1-B.
22. Associated Press, "Meningitis deaths spark panic, mass vaccinations," *The Tennessean,* 27 February 1998, 12-A.
23. Lara Santoro, "Killer Weed Strikes Lake Victoria," *The Christian Science Monitor,* 12 January 1998, 1.

Chapter 11
1. Paul Recer, Associated Press, "Mile-wide space rock headed for Earth," *The Tennessean,* 12 March 1998, 5-A.
2. Leon Jaroff, "Whew!" *Time,* 23 March 1998, 69.

3. Tennessean News Service, "Never mind, asteroid likely to miss Earth," 13 March 1998, 12-A.

4. "Headline News," Cable News Network, 11 May 1998.

5. Norma H. Dickey, ed., *Funk and Wagnalls New Encyclopedia,* vol. 3 (Funk and Wagnalls Corporation, 1996), 15.

6. Hilary McGlynn, ed. dir., *Webster's New Universal Encyclopedia,* (Helicon Publishing, Ltd., 1997), 74.

7. Video, *Fire from the Sky*

8. Ibid.

9. Ibid.

10. Ibid.

11. Adapted from Rich Christianson, *Scorched Earth: The Great Peshtigo Fire Remembered* (prepared by AACMsLinde, America On Line, Academic Assistance Center, document id:HHS5605; retrieved 25 January 1998).

12. Ibid.

13. Ibid.

14. Ibid.

15. Donald W. Cox and James H. Chestek, *Doomsday Asteroid* (Amherst, NY: Prometheus Books, 1996), 30.

16. Ibid., quoting Tom Gehrels, *Hazards of Comets and Asteroids* (Tucson, AZ: University of Arizona Press, 1994).

17. Ibid.

18. Video, *Asteroids—Deadly Impact* (National Geographic, © 1997; NGT Inc., 1145 17th St., Washington, DC 20036)

19. *Time,* 23 March 1998, 69.

20. Video, *Fire from the Sky.*

Chapter 12

1. David Jeremiah with C. C. Carlson, *Escape the Coming Night* (Dallas, TX: Word Publishing, 1990), 137.

Chapter 14

1. Arthur Katterjohn with Mark Fackler, *The Tribulation People* (Carol Stream, IL: Creation House, 1975), 15.